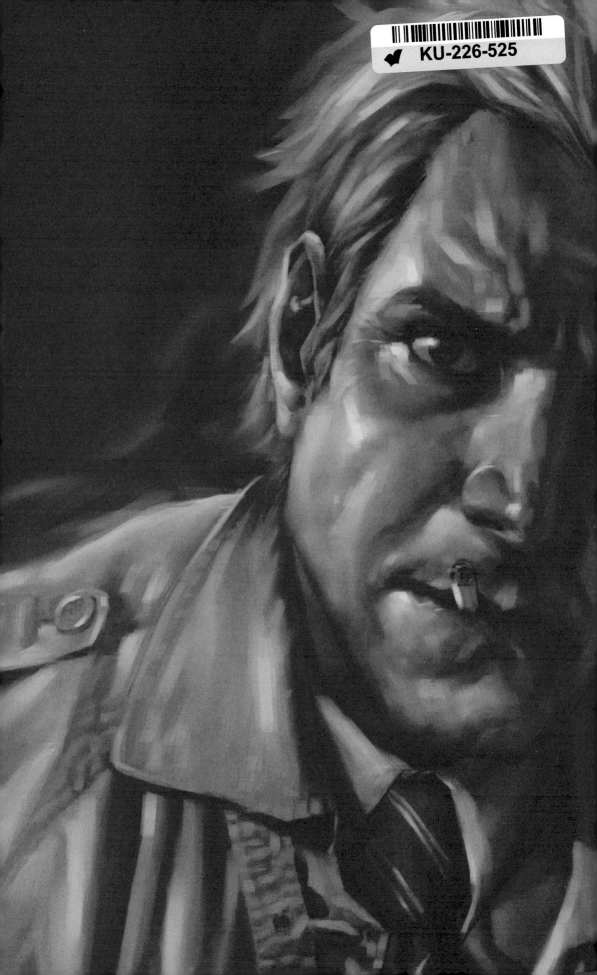

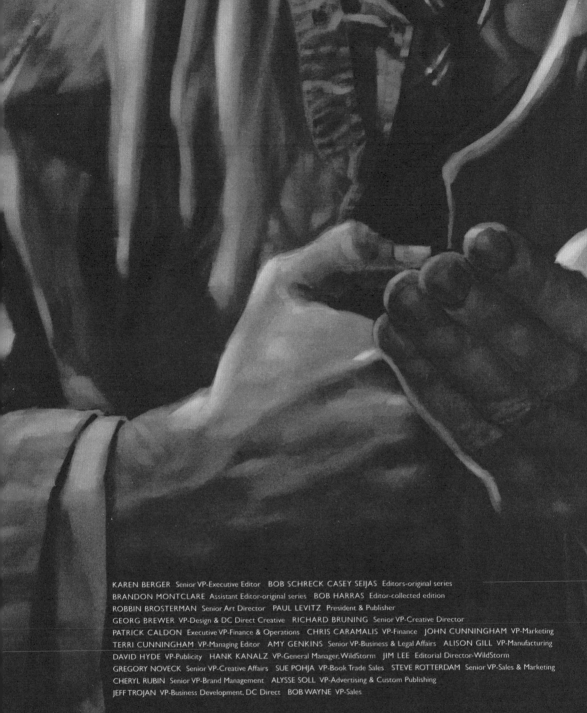

KAREN BERGER Senior VP-Executive Editor   BOB SCHRECK CASEY SEIJAS Editors-original series
BRANDON MONTCLARE Assistant Editor-original series   BOB HARRAS Editor-collected edition
ROBBIN BROSTERMAN Senior Art Director   PAUL LEVITZ President & Publisher
GEORG BREWER VP-Design & DC Direct Creative   RICHARD BRUNING Senior VP-Creative Director
PATRICK CALDON Executive VP-Finance & Operations   CHRIS CARAMALIS VP-Finance   JOHN CUNNINGHAM VP-Marketing
TERRI CUNNINGHAM VP-Managing Editor   AMY GENKINS Senior VP-Business & Legal Affairs   ALISON GILL VP-Manufacturing
DAVID HYDE VP-Publicity   HANK KANALZ VP-General Manager, WildStorm   JIM LEE Editorial Director-WildStorm
GREGORY NOVECK Senior VP-Creative Affairs   SUE POHJA VP-Book Trade Sales   STEVE ROTTERDAM Senior VP-Sales & Marketing
CHERYL RUBIN Senior VP-Brand Management   ALYSSE SOLL VP-Advertising & Custom Publishing
JEFF TROJAN VP-Business Development, DC Direct   BOB WAYNE VP-Sales

Cover illustration by Lee Bermejo.

JOHN CONSTANTINE, THE ROOTS OF COINCIDENCE
Published by DC Comics. Cover and compilation Copyright © 2009 DC Comics. All Rights Reserved. Originally published in single
magazine form as HELLBLAZER # 243-244, 247-249. Copyright © 2008 DC Comics. All Rights Reserved. VERTIGO and all characters,
their distinctive likenesses and related elements featured in this publication are trademarks of DC Comics. The stories, characters
and incidents featured in this publication are entirely fictional. DC Comics does not read or accept unsolicited submissions of ideas,
stories or artwork.

DC Comics, 1700 Broadway, New York, NY 10019
A Warner Bros. Entertainment Company
Printed in Canada. First Printing. ISBN: 978-1-4012-2251-2

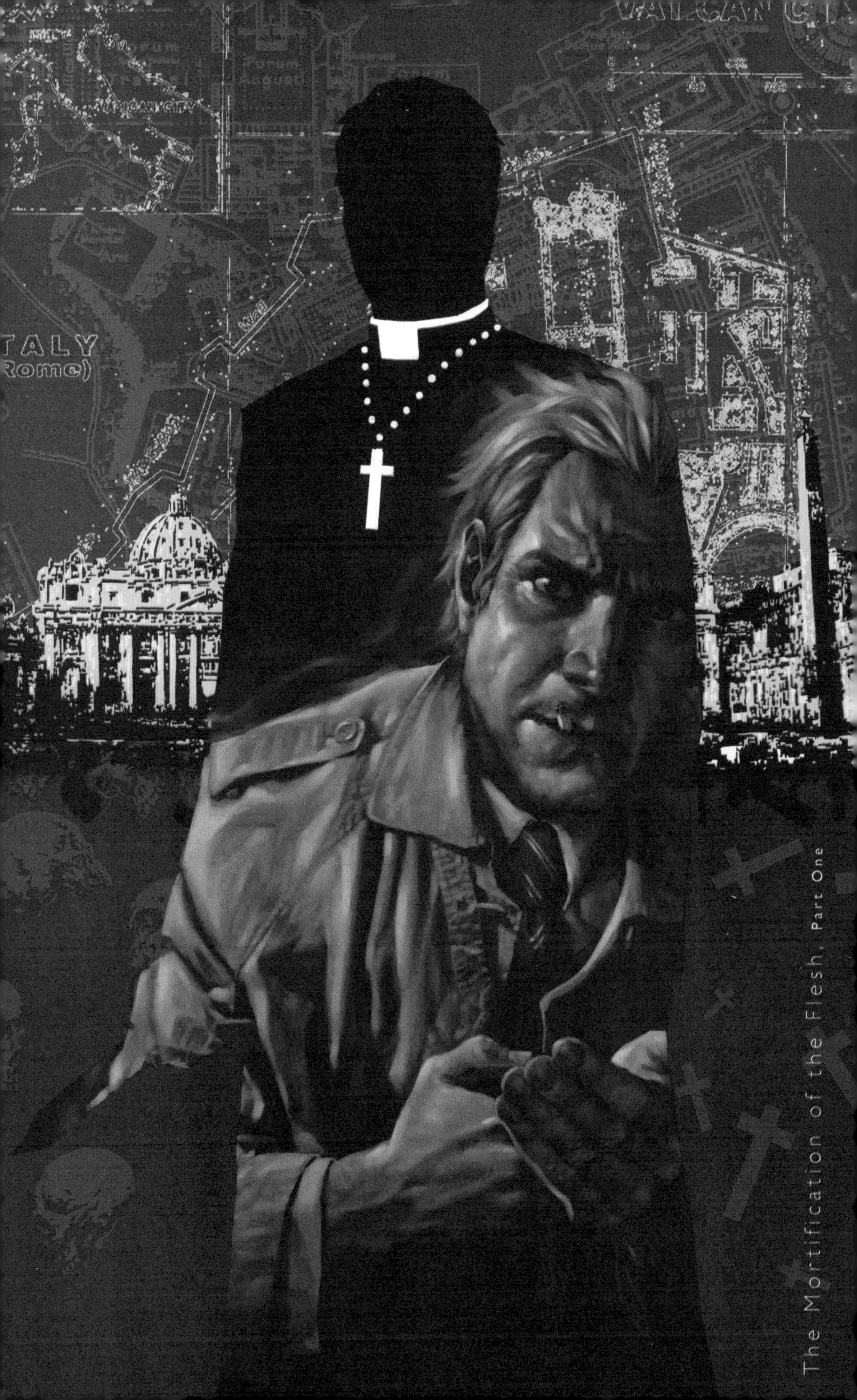
The Mortification of the Flesh, Part One

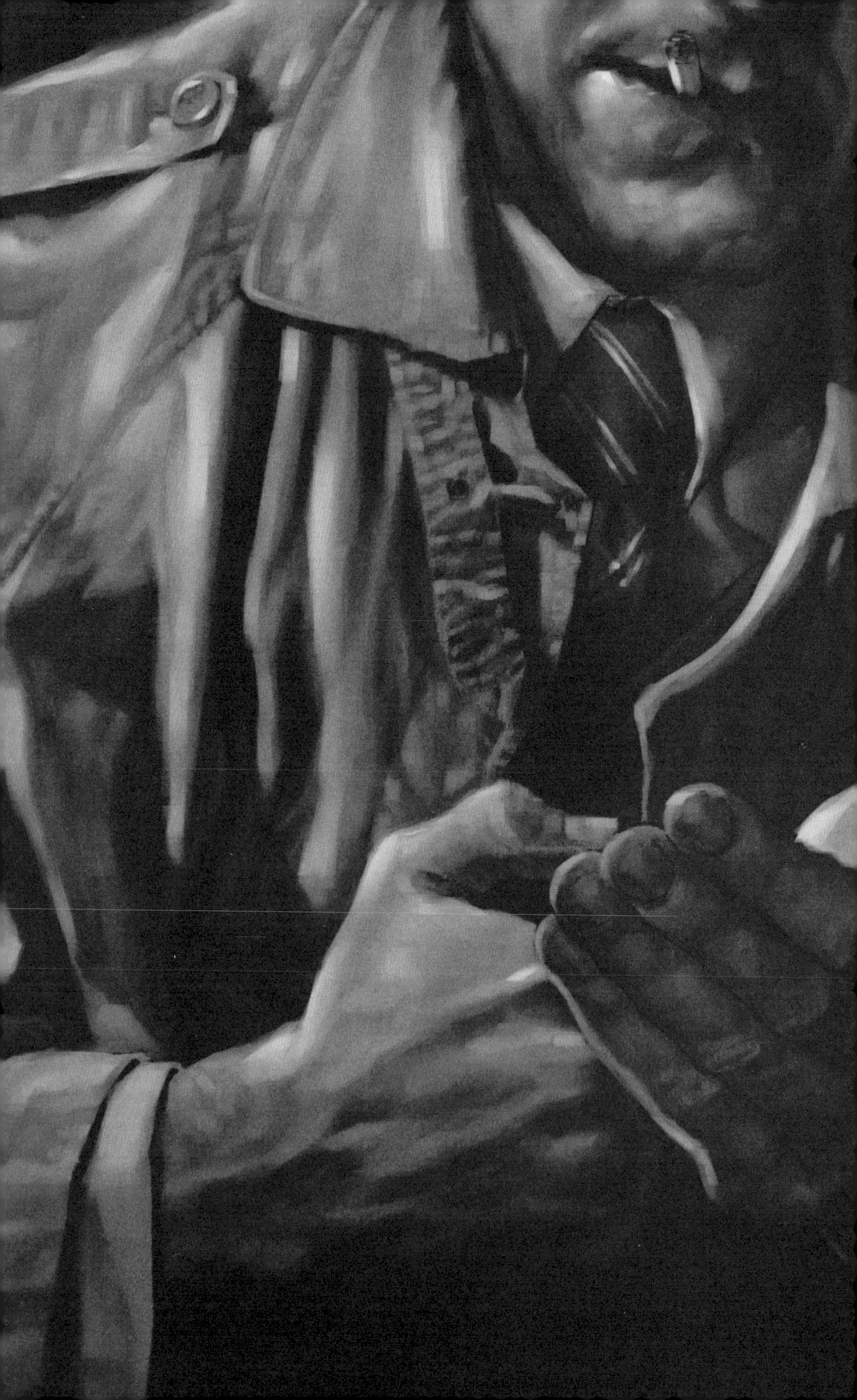

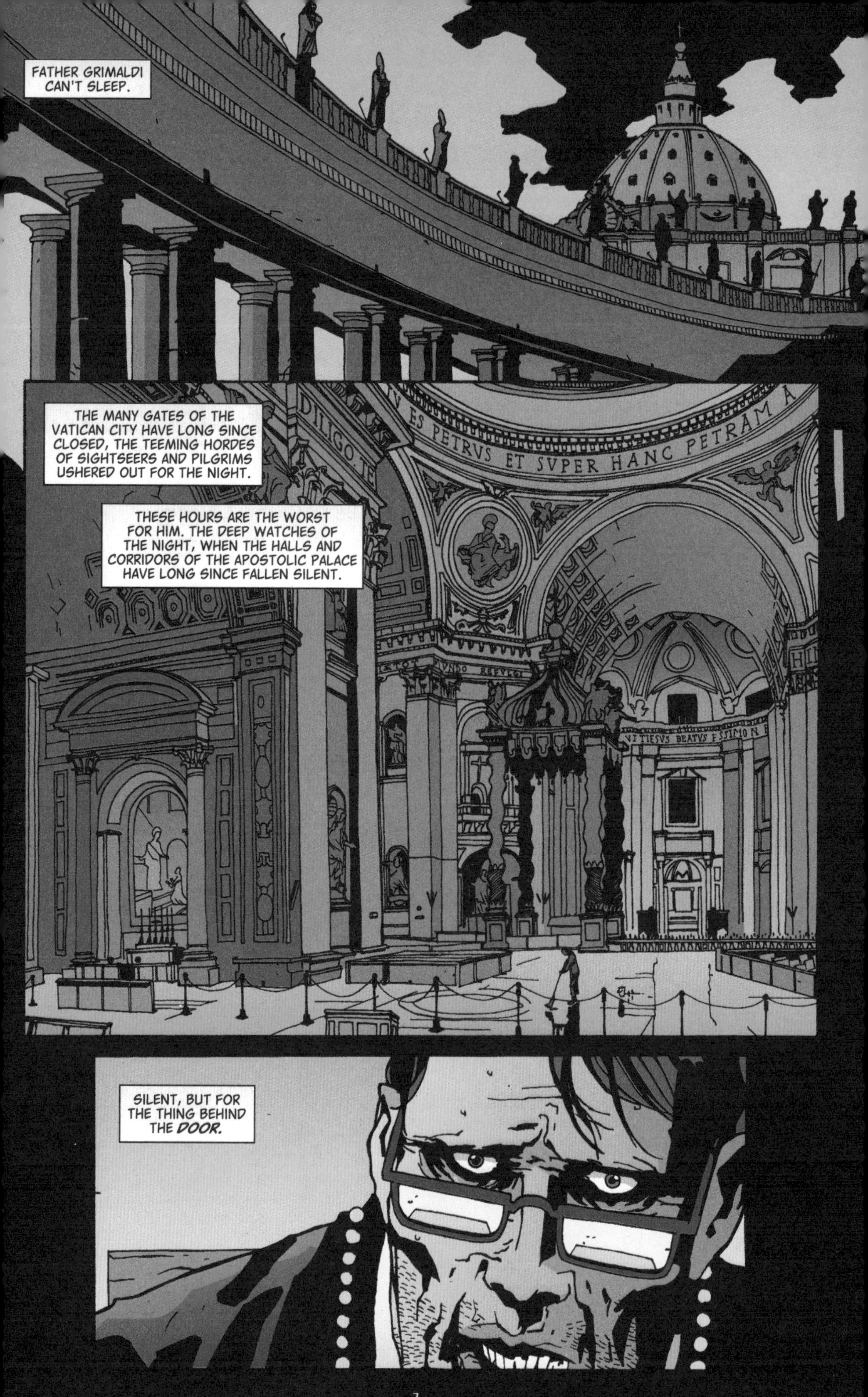
FATHER GRIMALDI CAN'T SLEEP.
THE MANY GATES OF THE VATICAN CITY HAVE LONG SINCE CLOSED, THE TEEMING HORDES OF SIGHTSEERS AND PILGRIMS USHERED OUT FOR THE NIGHT.
THESE HOURS ARE THE WORST FOR HIM. THE DEEP WATCHES OF THE NIGHT, WHEN THE HALLS AND CORRIDORS OF THE APOSTOLIC PALACE HAVE LONG SINCE FALLEN SILENT.
SILENT, BUT FOR THE THING BEHIND THE *DOOR.*

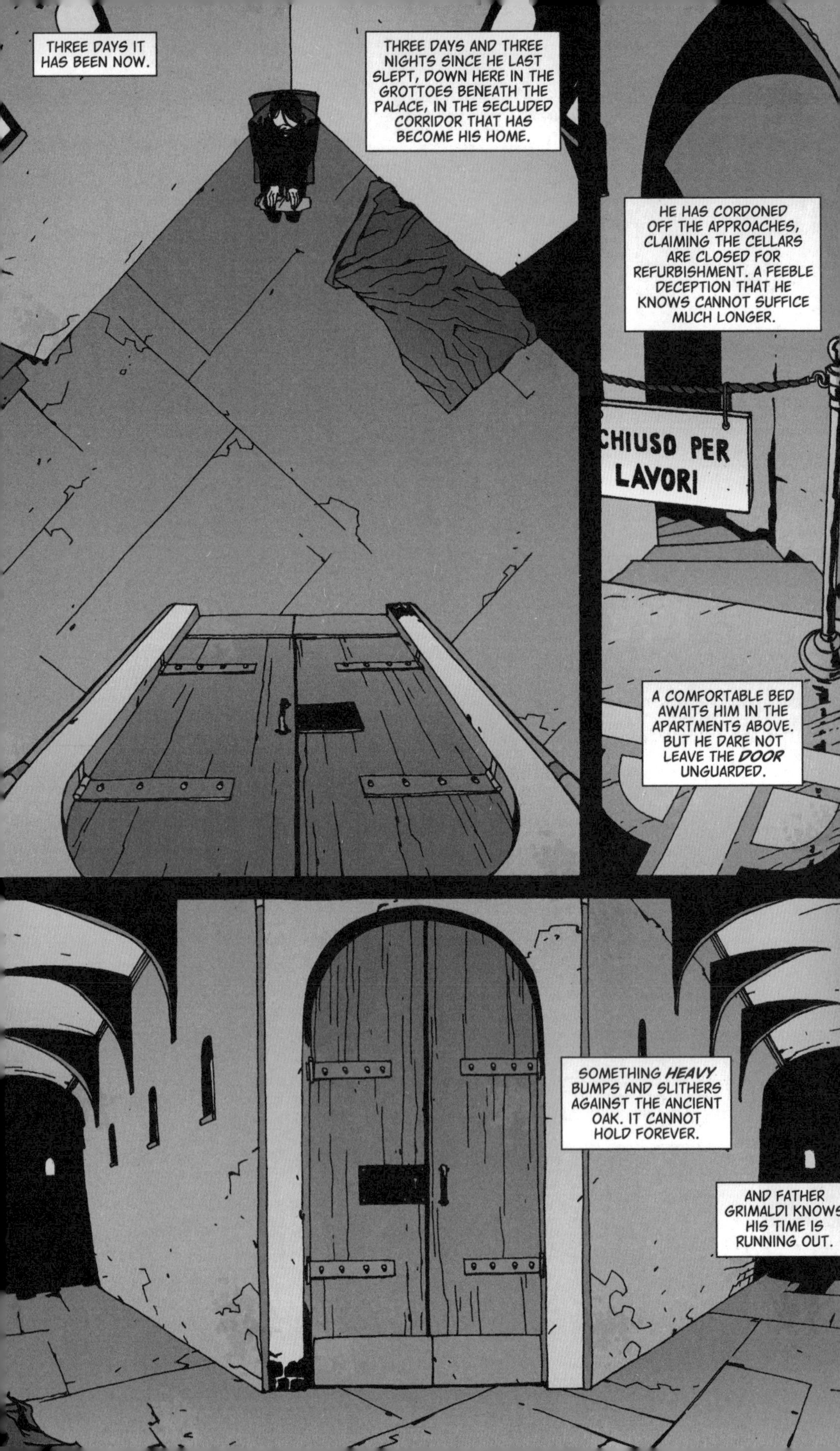
THREE DAYS IT HAS BEEN NOW.
THREE DAYS AND THREE NIGHTS SINCE HE LAST SLEPT, DOWN HERE IN THE GROTTOES BENEATH THE PALACE, IN THE SECLUDED CORRIDOR THAT HAS BECOME HIS HOME.
HE HAS CORDONED OFF THE APPROACHES, CLAIMING THE CELLARS ARE CLOSED FOR REFURBISHMENT. A FEEBLE DECEPTION THAT HE KNOWS CANNOT SUFFICE MUCH LONGER.
CHIUSO PER LAVORI
A COMFORTABLE BED AWAITS HIM IN THE APARTMENTS ABOVE. BUT HE DARE NOT LEAVE THE ***DOOR*** UNGUARDED.
SOMETHING ***HEAVY*** BUMPS AND SLITHERS AGAINST THE ANCIENT OAK. IT CANNOT HOLD FOREVER.
AND FATHER GRIMALDI KNOWS HIS TIME IS RUNNING OUT.

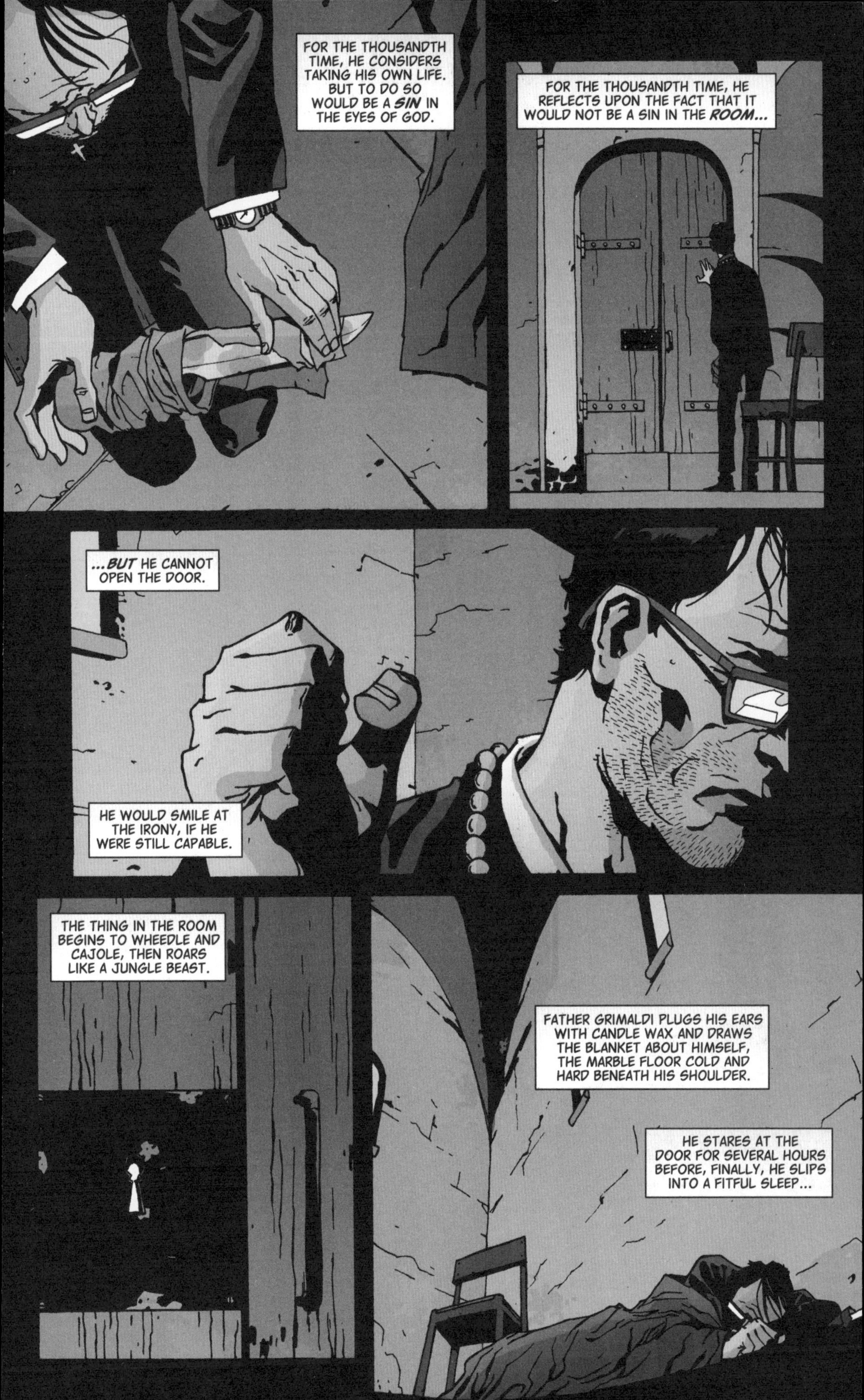

FOR THE THOUSANDTH TIME, HE CONSIDERS TAKING HIS OWN LIFE. BUT TO DO SO WOULD BE A *SIN* IN THE EYES OF GOD.
FOR THE THOUSANDTH TIME, HE REFLECTS UPON THE FACT THAT IT WOULD NOT BE A SIN IN THE *ROOM*...
...*BUT* HE CANNOT OPEN THE DOOR.
HE WOULD SMILE AT THE IRONY, IF HE WERE STILL CAPABLE.
THE THING IN THE ROOM BEGINS TO WHEEDLE AND CAJOLE, THEN ROARS LIKE A JUNGLE BEAST.
FATHER GRIMALDI PLUGS HIS EARS WITH CANDLE WAX AND DRAWS THE BLANKET ABOUT HIMSELF, THE MARBLE FLOOR COLD AND HARD BENEATH HIS SHOULDER.
HE STARES AT THE DOOR FOR SEVERAL HOURS BEFORE, FINALLY, HE SLIPS INTO A FITFUL SLEEP...

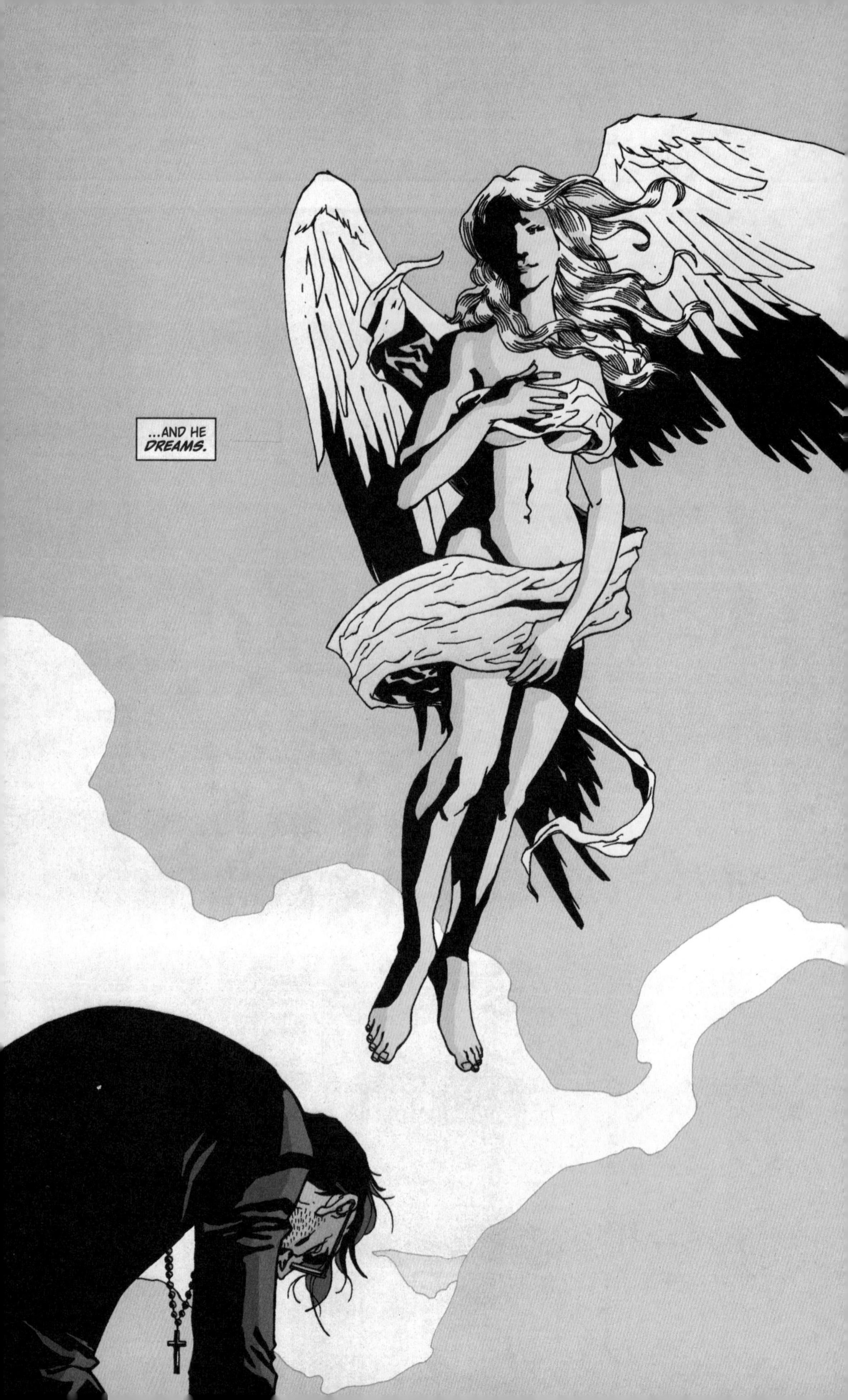
...AND HE DREAMS.

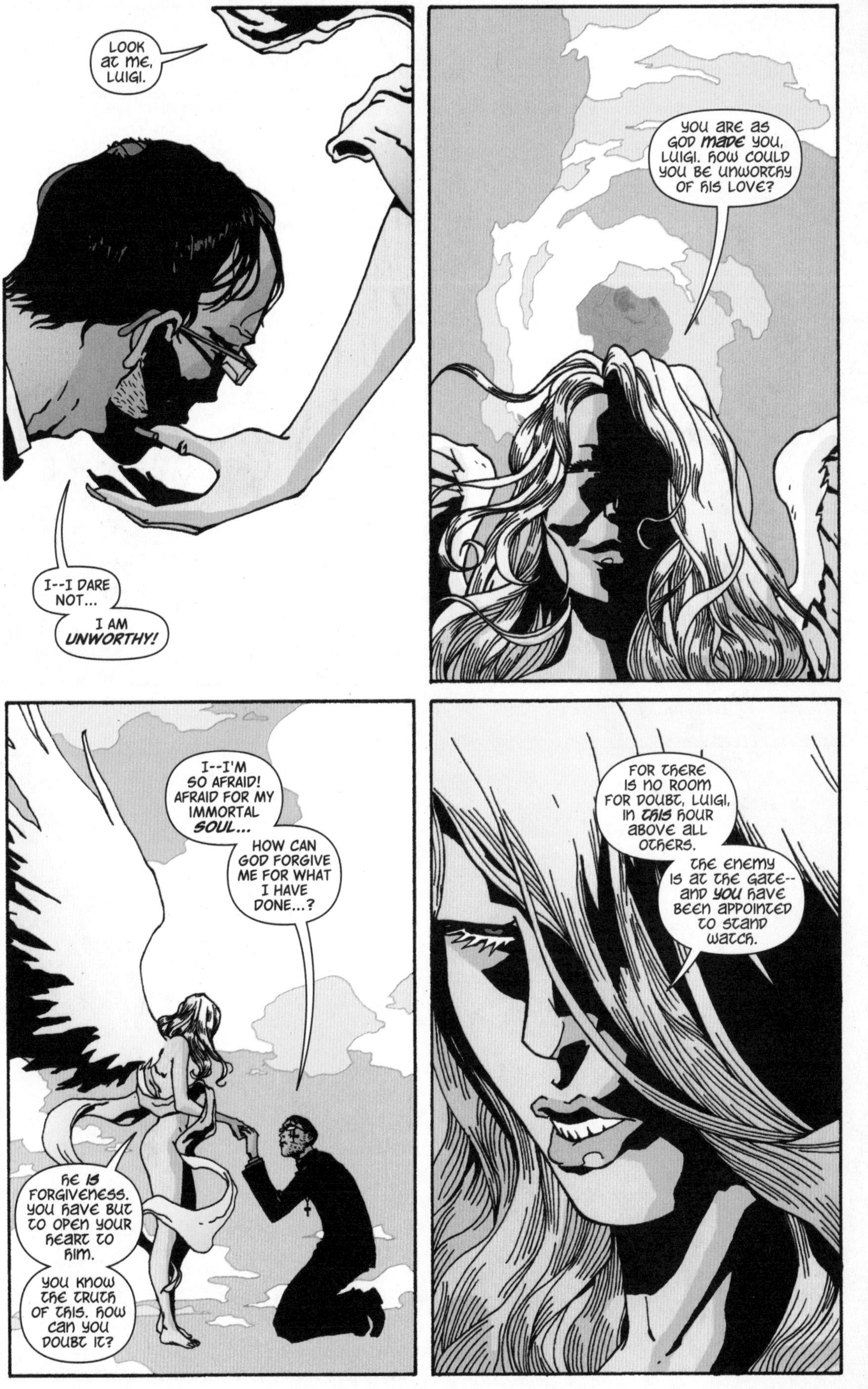
LOOK AT ME, LUIGI.
I--I DARE NOT...
I AM UNWORTHY!
YOU ARE AS GOD MADE YOU, LUIGI. HOW COULD YOU BE UNWORTHY OF HIS LOVE?
I--I'M SO AFRAID! AFRAID FOR MY IMMORTAL SOUL...
HOW CAN GOD FORGIVE ME FOR WHAT I HAVE DONE...?
HE IS FORGIVENESS. YOU HAVE BUT TO OPEN YOUR HEART TO HIM.
YOU KNOW THE TRUTH OF THIS. HOW CAN YOU DOUBT IT?
FOR THERE IS NO ROOM FOR DOUBT, LUIGI, IN THIS HOUR ABOVE ALL OTHERS.
THE ENEMY IS AT THE GATE-- AND YOU HAVE BEEN APPOINTED TO STAND WATCH.

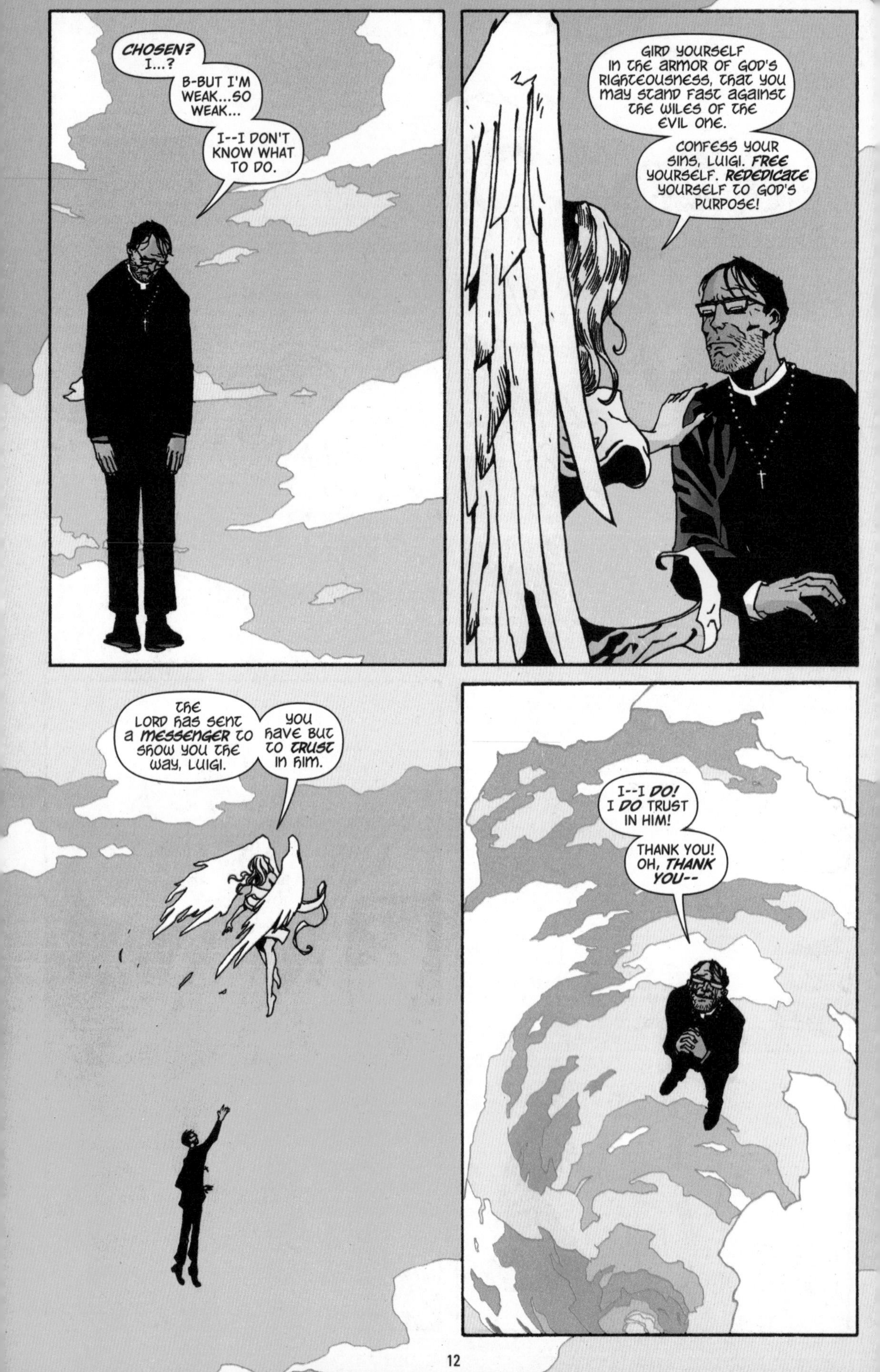
CHOSEN? I...?
B-BUT I'M WEAK...SO WEAK...
I--I DON'T KNOW WHAT TO DO.
GIRD YOURSELF IN THE ARMOR OF GOD'S RIGHTEOUSNESS, THAT YOU MAY STAND FAST AGAINST THE WILES OF THE EVIL ONE.
CONFESS YOUR SINS, LUIGI. FREE YOURSELF. REDEDICATE YOURSELF TO GOD'S PURPOSE!
THE LORD HAS SENT A MESSENGER TO SHOW YOU THE WAY, LUIGI.
YOU HAVE BUT TO TRUST IN HIM.
I--I DO! I DO TRUST IN HIM!
THANK YOU! OH, THANK YOU--

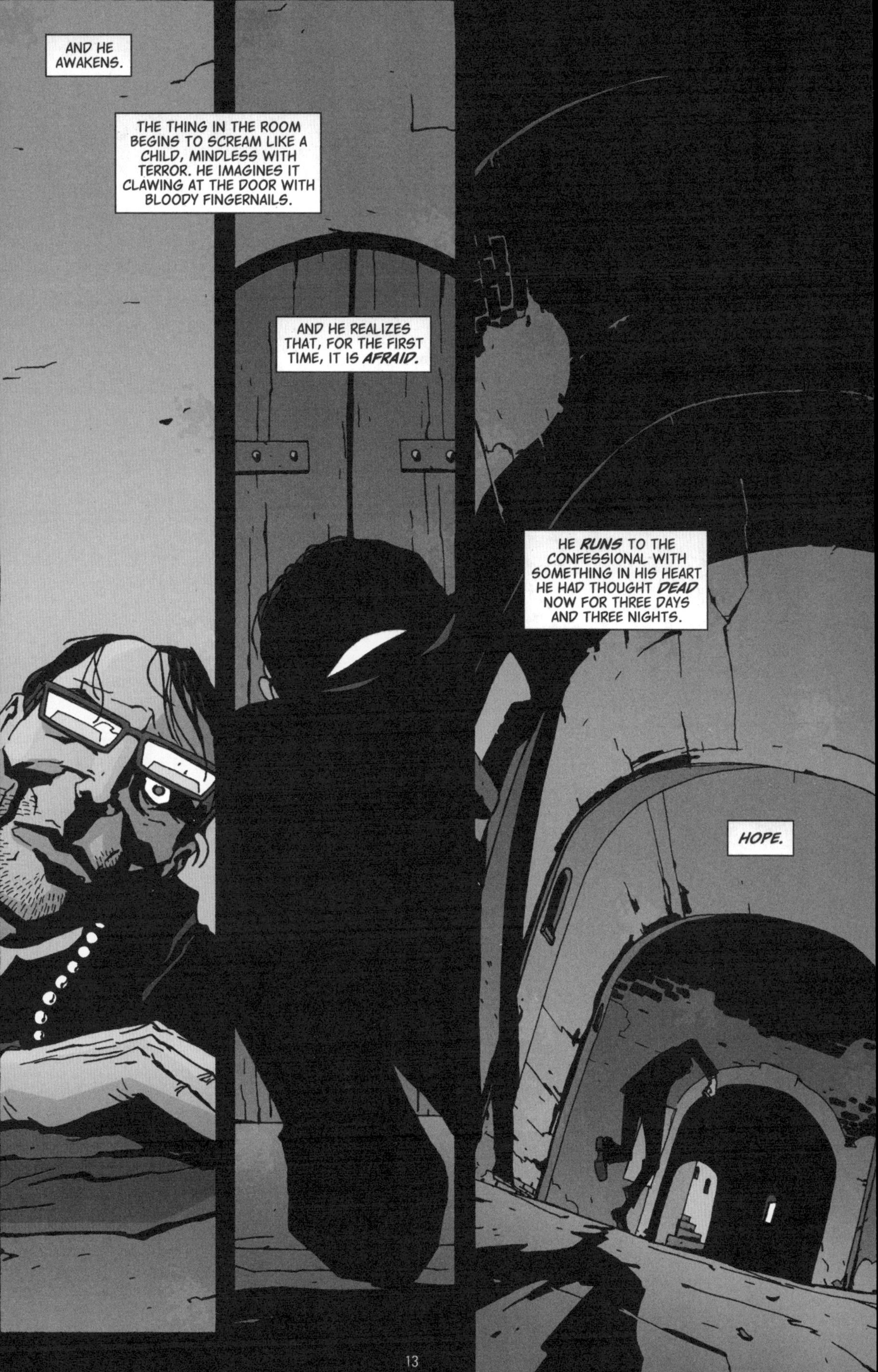
AND HE AWAKENS.
THE THING IN THE ROOM BEGINS TO SCREAM LIKE A CHILD, MINDLESS WITH TERROR. HE IMAGINES IT CLAWING AT THE DOOR WITH BLOODY FINGERNAILS.
AND HE REALIZES THAT, FOR THE FIRST TIME, IT IS *AFRAID.*
HE ***RUNS*** TO THE CONFESSIONAL WITH SOMETHING IN HIS HEART HE HAD THOUGHT ***DEAD*** NOW FOR THREE DAYS AND THREE NIGHTS.
HOPE.

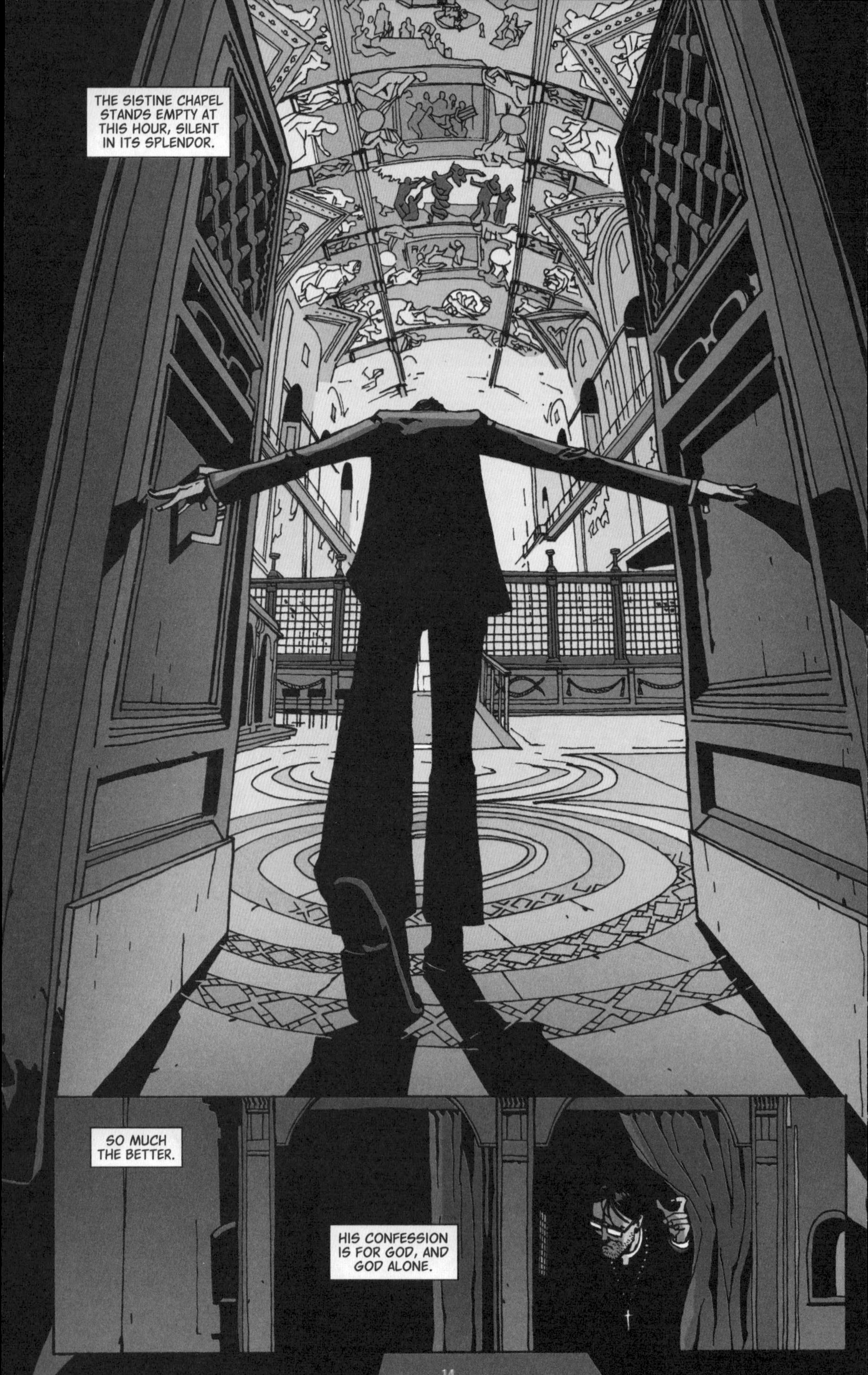
THE SISTINE CHAPEL STANDS EMPTY AT THIS HOUR, SILENT IN ITS SPLENDOR.
SO MUCH THE BETTER.
HIS CONFESSION IS FOR GOD, AND GOD ALONE.

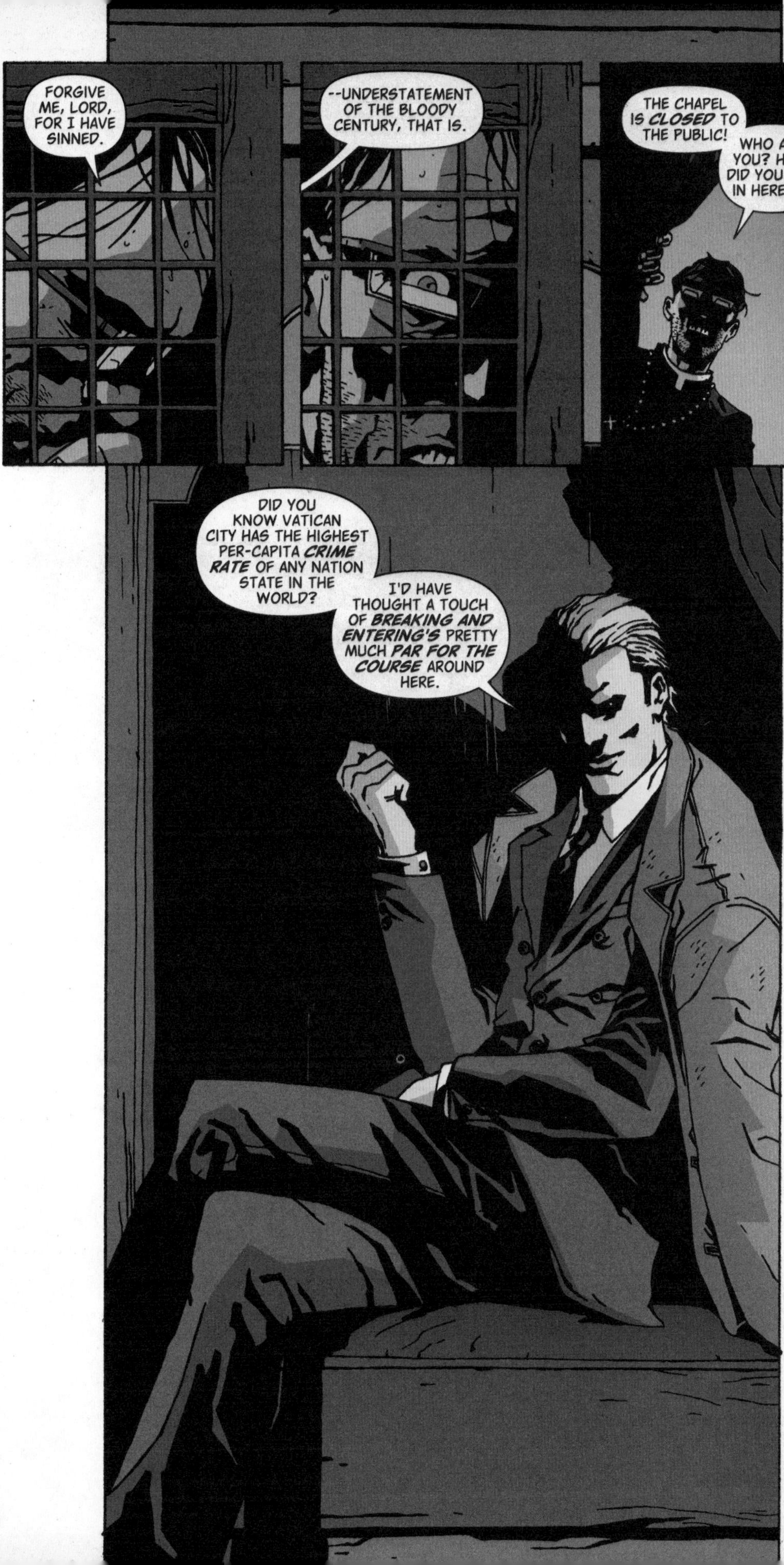
FORGIVE ME, LORD, FOR I HAVE SINNED.
--UNDERSTATEMENT OF THE BLOODY CENTURY, THAT IS.
THE CHAPEL IS CLOSED TO THE PUBLIC!
WHO ARE YOU? HOW DID YOU GET IN HERE...?
DID YOU KNOW VATICAN CITY HAS THE HIGHEST PER-CAPITA CRIME RATE OF ANY NATION STATE IN THE WORLD?
I'D HAVE THOUGHT A TOUCH OF BREAKING AND ENTERING'S PRETTY MUCH PAR FOR THE COURSE AROUND HERE.

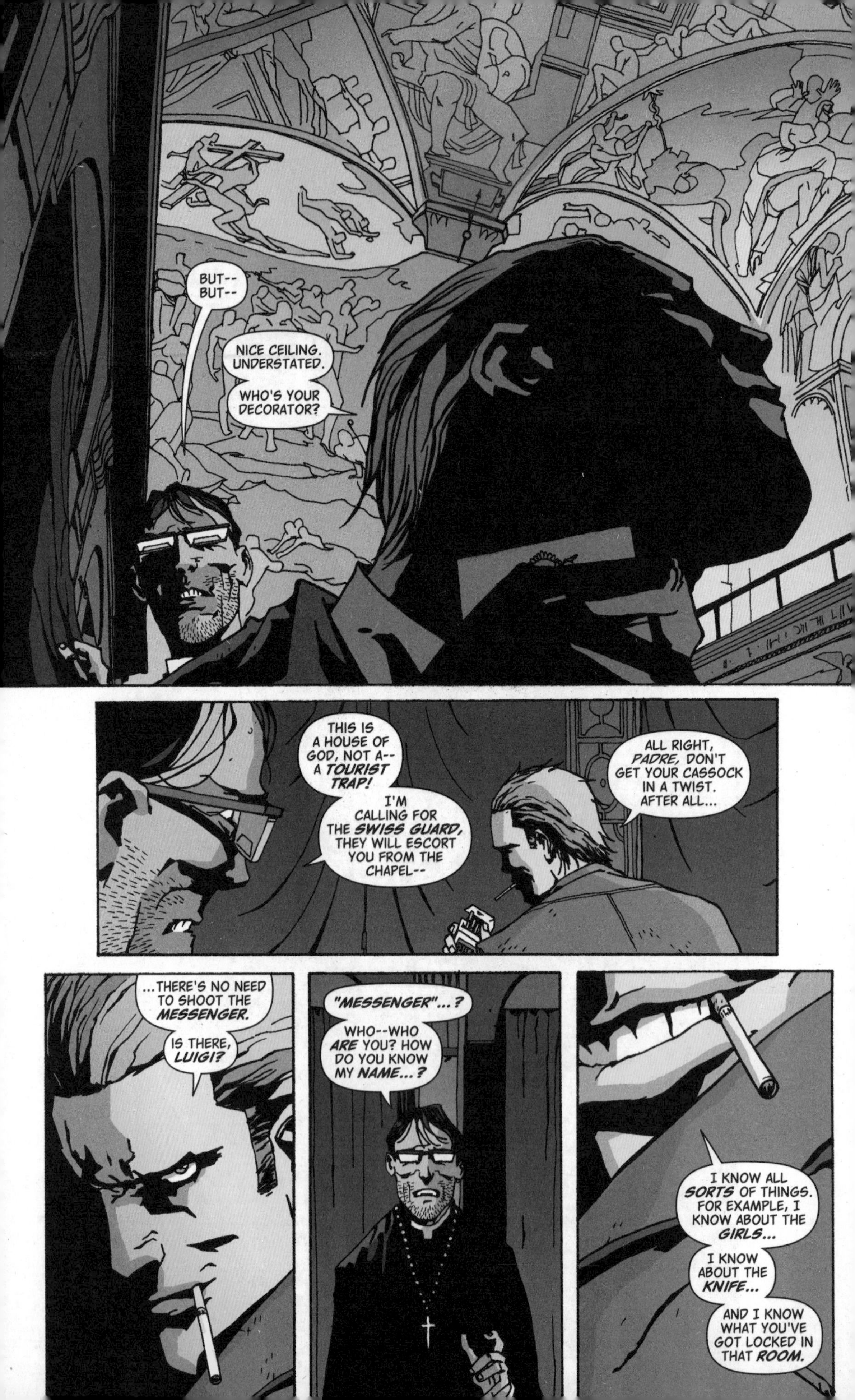
BUT-- BUT--
NICE CEILING. UNDERSTATED.
WHO'S YOUR DECORATOR?
THIS IS A HOUSE OF GOD, NOT A-- A *TOURIST TRAP!*
I'M CALLING FOR THE *SWISS GUARD,* THEY WILL ESCORT YOU FROM THE CHAPEL--
ALL RIGHT, *PADRE,* DON'T GET YOUR CASSOCK IN A TWIST. AFTER ALL...
...THERE'S NO NEED TO SHOOT THE *MESSENGER.*
IS THERE, *LUIGI?*
"MESSENGER"...?
WHO--WHO *ARE* YOU? HOW DO YOU KNOW MY *NAME...?*
I KNOW ALL *SORTS* OF THINGS. FOR EXAMPLE, I KNOW ABOUT THE *GIRLS...*
I KNOW ABOUT THE *KNIFE...*
AND I KNOW WHAT YOU'VE GOT LOCKED IN THAT *ROOM.*

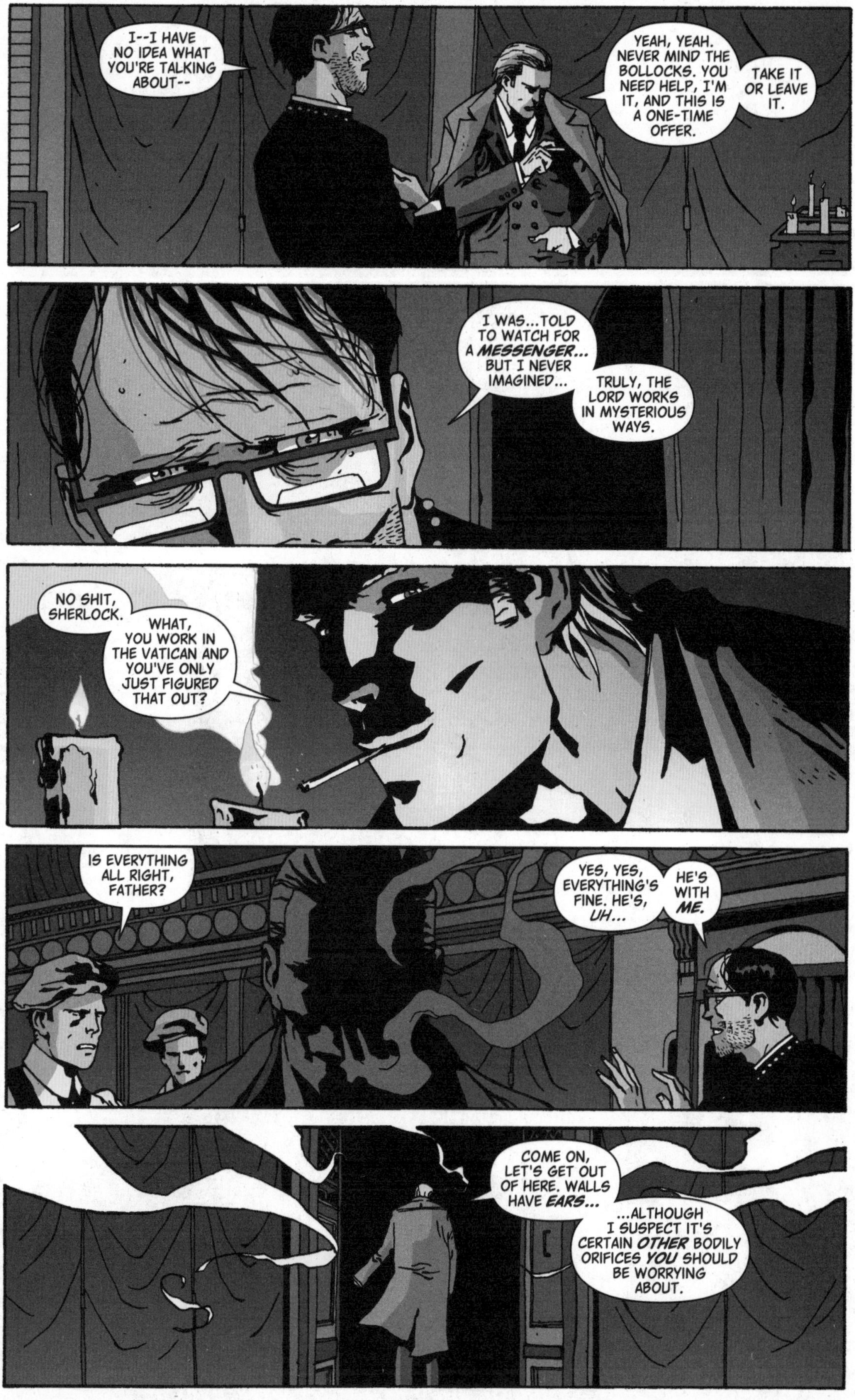
I--I HAVE NO IDEA WHAT YOU'RE TALKING ABOUT--
YEAH, YEAH. NEVER MIND THE BOLLOCKS. YOU NEED HELP, I'M IT, AND THIS IS A ONE-TIME OFFER.
TAKE IT OR LEAVE IT.
I WAS...TOLD TO WATCH FOR A *MESSENGER...* BUT I NEVER IMAGINED...
TRULY, THE LORD WORKS IN MYSTERIOUS WAYS.
NO SHIT, SHERLOCK.
WHAT, YOU WORK IN THE VATICAN AND YOU'VE ONLY JUST FIGURED THAT OUT?
IS EVERYTHING ALL RIGHT, FATHER?
YES, YES, EVERYTHING'S FINE. HE'S, *UH...*
HE'S WITH *ME.*
COME ON, LET'S GET OUT OF HERE. WALLS HAVE *EARS...*
...ALTHOUGH I SUSPECT IT'S CERTAIN *OTHER* BODILY ORIFICES *YOU* SHOULD BE WORRYING ABOUT.

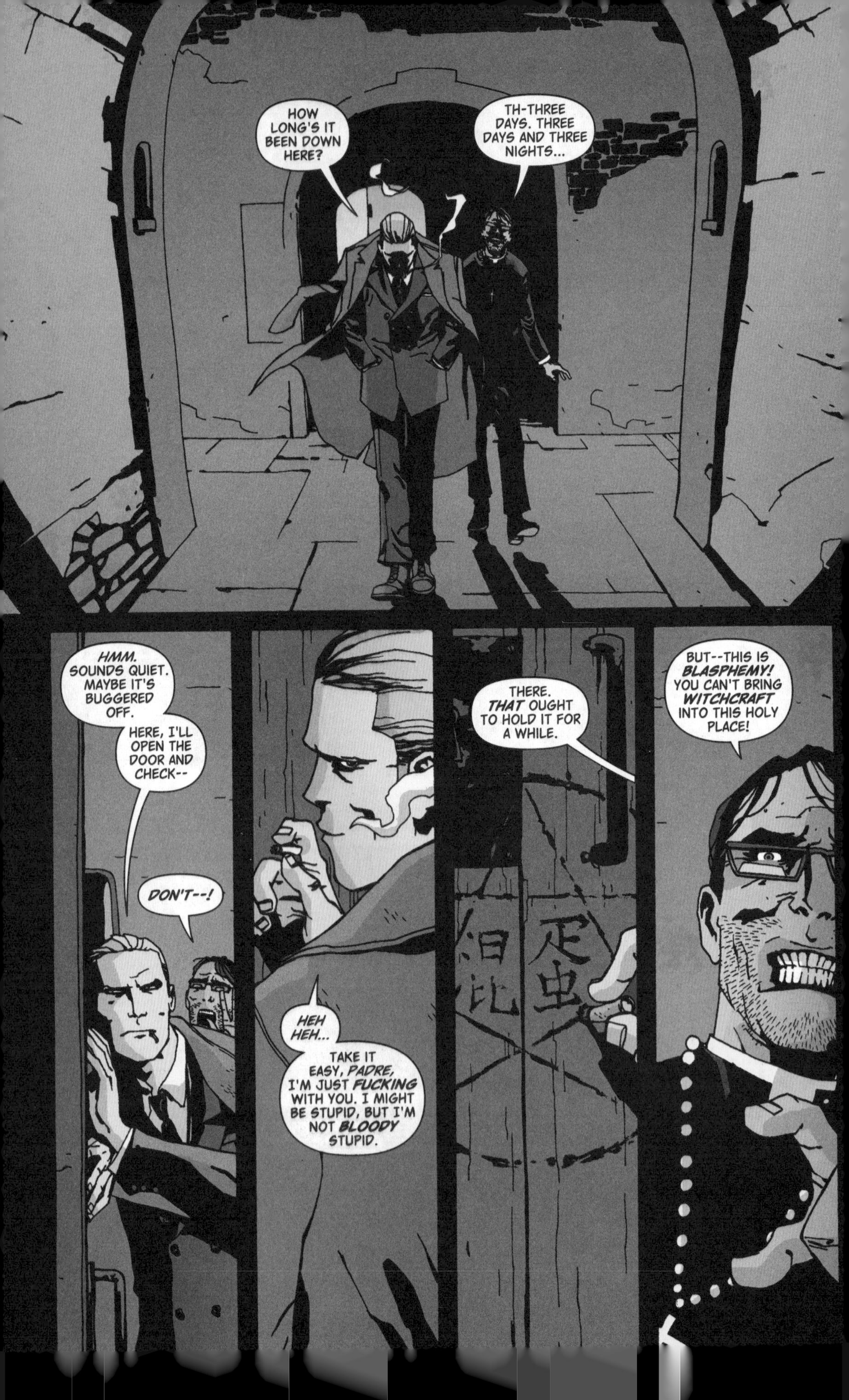
HOW LONG'S IT BEEN DOWN HERE?
TH-THREE DAYS. THREE DAYS AND THREE NIGHTS...
HMM. SOUNDS QUIET. MAYBE IT'S BUGGERED OFF.
HERE, I'LL OPEN THE DOOR AND CHECK--
DON'T--!
HEH HEH...
TAKE IT EASY, PADRE, I'M JUST FUCKING WITH YOU. I MIGHT BE STUPID, BUT I'M NOT BLOODY STUPID.
THERE. THAT OUGHT TO HOLD IT FOR A WHILE.
BUT--THIS IS BLASPHEMY! YOU CAN'T BRING WITCHCRAFT INTO THIS HOLY PLACE!

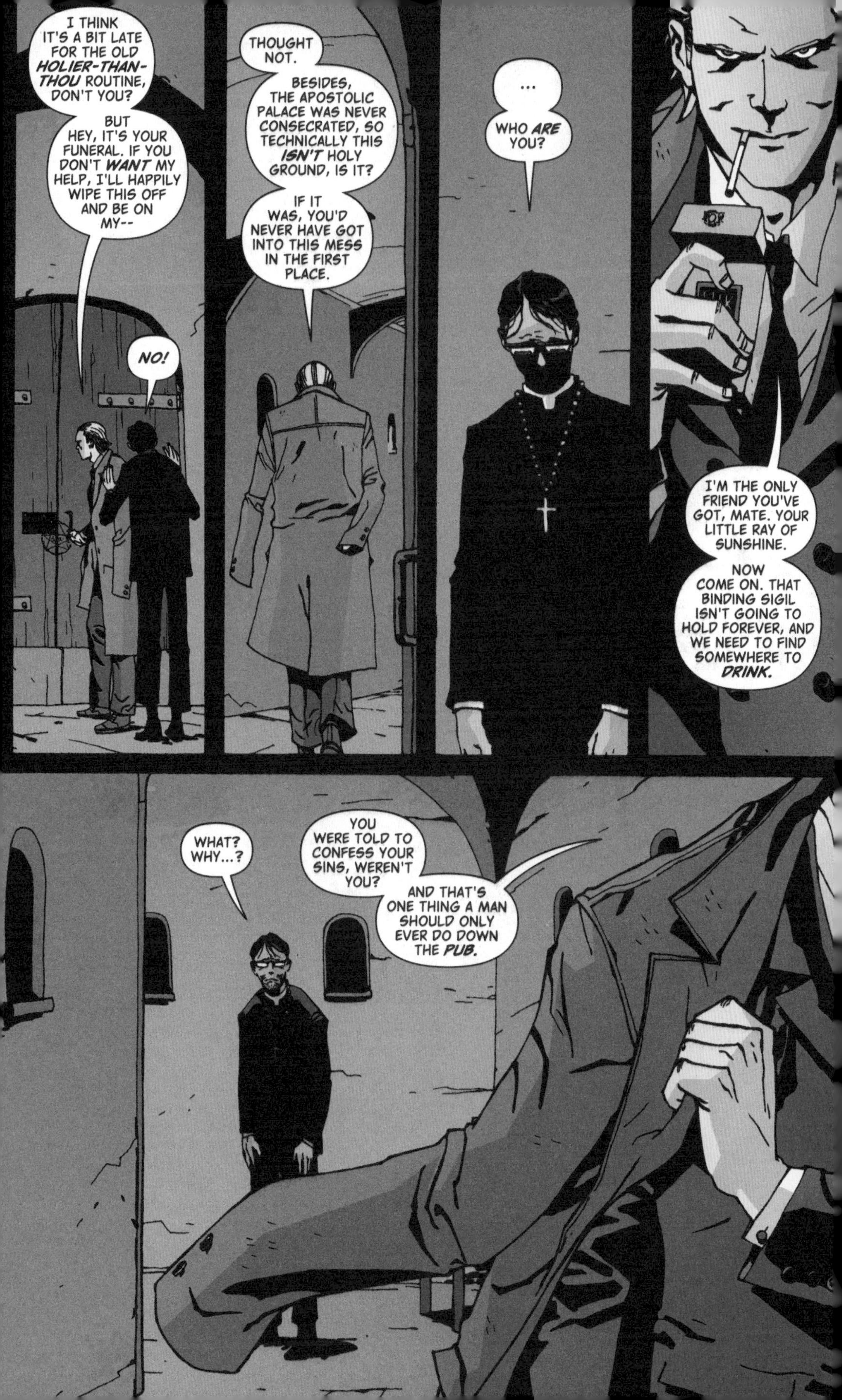

I THINK IT'S A BIT LATE FOR THE OLD HOLIER-THAN-THOU ROUTINE, DON'T YOU?
BUT HEY, IT'S YOUR FUNERAL. IF YOU DON'T WANT MY HELP, I'LL HAPPILY WIPE THIS OFF AND BE ON MY--
NO!
THOUGHT NOT.
BESIDES, THE APOSTOLIC PALACE WAS NEVER CONSECRATED, SO TECHNICALLY THIS ISN'T HOLY GROUND, IS IT?
IF IT WAS, YOU'D NEVER HAVE GOT INTO THIS MESS IN THE FIRST PLACE.
...
WHO ARE YOU?
I'M THE ONLY FRIEND YOU'VE GOT, MATE. YOUR LITTLE RAY OF SUNSHINE.
NOW COME ON. THAT BINDING SIGIL ISN'T GOING TO HOLD FOREVER, AND WE NEED TO FIND SOMEWHERE TO DRINK.
WHAT? WHY...?
YOU WERE TOLD TO CONFESS YOUR SINS, WEREN'T YOU?
AND THAT'S ONE THING A MAN SHOULD ONLY EVER DO DOWN THE PUB.

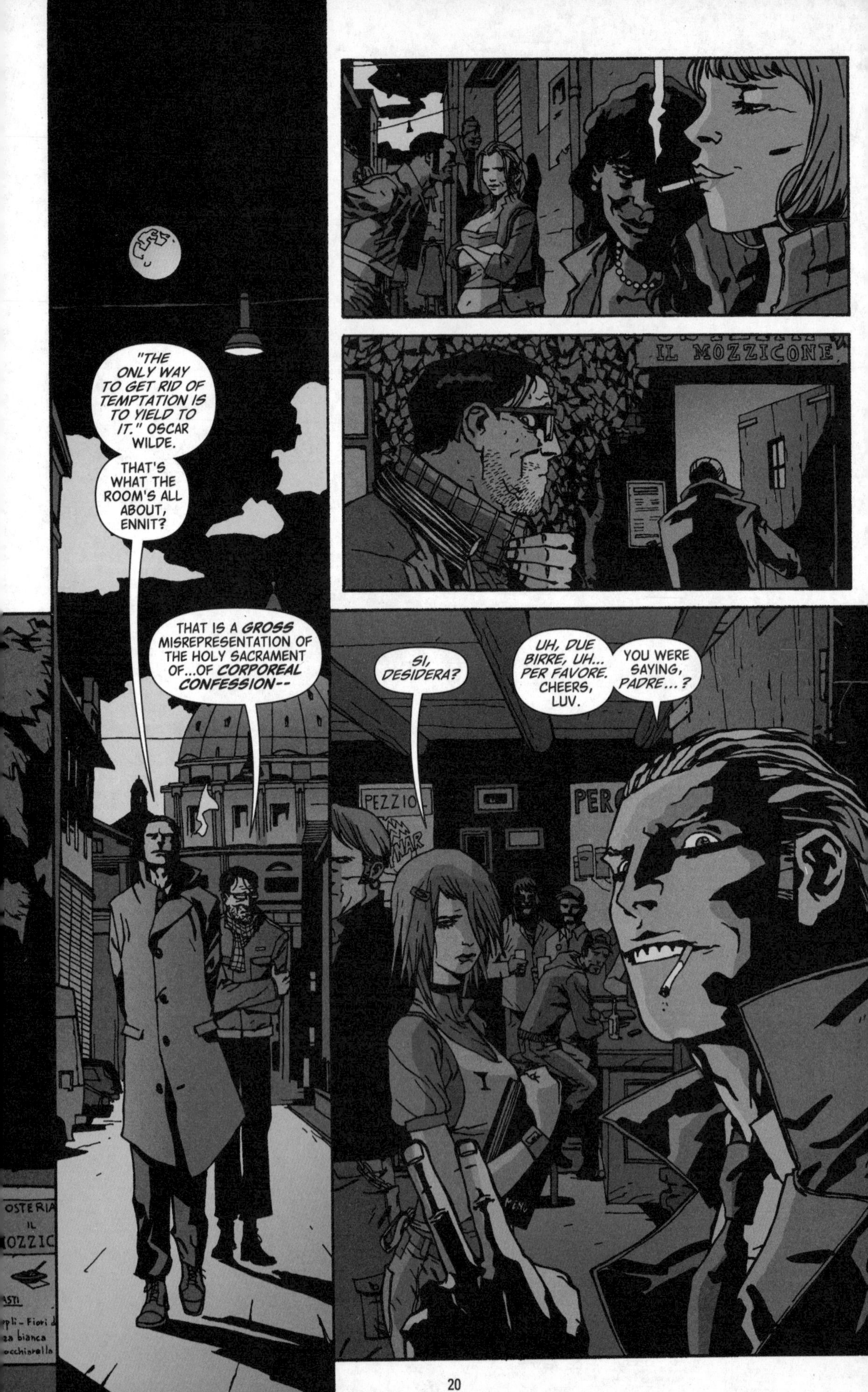
"THE ONLY WAY TO GET RID OF TEMPTATION IS TO YIELD TO IT." OSCAR WILDE.
THAT'S WHAT THE ROOM'S ALL ABOUT, ENNIT?
THAT IS A GROSS MISREPRESENTATION OF THE HOLY SACRAMENT OF...OF CORPOREAL CONFESSION--
IL MOZZICONE
OSTERIA
SI, DESIDERA?
UH, DUE BIRRE, UH... PER FAVORE. CHEERS, LUV.
YOU WERE SAYING, PADRE...?

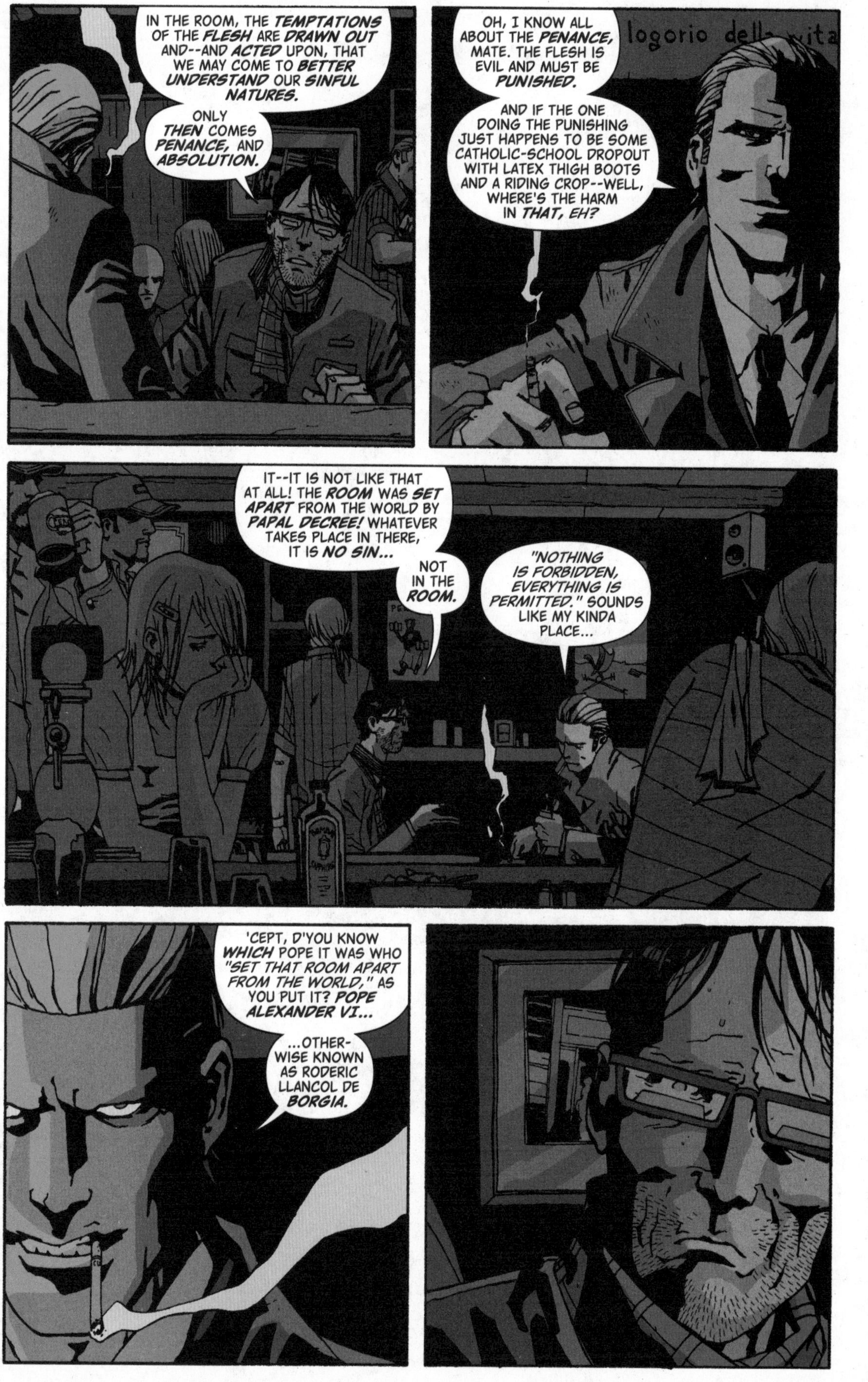
IN THE ROOM, THE TEMPTATIONS OF THE FLESH ARE DRAWN OUT AND--AND ACTED UPON, THAT WE MAY COME TO BETTER UNDERSTAND OUR SINFUL NATURES.
ONLY THEN COMES PENANCE, AND ABSOLUTION.
logorio della vita
OH, I KNOW ALL ABOUT THE PENANCE, MATE. THE FLESH IS EVIL AND MUST BE PUNISHED.
AND IF THE ONE DOING THE PUNISHING JUST HAPPENS TO BE SOME CATHOLIC-SCHOOL DROPOUT WITH LATEX THIGH BOOTS AND A RIDING CROP--WELL, WHERE'S THE HARM IN THAT, EH?
IT--IT IS NOT LIKE THAT AT ALL! THE ROOM WAS SET APART FROM THE WORLD BY PAPAL DECREE! WHATEVER TAKES PLACE IN THERE, IT IS NO SIN...
NOT IN THE ROOM.
"NOTHING IS FORBIDDEN, EVERYTHING IS PERMITTED." SOUNDS LIKE MY KINDA PLACE...
'CEPT, D'YOU KNOW WHICH POPE IT WAS WHO "SET THAT ROOM APART FROM THE WORLD," AS YOU PUT IT? POPE ALEXANDER VI...
...OTHER-WISE KNOWN AS RODERIC LLANCOL DE BORGIA.

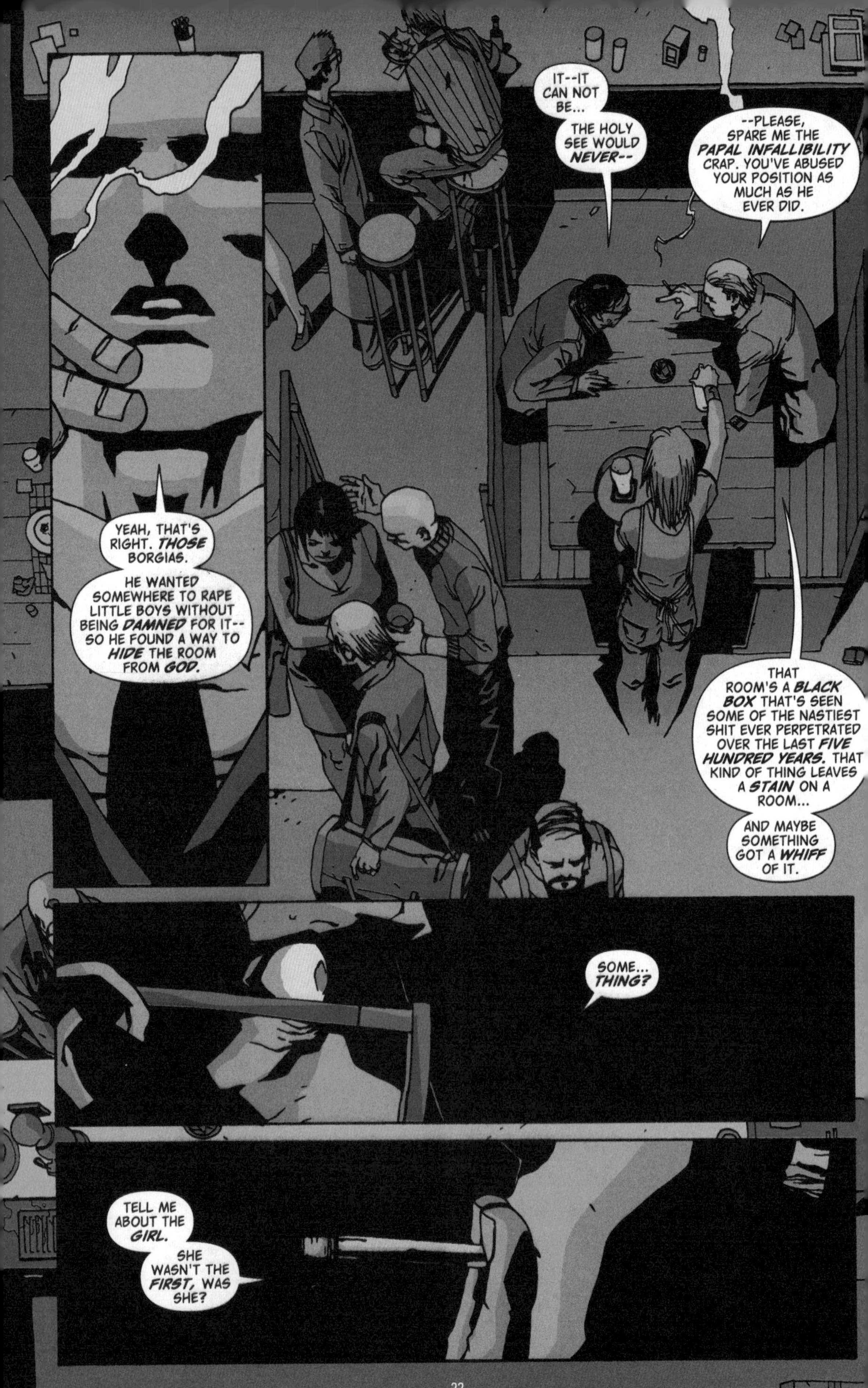
IT--IT CAN NOT BE...
THE HOLY SEE WOULD NEVER--
--PLEASE, SPARE ME THE PAPAL INFALLIBILITY CRAP. YOU'VE ABUSED YOUR POSITION AS MUCH AS HE EVER DID.
YEAH, THAT'S RIGHT. THOSE BORGIAS.
HE WANTED SOMEWHERE TO RAPE LITTLE BOYS WITHOUT BEING DAMNED FOR IT--SO HE FOUND A WAY TO HIDE THE ROOM FROM GOD.
THAT ROOM'S A BLACK BOX THAT'S SEEN SOME OF THE NASTIEST SHIT EVER PERPETRATED OVER THE LAST FIVE HUNDRED YEARS. THAT KIND OF THING LEAVES A STAIN ON A ROOM...
AND MAYBE SOMETHING GOT A WHIFF OF IT.
SOME... THING?
TELL ME ABOUT THE GIRL.
SHE WASN'T THE FIRST, WAS SHE?

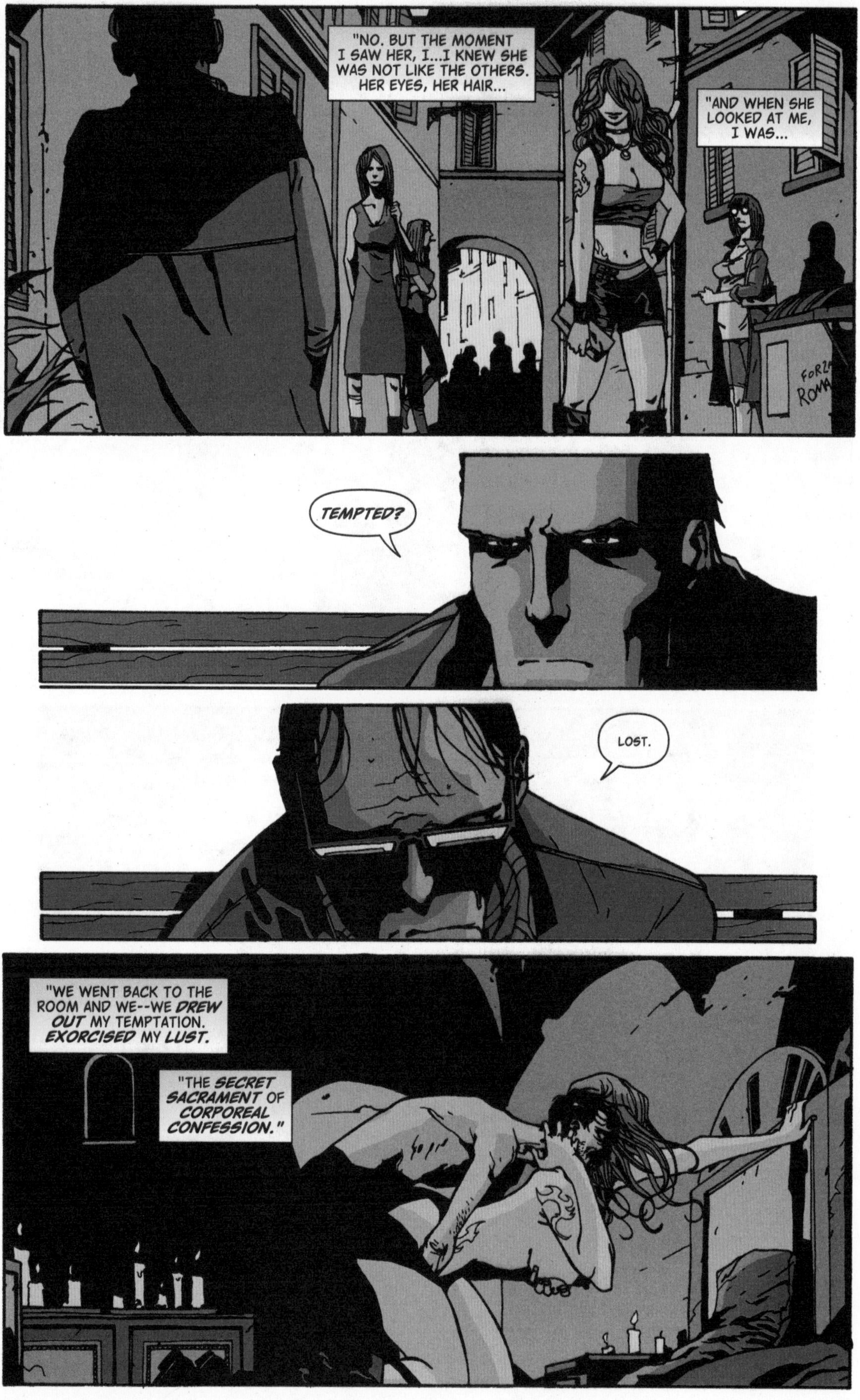
"NO. BUT THE MOMENT I SAW HER, I...I KNEW SHE WAS NOT LIKE THE OTHERS. HER EYES, HER HAIR...
"AND WHEN SHE LOOKED AT ME, I WAS...
FORZA ROMA
TEMPTED?
LOST.
"WE WENT BACK TO THE ROOM AND WE--WE DREW OUT MY TEMPTATION. EXORCISED MY LUST.
"THE SECRET SACRAMENT OF CORPOREAL CONFESSION."

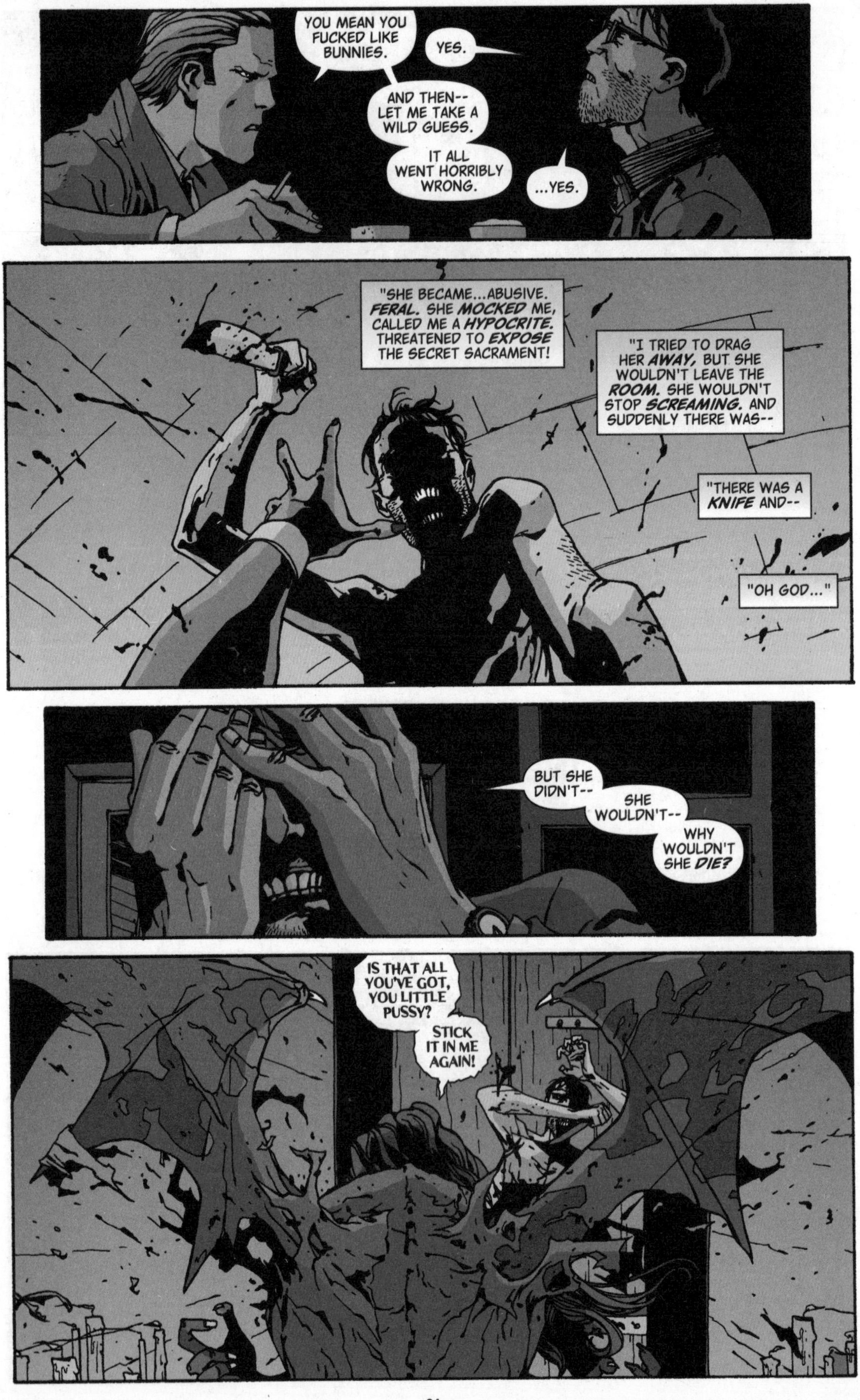
YOU MEAN YOU FUCKED LIKE BUNNIES.
YES.
AND THEN-- LET ME TAKE A WILD GUESS.
IT ALL WENT HORRIBLY WRONG.
...YES.
"SHE BECAME...ABUSIVE. FERAL. SHE MOCKED ME, CALLED ME A HYPOCRITE. THREATENED TO EXPOSE THE SECRET SACRAMENT!
"I TRIED TO DRAG HER AWAY, BUT SHE WOULDN'T LEAVE THE ROOM. SHE WOULDN'T STOP SCREAMING. AND SUDDENLY THERE WAS--
"THERE WAS A KNIFE AND--
"OH GOD..."
BUT SHE DIDN'T--
SHE WOULDN'T--
WHY WOULDN'T SHE DIE?
IS THAT ALL YOU'VE GOT, YOU LITTLE PUSSY?
STICK IT IN ME AGAIN!

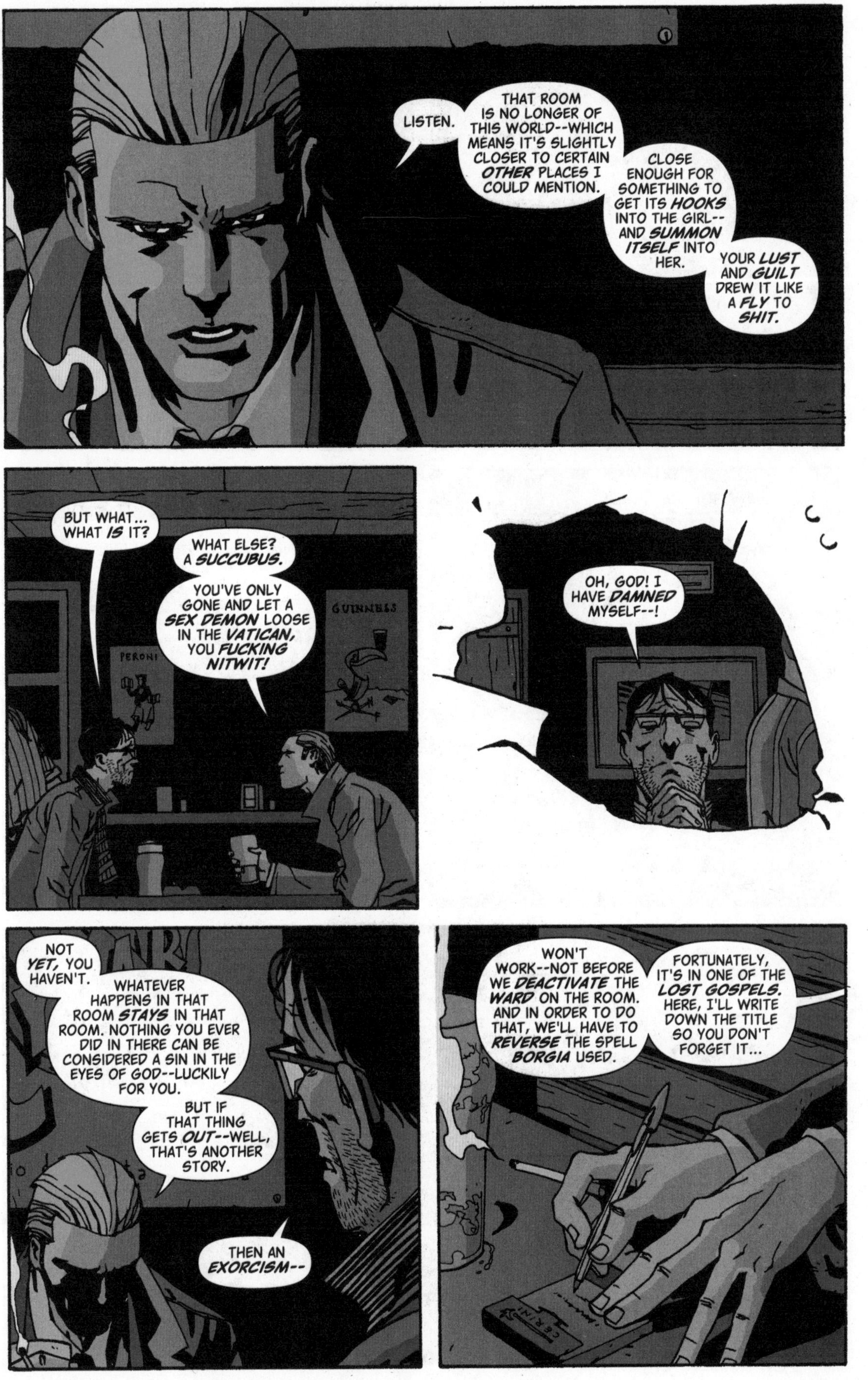
LISTEN.
THAT ROOM IS NO LONGER OF THIS WORLD--WHICH MEANS IT'S SLIGHTLY CLOSER TO CERTAIN OTHER PLACES I COULD MENTION.
CLOSE ENOUGH FOR SOMETHING TO GET ITS HOOKS INTO THE GIRL--AND SUMMON ITSELF INTO HER.
YOUR LUST AND GUILT DREW IT LIKE A FLY TO SHIT.
BUT WHAT... WHAT IS IT?
WHAT ELSE? A SUCCUBUS.
YOU'VE ONLY GONE AND LET A SEX DEMON LOOSE IN THE VATICAN, YOU FUCKING NITWIT!
PERONI
GUINNESS
OH, GOD! I HAVE DAMNED MYSELF--!
NOT YET, YOU HAVEN'T.
WHATEVER HAPPENS IN THAT ROOM STAYS IN THAT ROOM. NOTHING YOU EVER DID IN THERE CAN BE CONSIDERED A SIN IN THE EYES OF GOD--LUCKILY FOR YOU.
BUT IF THAT THING GETS OUT--WELL, THAT'S ANOTHER STORY.
THEN AN EXORCISM--
WON'T WORK--NOT BEFORE WE DEACTIVATE THE WARD ON THE ROOM. AND IN ORDER TO DO THAT, WE'LL HAVE TO REVERSE THE SPELL BORGIA USED.
FORTUNATELY, IT'S IN ONE OF THE LOST GOSPELS. HERE, I'LL WRITE DOWN THE TITLE SO YOU DON'T FORGET IT...

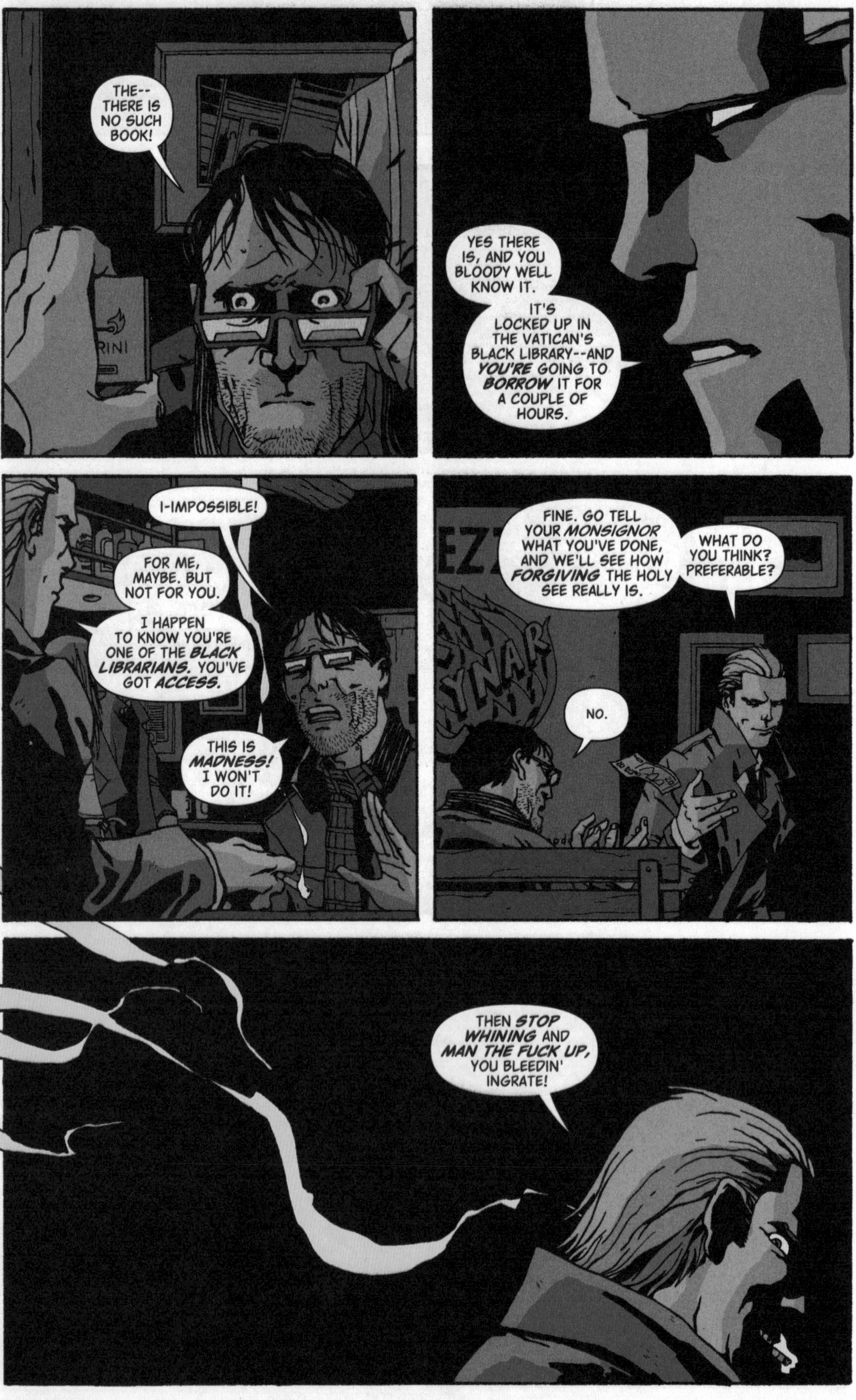
THE-- THERE IS NO SUCH BOOK!
YES THERE IS, AND YOU BLOODY WELL KNOW IT.
IT'S LOCKED UP IN THE VATICAN'S BLACK LIBRARY--AND YOU'RE GOING TO BORROW IT FOR A COUPLE OF HOURS.
I-IMPOSSIBLE!
FOR ME, MAYBE. BUT NOT FOR YOU.
I HAPPEN TO KNOW YOU'RE ONE OF THE BLACK LIBRARIANS. YOU'VE GOT ACCESS.
THIS IS MADNESS! I WON'T DO IT!
FINE. GO TELL YOUR MONSIGNOR WHAT YOU'VE DONE, AND WE'LL SEE HOW FORGIVING THE HOLY SEE REALLY IS.
WHAT DO YOU THINK? PREFERABLE?
NO.
THEN STOP WHINING AND MAN THE FUCK UP, YOU BLEEDIN' INGRATE!

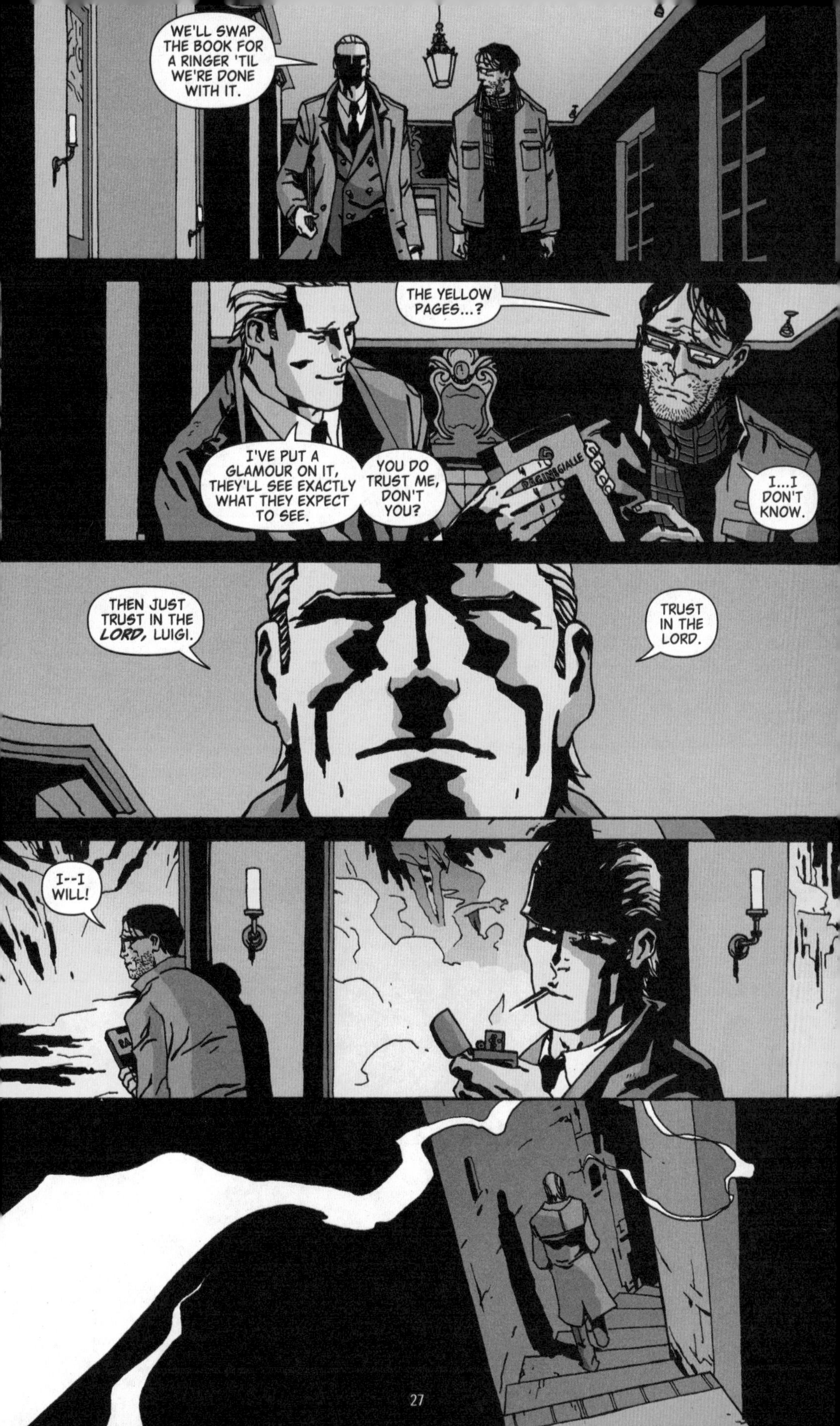
WE'LL SWAP THE BOOK FOR A RINGER 'TIL WE'RE DONE WITH IT.
THE YELLOW PAGES...?
I'VE PUT A GLAMOUR ON IT, THEY'LL SEE EXACTLY WHAT THEY EXPECT TO SEE.
YOU DO TRUST ME, DON'T YOU?
I...I DON'T KNOW.
THEN JUST TRUST IN THE LORD, LUIGI.
TRUST IN THE LORD.
I--I WILL!

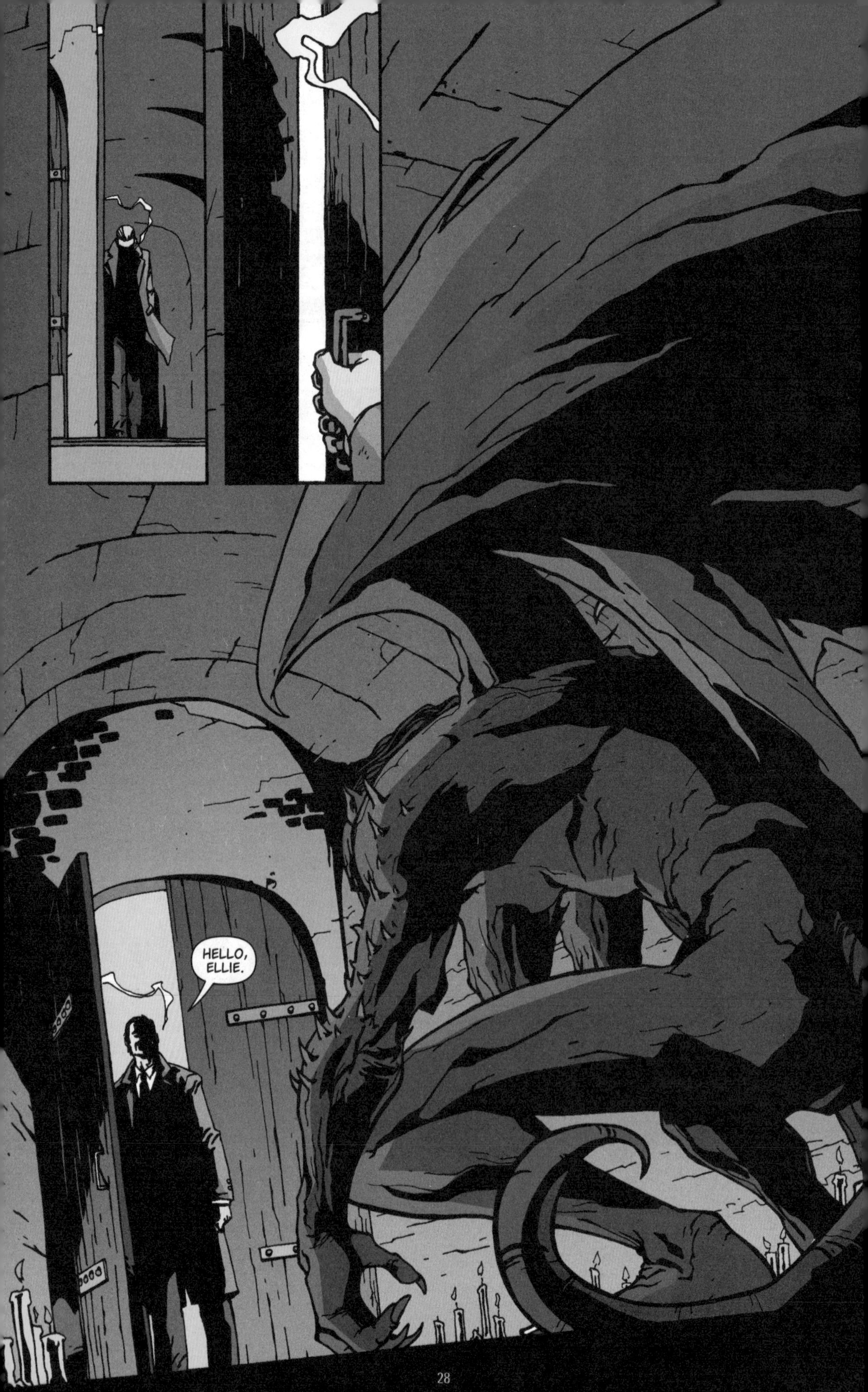
HELLO, ELLIE.

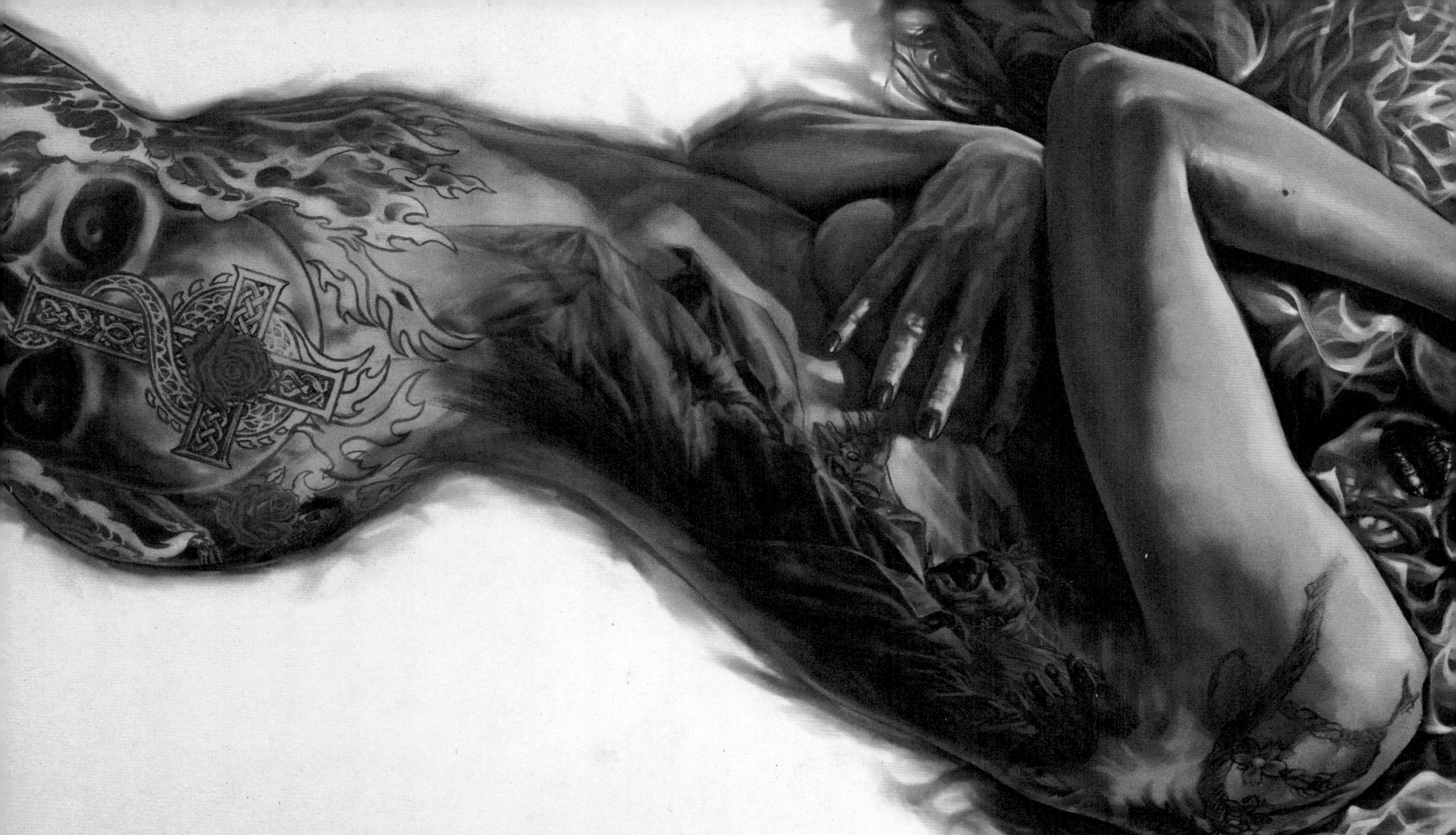

The Mortification of the Flesh, **Part Two**

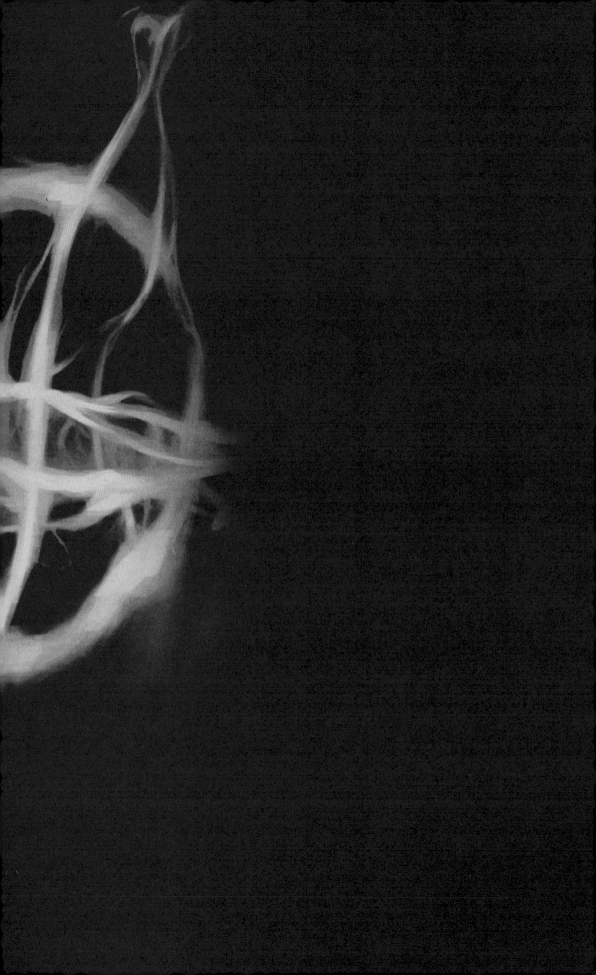

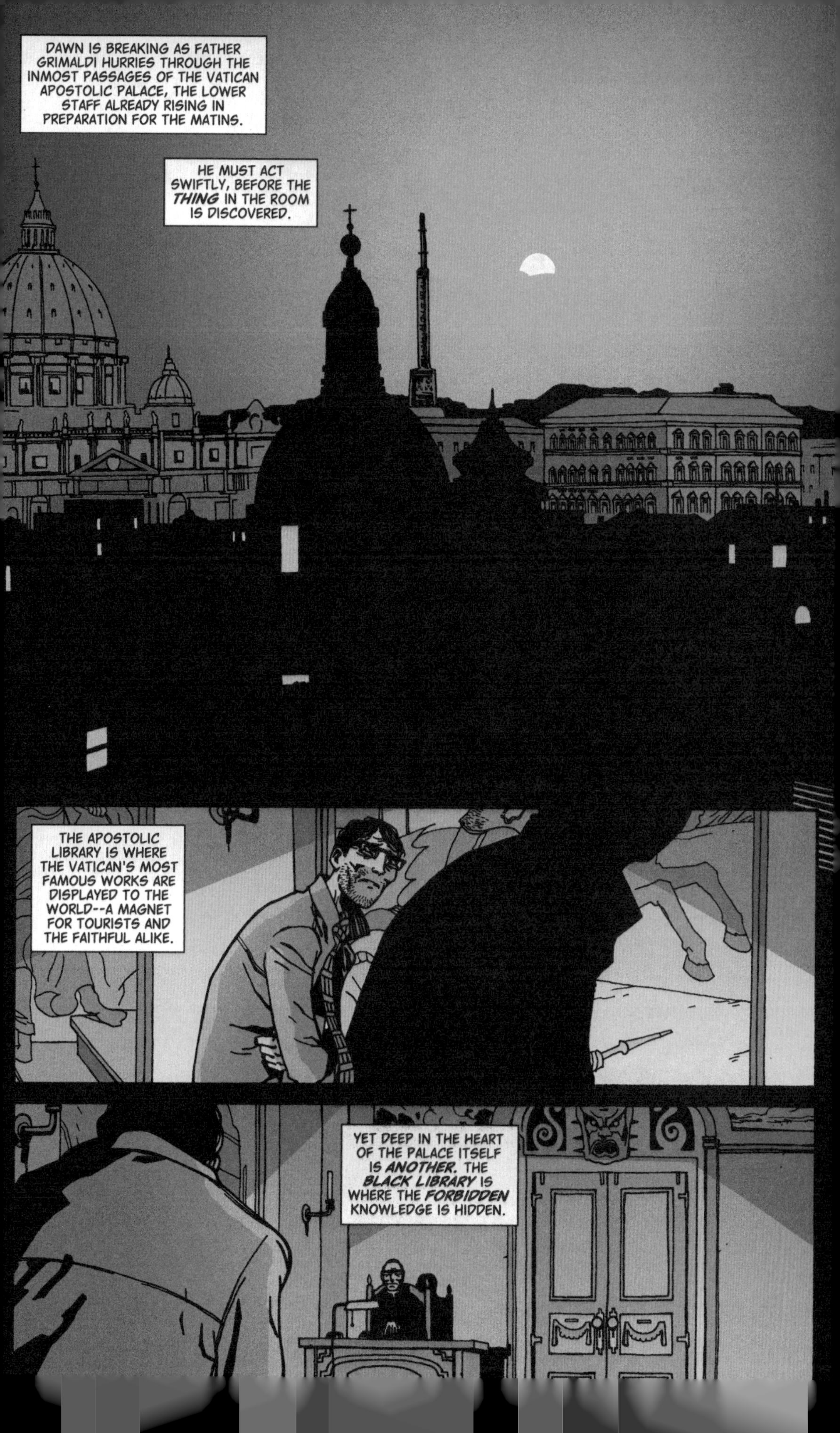
DAWN IS BREAKING AS FATHER GRIMALDI HURRIES THROUGH THE INMOST PASSAGES OF THE VATICAN APOSTOLIC PALACE, THE LOWER STAFF ALREADY RISING IN PREPARATION FOR THE MATINS.
HE MUST ACT SWIFTLY, BEFORE THE *THING* IN THE ROOM IS DISCOVERED.
THE APOSTOLIC LIBRARY IS WHERE THE VATICAN'S MOST FAMOUS WORKS ARE DISPLAYED TO THE WORLD--A MAGNET FOR TOURISTS AND THE FAITHFUL ALIKE.
YET DEEP IN THE HEART OF THE PALACE ITSELF IS *ANOTHER*. THE *BLACK LIBRARY* IS WHERE THE *FORBIDDEN* KNOWLEDGE IS HIDDEN.

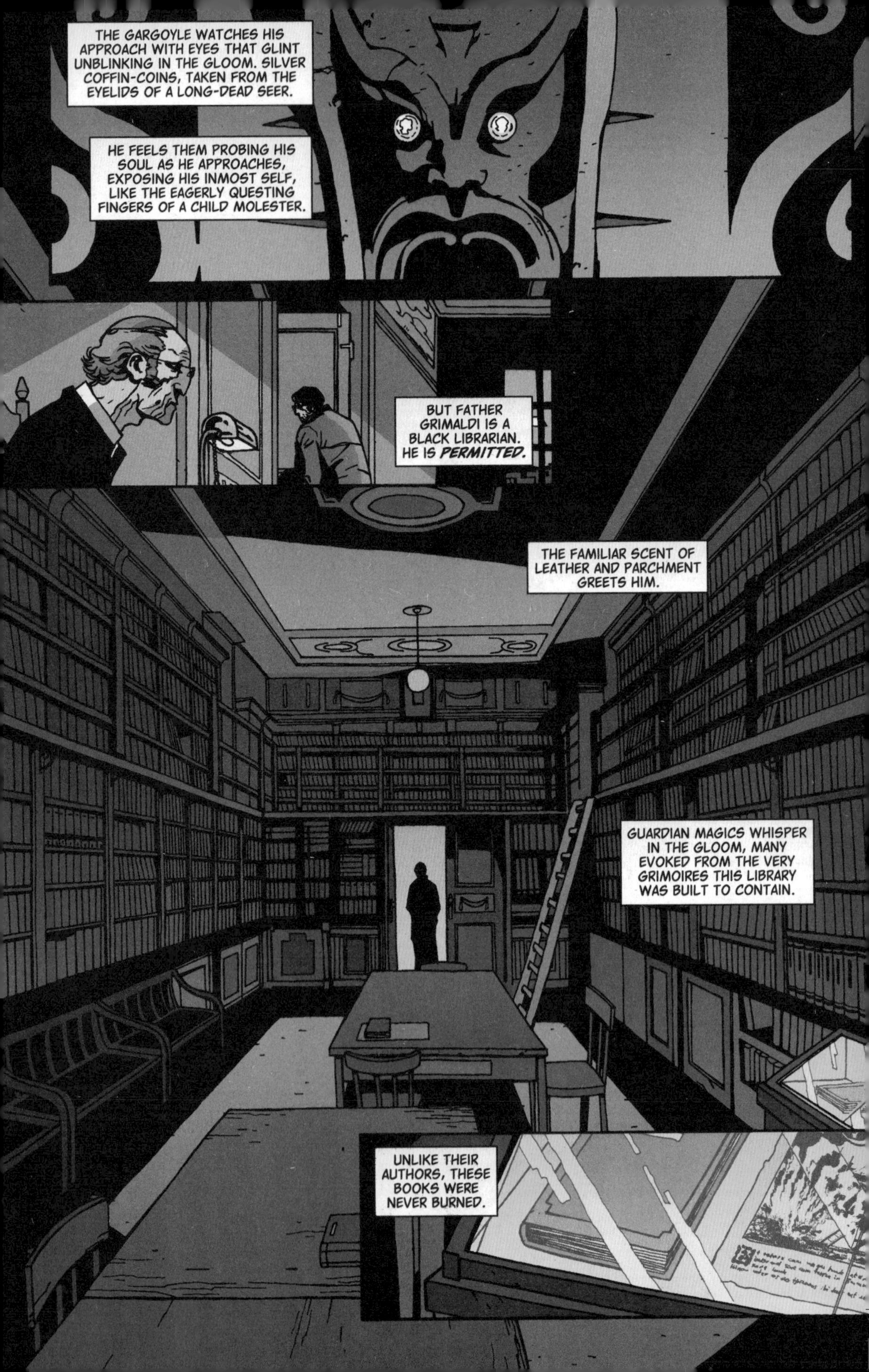
THE GARGOYLE WATCHES HIS APPROACH WITH EYES THAT GLINT UNBLINKING IN THE GLOOM. SILVER COFFIN-COINS, TAKEN FROM THE EYELIDS OF A LONG-DEAD SEER.
HE FEELS THEM PROBING HIS SOUL AS HE APPROACHES, EXPOSING HIS INMOST SELF, LIKE THE EAGERLY QUESTING FINGERS OF A CHILD MOLESTER.
BUT FATHER GRIMALDI IS A BLACK LIBRARIAN. HE IS *PERMITTED.*
THE FAMILIAR SCENT OF LEATHER AND PARCHMENT GREETS HIM.
GUARDIAN MAGICS WHISPER IN THE GLOOM, MANY EVOKED FROM THE VERY GRIMOIRES THIS LIBRARY WAS BUILT TO CONTAIN.
UNLIKE THEIR AUTHORS, THESE BOOKS WERE NEVER BURNED.

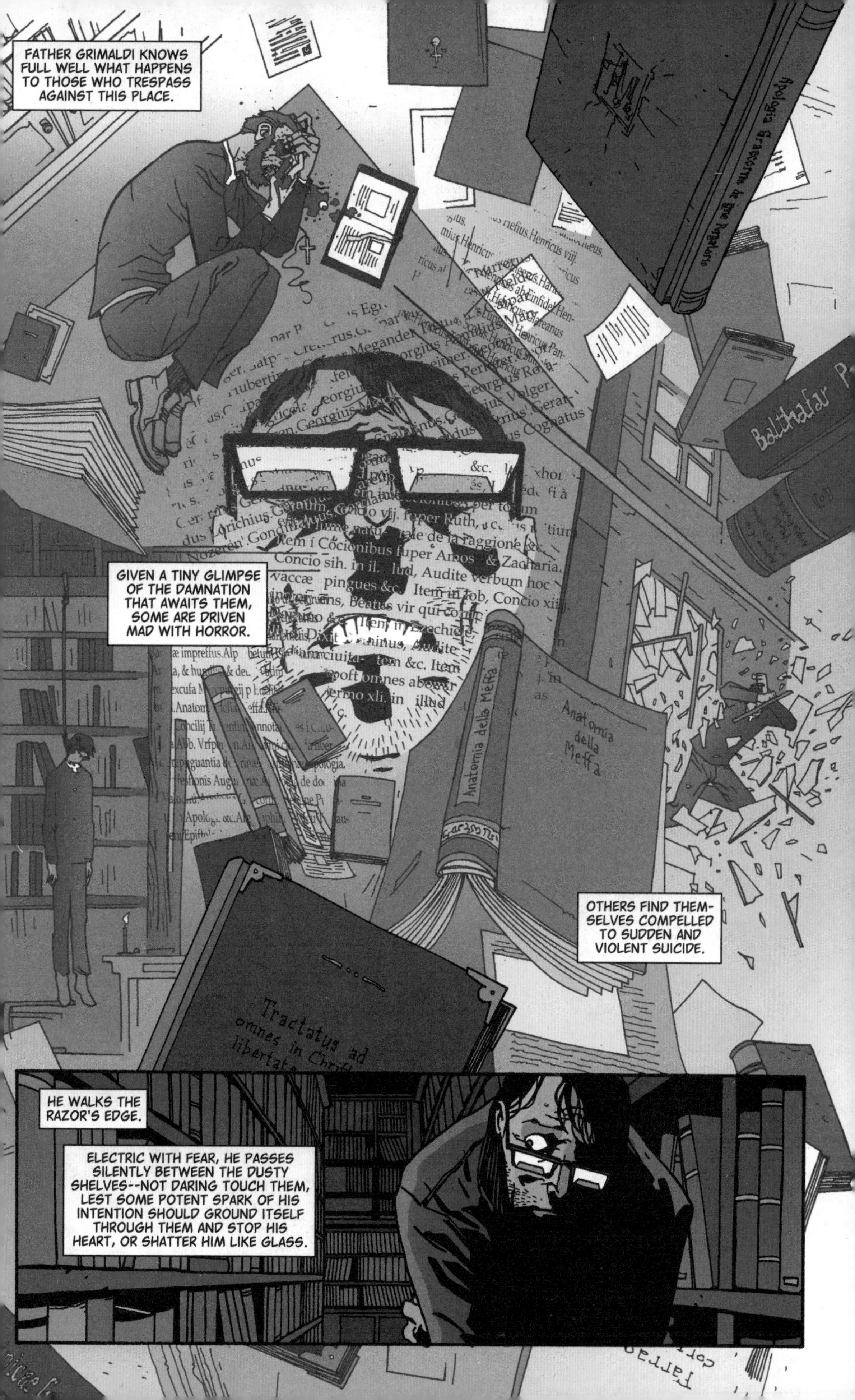
FATHER GRIMALDI KNOWS FULL WELL WHAT HAPPENS TO THOSE WHO TRESPASS AGAINST THIS PLACE.
GIVEN A TINY GLIMPSE OF THE DAMNATION THAT AWAITS THEM, SOME ARE DRIVEN MAD WITH HORROR.
OTHERS FIND THEMSELVES COMPELLED TO SUDDEN AND VIOLENT SUICIDE.
HE WALKS THE RAZOR'S EDGE.
ELECTRIC WITH FEAR, HE PASSES SILENTLY BETWEEN THE DUSTY SHELVES--NOT DARING TOUCH THEM, LEST SOME POTENT SPARK OF HIS INTENTION SHOULD GROUND ITSELF THROUGH THEM AND STOP HIS HEART, OR SHATTER HIM LIKE GLASS.

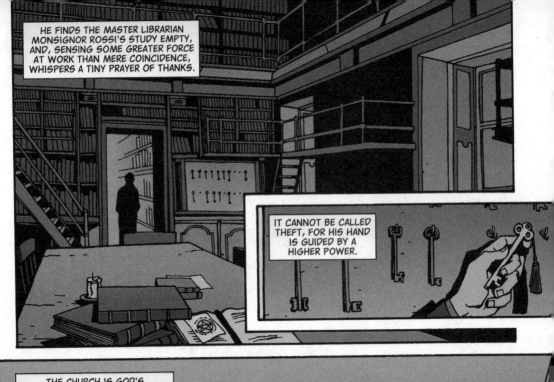

HE FINDS THE MASTER LIBRARIAN MONSIGNOR ROSSI'S STUDY EMPTY, AND, SENSING SOME GREATER FORCE AT WORK THAN MERE COINCIDENCE, WHISPERS A TINY PRAYER OF THANKS.

IT CANNOT BE CALLED THEFT, FOR HIS HAND IS GUIDED BY A HIGHER POWER.

THE CHURCH IS GOD'S INSTRUMENT ON THIS EARTH, AND IT MUST BE PROTECTED AT ALL COSTS--EVEN FROM ITSELF.

KNOWLEDGE IS POWER, AND THE MOST DANGEROUS BOOKS ARE CAGED LIKE JUNGLE BEASTS.

SOME ARE BOUND IN THE SKIN OF THEIR AUTHORS, FLAYED FROM THEIR LIVING FLESH BY SKILLFUL INTERROGATORS...

BUT NOT THIS BOOK. IT IS ONE OF THE LOST GOSPELS THAT FATHER GRIMALDI HAS COME FOR.

THE LAST REMAINING COPY OF A HERETICAL WORK PASSED DOWN THROUGH THE SHADOWS OF THE CENTURIES. ITS COVER BEARS NO TITLE, ITS VERY EXISTENCE DENIED.

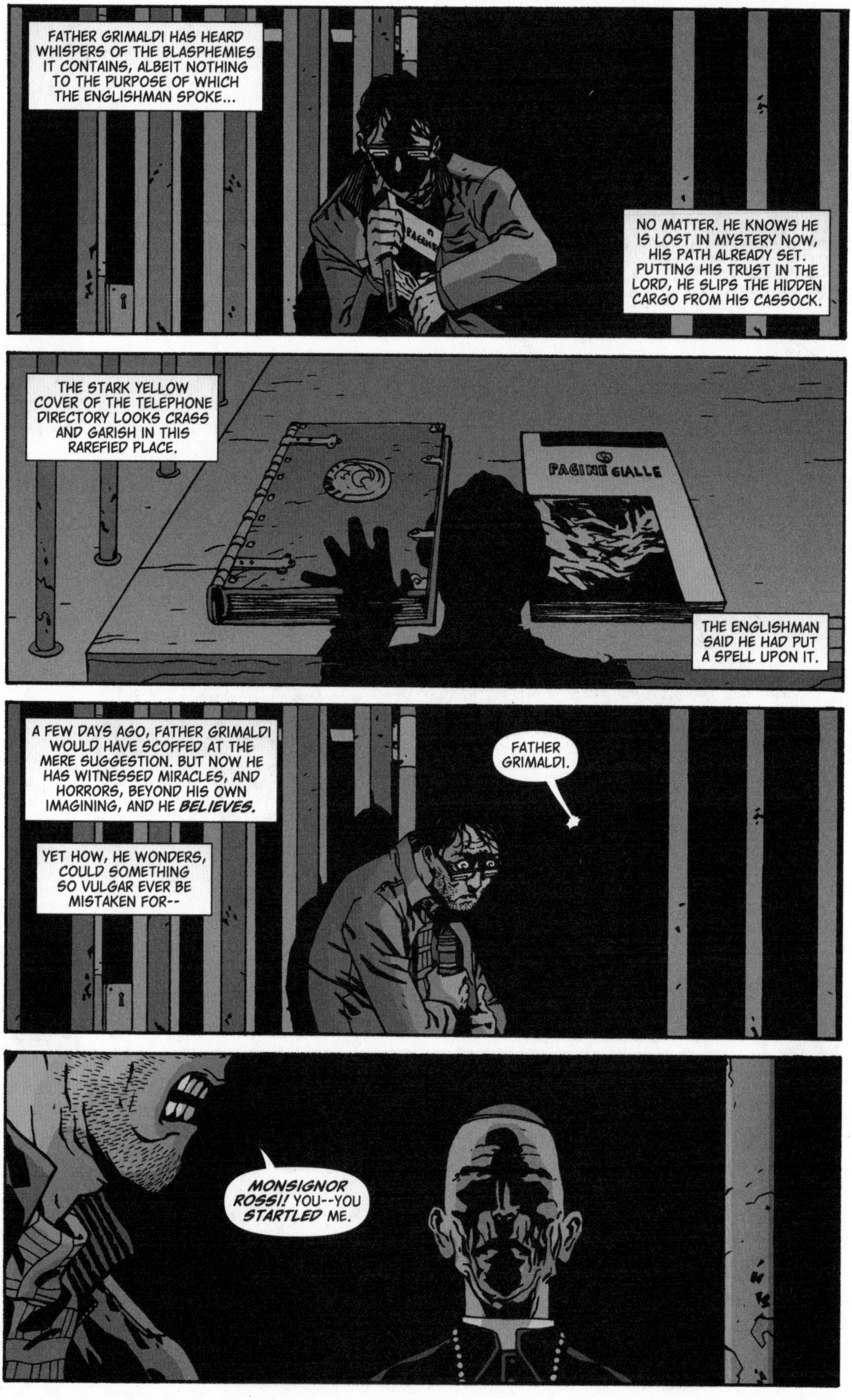
FATHER GRIMALDI HAS HEARD WHISPERS OF THE BLASPHEMIES IT CONTAINS, ALBEIT NOTHING TO THE PURPOSE OF WHICH THE ENGLISHMAN SPOKE...
NO MATTER. HE KNOWS HE IS LOST IN MYSTERY NOW, HIS PATH ALREADY SET. PUTTING HIS TRUST IN THE LORD, HE SLIPS THE HIDDEN CARGO FROM HIS CASSOCK.
THE STARK YELLOW COVER OF THE TELEPHONE DIRECTORY LOOKS CRASS AND GARISH IN THIS RAREFIED PLACE.
PAGINE GIALLE
THE ENGLISHMAN SAID HE HAD PUT A SPELL UPON IT.
A FEW DAYS AGO, FATHER GRIMALDI WOULD HAVE SCOFFED AT THE MERE SUGGESTION. BUT NOW HE HAS WITNESSED MIRACLES, AND HORRORS, BEYOND HIS OWN IMAGINING, AND HE ***BELIEVES.***
YET HOW, HE WONDERS, COULD SOMETHING SO VULGAR EVER BE MISTAKEN FOR--
FATHER GRIMALDI.
MONSIGNOR ROSSI! YOU--YOU ***STARTLED*** ME.

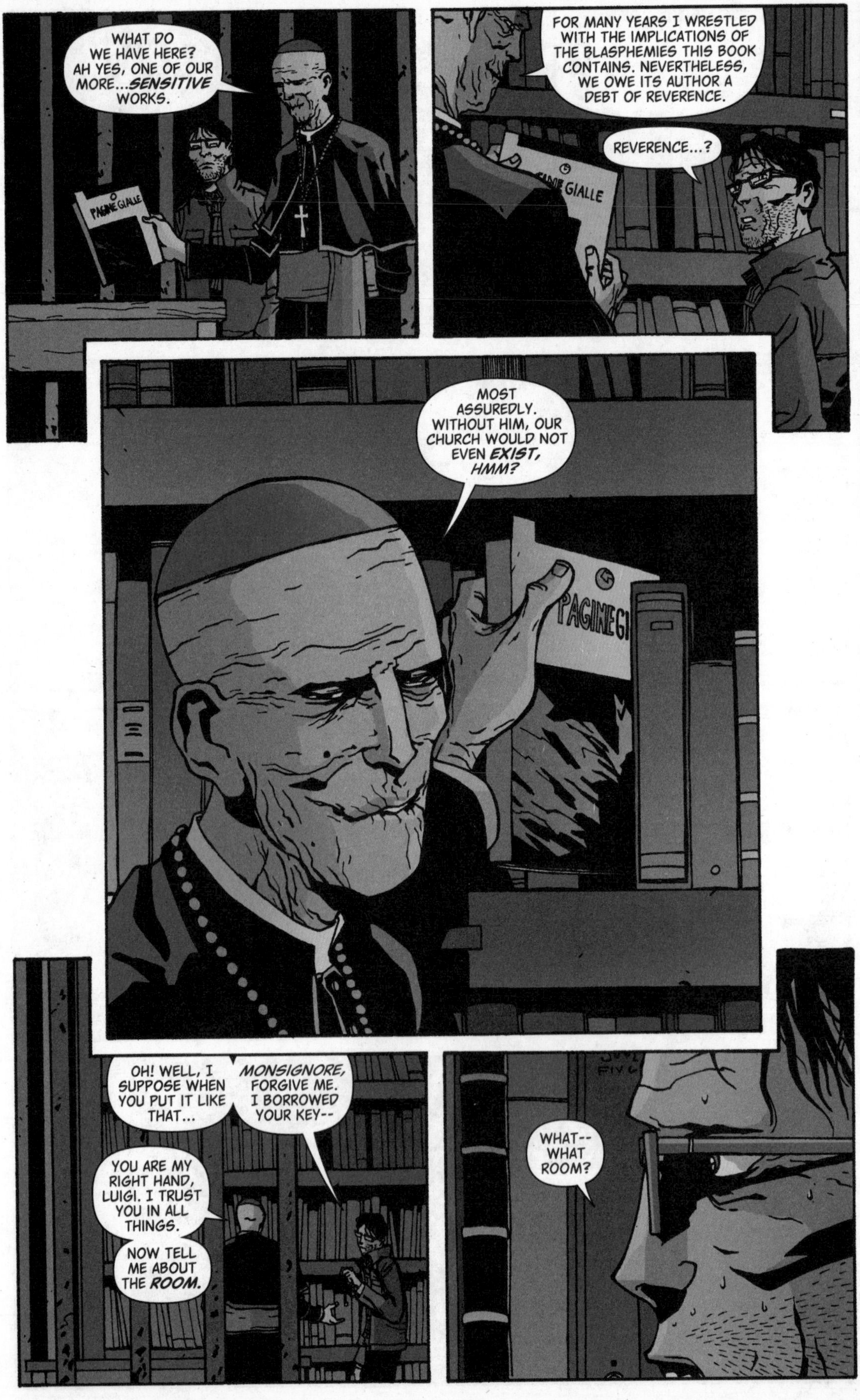
WHAT DO WE HAVE HERE? AH YES, ONE OF OUR MORE...SENSITIVE WORKS.
PAGINE GIALLE
FOR MANY YEARS I WRESTLED WITH THE IMPLICATIONS OF THE BLASPHEMIES THIS BOOK CONTAINS. NEVERTHELESS, WE OWE ITS AUTHOR A DEBT OF REVERENCE.
REVERENCE...?
MOST ASSUREDLY. WITHOUT HIM, OUR CHURCH WOULD NOT EVEN EXIST, HMM?
OH! WELL, I SUPPOSE WHEN YOU PUT IT LIKE THAT...
MONSIGNORE, FORGIVE ME. I BORROWED YOUR KEY--
YOU ARE MY RIGHT HAND, LUIGI. I TRUST YOU IN ALL THINGS.
NOW TELL ME ABOUT THE ROOM.
WHAT-- WHAT ROOM?

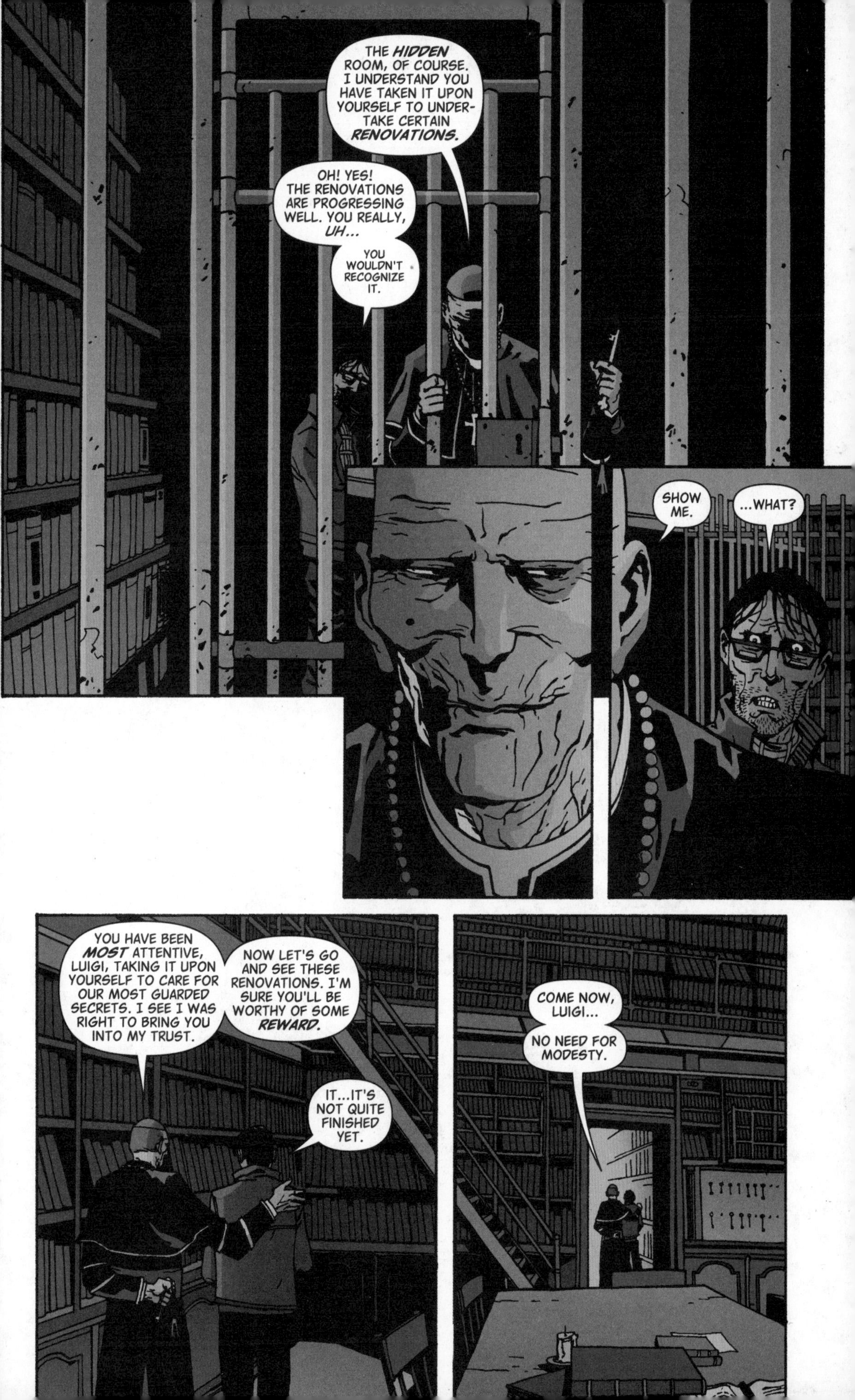

THE HIDDEN ROOM, OF COURSE. I UNDERSTAND YOU HAVE TAKEN IT UPON YOURSELF TO UNDER-TAKE CERTAIN RENOVATIONS.
OH! YES! THE RENOVATIONS ARE PROGRESSING WELL. YOU REALLY, UH...
YOU WOULDN'T RECOGNIZE IT.
SHOW ME.
...WHAT?
YOU HAVE BEEN MOST ATTENTIVE, LUIGI, TAKING IT UPON YOURSELF TO CARE FOR OUR MOST GUARDED SECRETS. I SEE I WAS RIGHT TO BRING YOU INTO MY TRUST.
NOW LET'S GO AND SEE THESE RENOVATIONS. I'M SURE YOU'LL BE WORTHY OF SOME REWARD.
IT...IT'S NOT QUITE FINISHED YET.
COME NOW, LUIGI...
NO NEED FOR MODESTY.

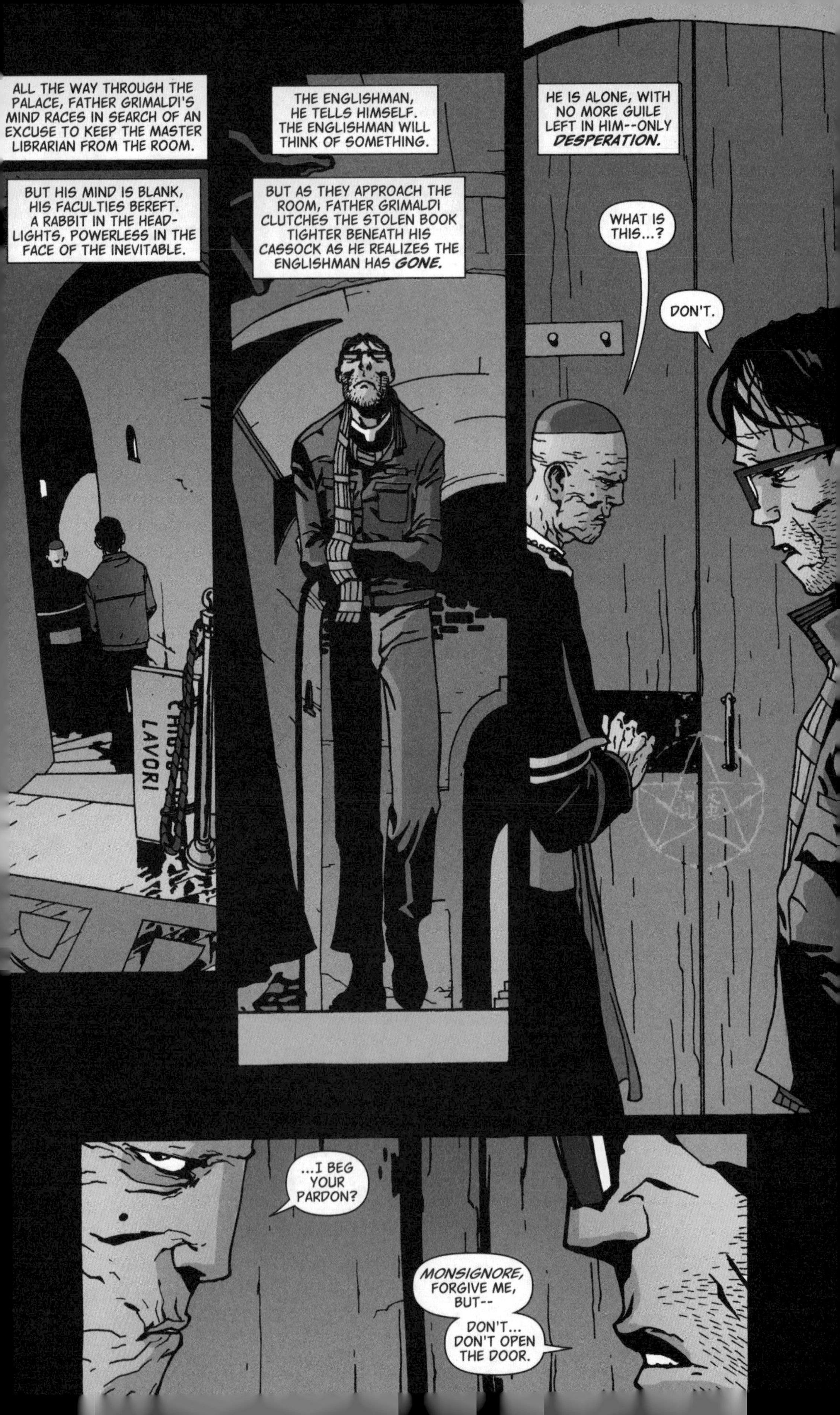
ALL THE WAY THROUGH THE PALACE, FATHER GRIMALDI'S MIND RACES IN SEARCH OF AN EXCUSE TO KEEP THE MASTER LIBRARIAN FROM THE ROOM.
BUT HIS MIND IS BLANK, HIS FACULTIES BEREFT. A RABBIT IN THE HEAD-LIGHTS, POWERLESS IN THE FACE OF THE INEVITABLE.
LAVORI
THE ENGLISHMAN, HE TELLS HIMSELF. THE ENGLISHMAN WILL THINK OF SOMETHING.
BUT AS THEY APPROACH THE ROOM, FATHER GRIMALDI CLUTCHES THE STOLEN BOOK TIGHTER BENEATH HIS CASSOCK AS HE REALIZES THE ENGLISHMAN HAS *GONE.*
HE IS ALONE, WITH NO MORE GUILE LEFT IN HIM--ONLY *DESPERATION.*
WHAT IS THIS...?
DON'T.
...I BEG YOUR PARDON?
MONSIGNORE, FORGIVE ME, BUT--
DON'T... DON'T OPEN THE DOOR.

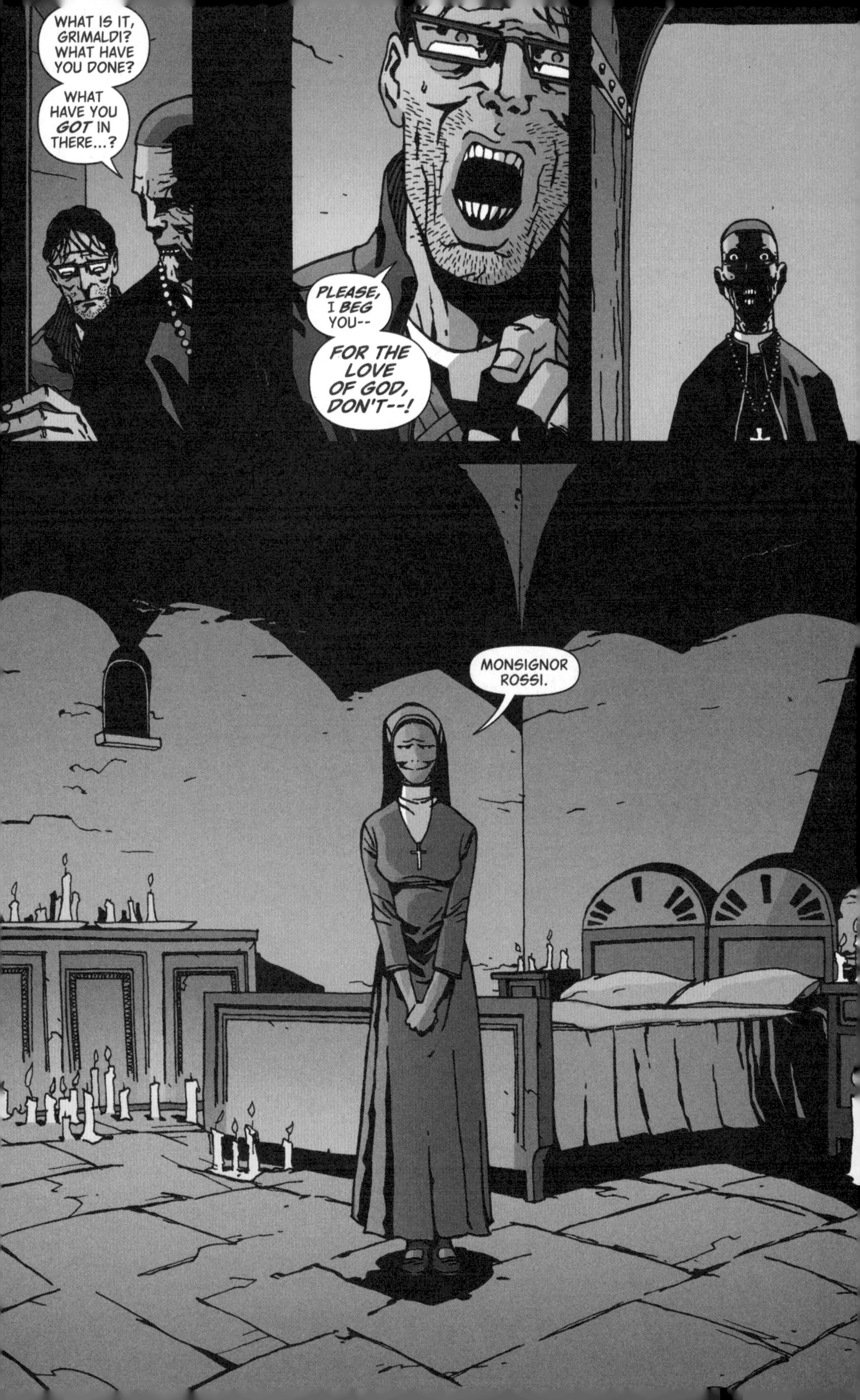
WHAT IS IT, GRIMALDI? WHAT HAVE YOU DONE?
WHAT HAVE YOU GOT IN THERE...?
PLEASE, I BEG YOU--
FOR THE LOVE OF GOD, DON'T--!
MONSIGNOR ROSSI.

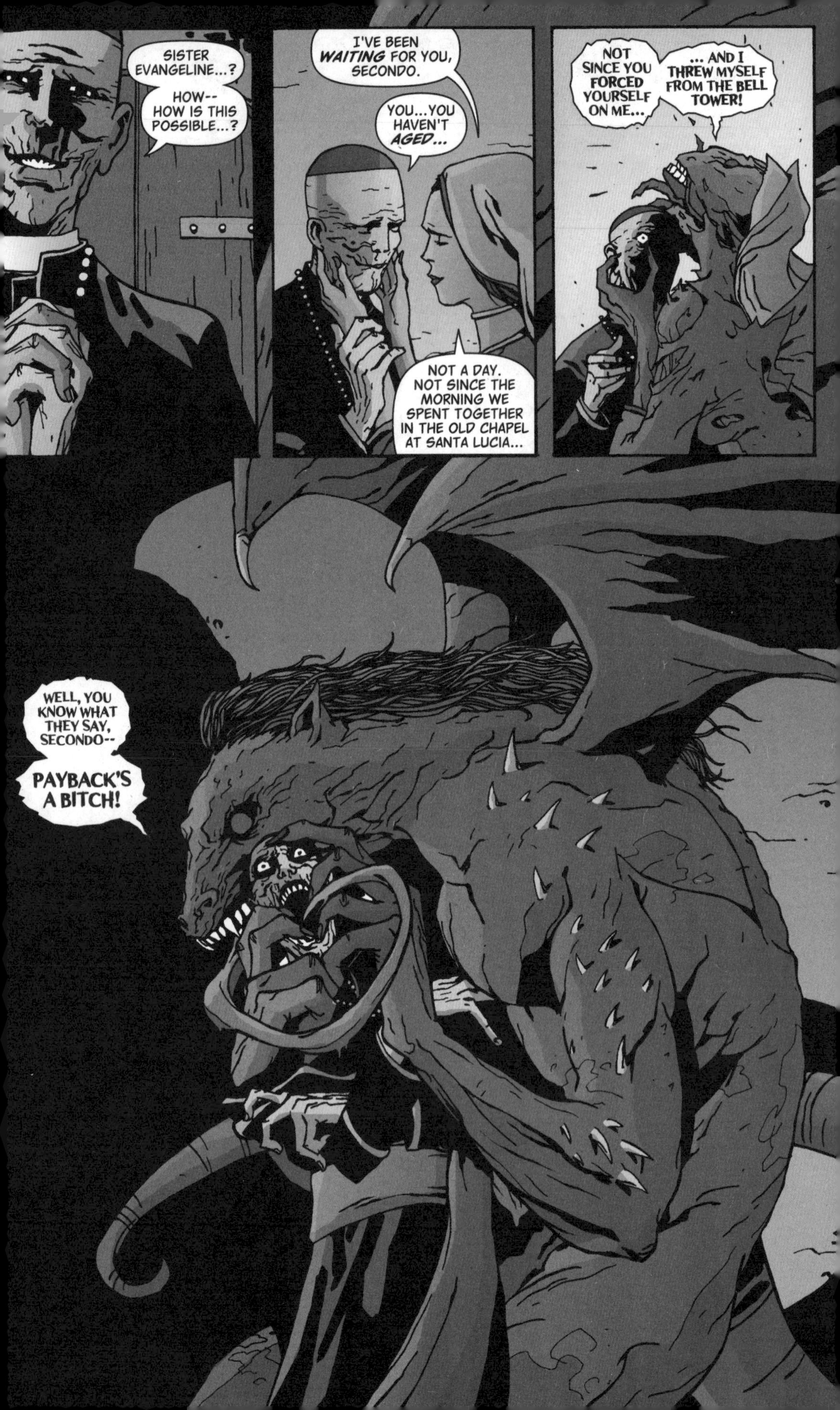
SISTER EVANGELINE...?
HOW-- HOW IS THIS POSSIBLE...?
I'VE BEEN WAITING FOR YOU, SECONDO.
YOU...YOU HAVEN'T AGED...
NOT A DAY. NOT SINCE THE MORNING WE SPENT TOGETHER IN THE OLD CHAPEL AT SANTA LUCIA...
NOT SINCE YOU FORCED YOURSELF ON ME...
... AND I THREW MYSELF FROM THE BELL TOWER!
WELL, YOU KNOW WHAT THEY SAY, SECONDO--
PAYBACK'S A BITCH!

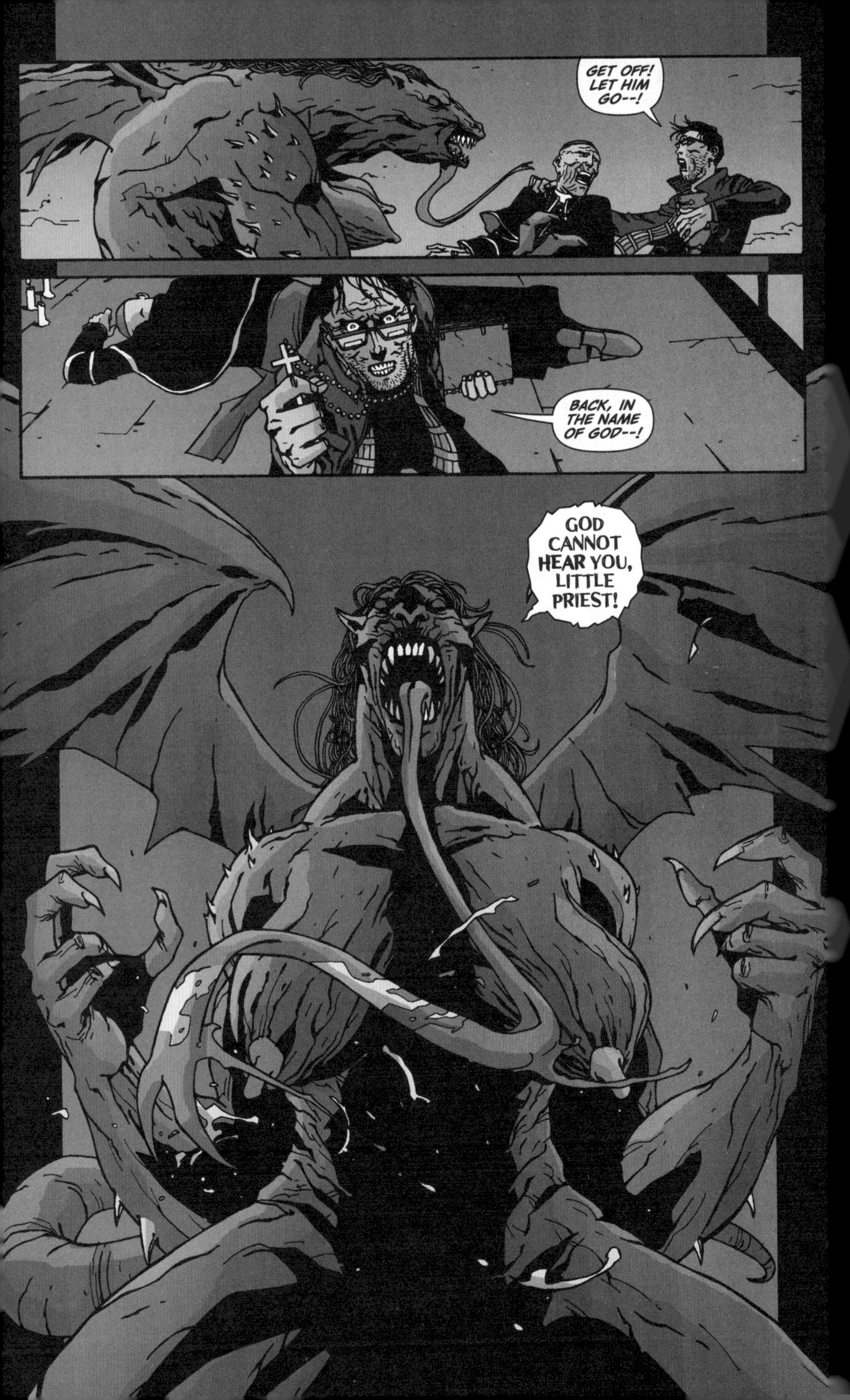
GET OFF! LET HIM GO--!
BACK, IN THE NAME OF GOD--!
GOD CANNOT HEAR YOU, LITTLE PRIEST!

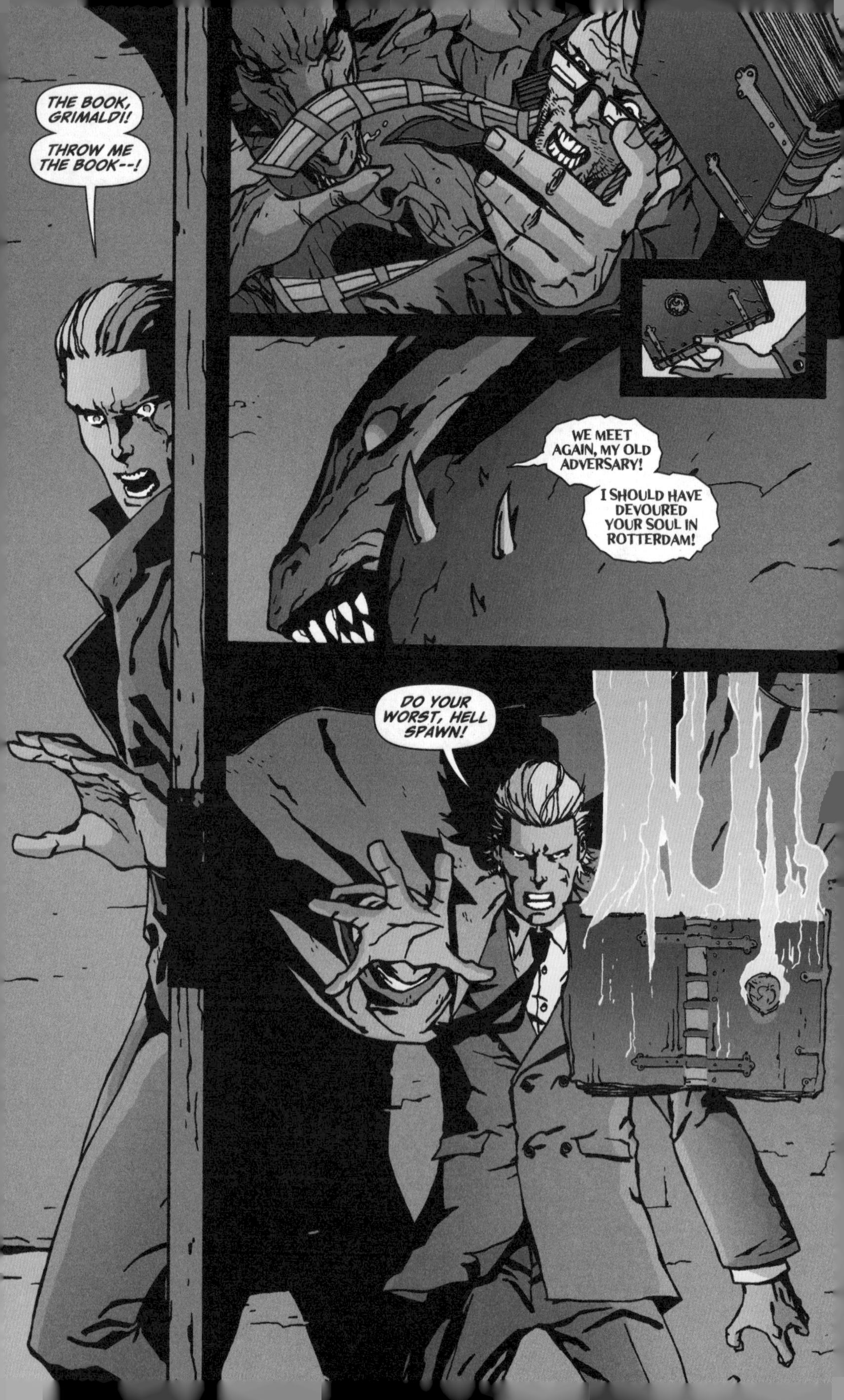
THE BOOK, GRIMALDI!
THROW ME THE BOOK--!
WE MEET AGAIN, MY OLD ADVERSARY!
I SHOULD HAVE DEVOURED YOUR SOUL IN ROTTERDAM!
DO YOUR WORST, HELL SPAWN!

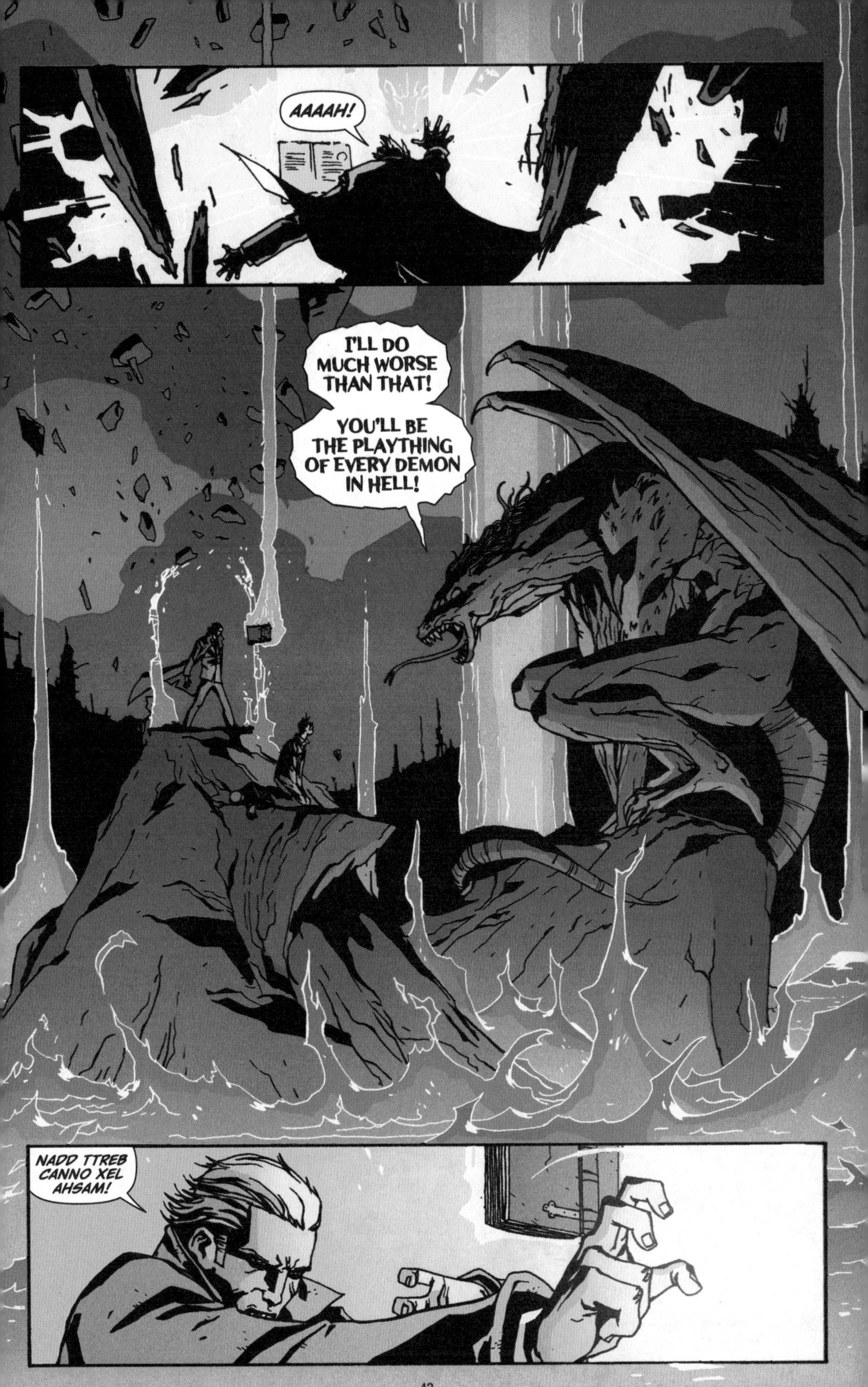
AAAAH!
I'LL DO MUCH WORSE THAN THAT!
YOU'LL BE THE PLAYTHING OF EVERY DEMON IN HELL!
NADD TTREB CANNO XEL AHSAM!

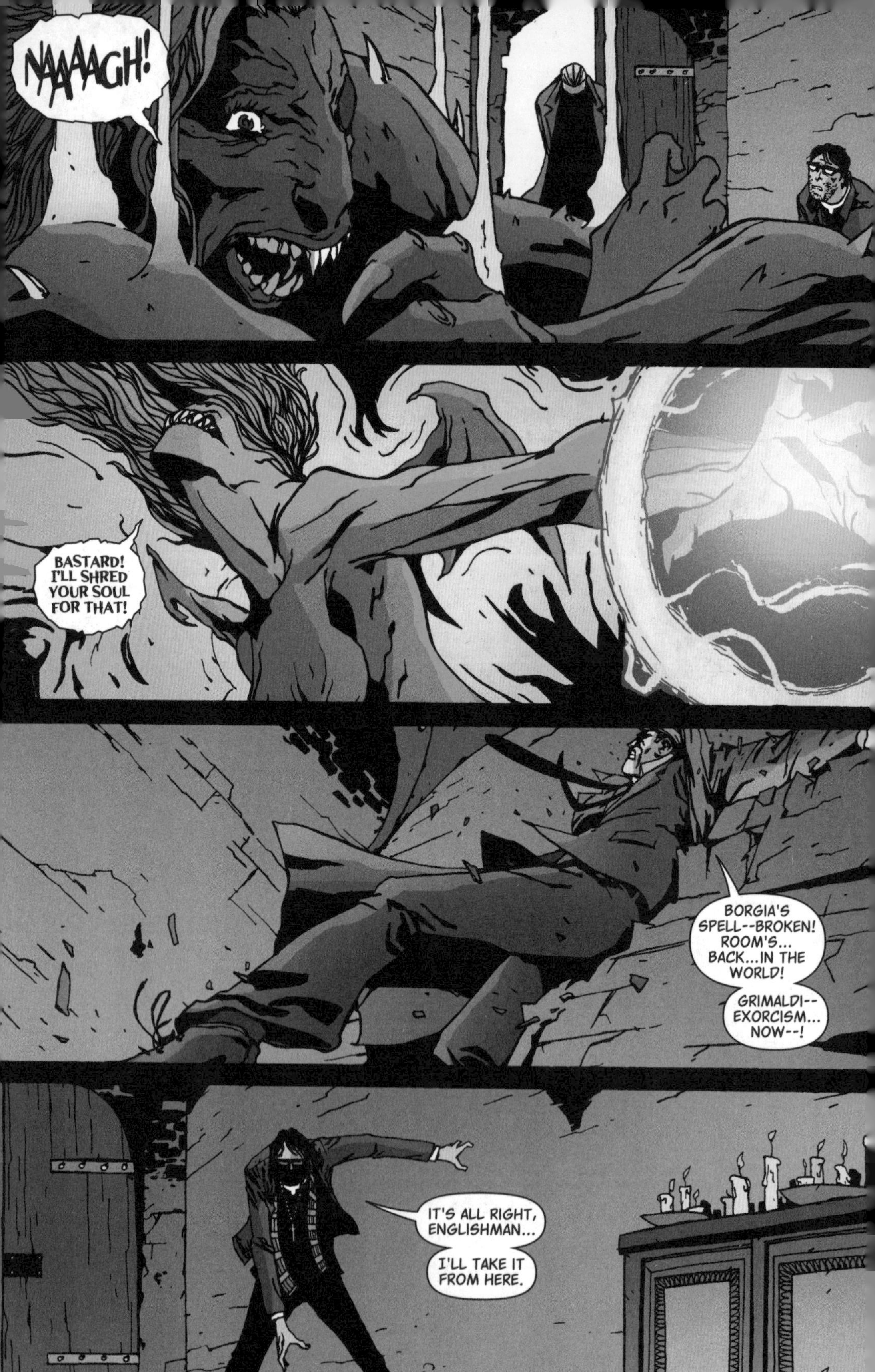
NAAAAGH!
BASTARD! I'LL SHRED YOUR SOUL FOR THAT!
BORGIA'S SPELL--BROKEN! ROOM'S... BACK...IN THE WORLD!
GRIMALDI-- EXORCISM... NOW--!
IT'S ALL RIGHT, ENGLISHMAN...
I'LL TAKE IT FROM HERE.

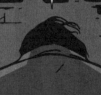

WHAT DO YOU SAY, LOVERBOY-- READY TO GO AGAIN?

MY GOD *IS* FORGIVENESS.

AMEN.

IT'S NOT OVER, LITTLE PRIEST!

YOUR GOD WILL NOT FORGIVE YOU FOR WHAT YOU HAVE DONE! HE WILL NEVER FORGIVE YOU--!

EXORCISO TE, IMMUNDISSIME SPIRITUS, OMNIS INCURSIO ADVERSARII, OMNE PHANTASMA, OMNIS LEGIO, IN NOMINE DOMINI NOSTRI JESU CHRISTI ERADICARE, ET EFFUGARE AB HOC PLASMATE DEI!

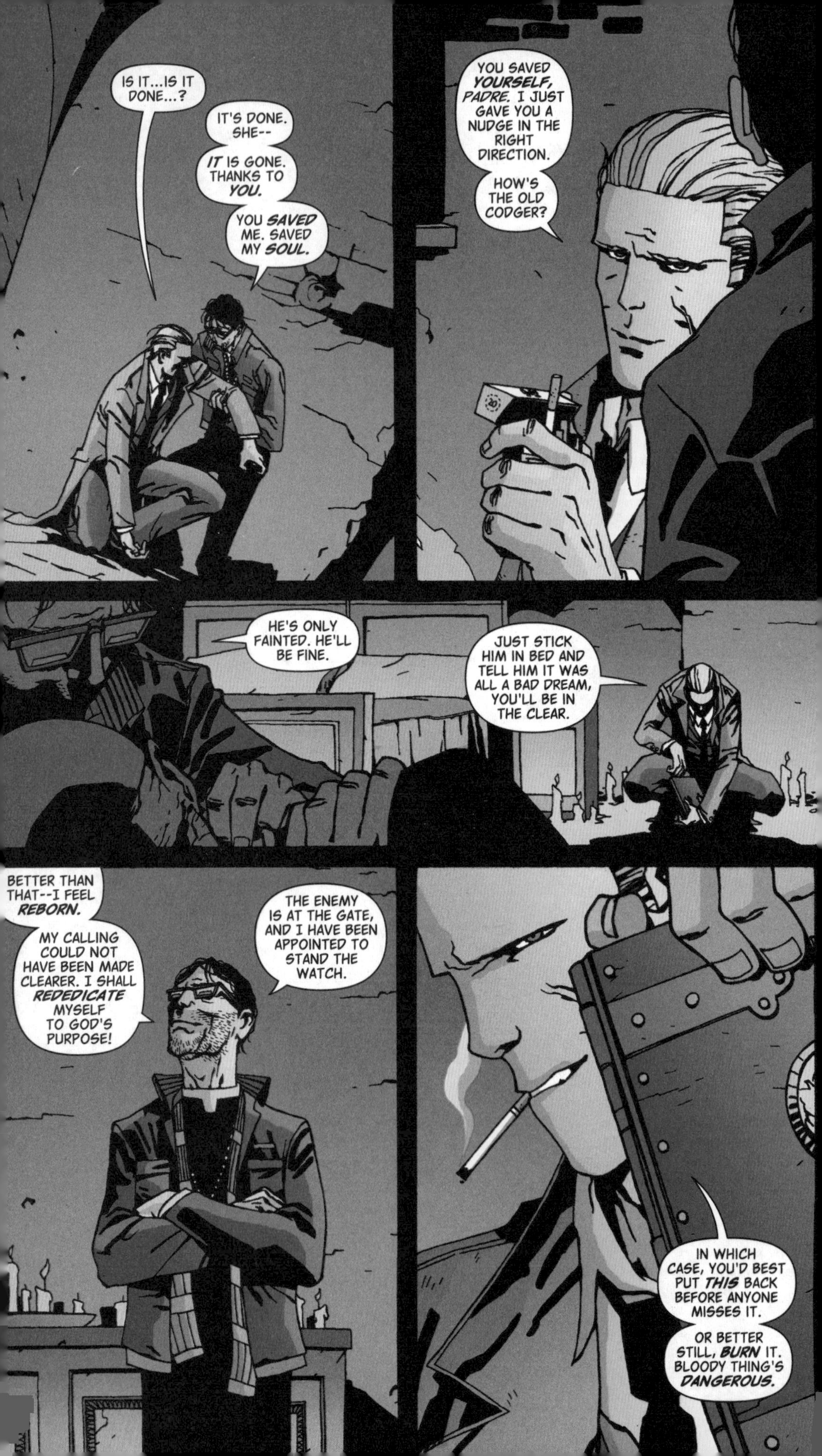
IS IT...IS IT DONE...?
IT'S DONE. SHE--
IT IS GONE. THANKS TO YOU.
YOU SAVED ME. SAVED MY SOUL.
YOU SAVED YOURSELF, PADRE. I JUST GAVE YOU A NUDGE IN THE RIGHT DIRECTION.
HOW'S THE OLD CODGER?
HE'S ONLY FAINTED. HE'LL BE FINE.
JUST STICK HIM IN BED AND TELL HIM IT WAS ALL A BAD DREAM, YOU'LL BE IN THE CLEAR.
BETTER THAN THAT--I FEEL REBORN.
MY CALLING COULD NOT HAVE BEEN MADE CLEARER. I SHALL REDEDICATE MYSELF TO GOD'S PURPOSE!
THE ENEMY IS AT THE GATE, AND I HAVE BEEN APPOINTED TO STAND THE WATCH.
IN WHICH CASE, YOU'D BEST PUT THIS BACK BEFORE ANYONE MISSES IT.
OR BETTER STILL, BURN IT. BLOODY THING'S DANGEROUS.

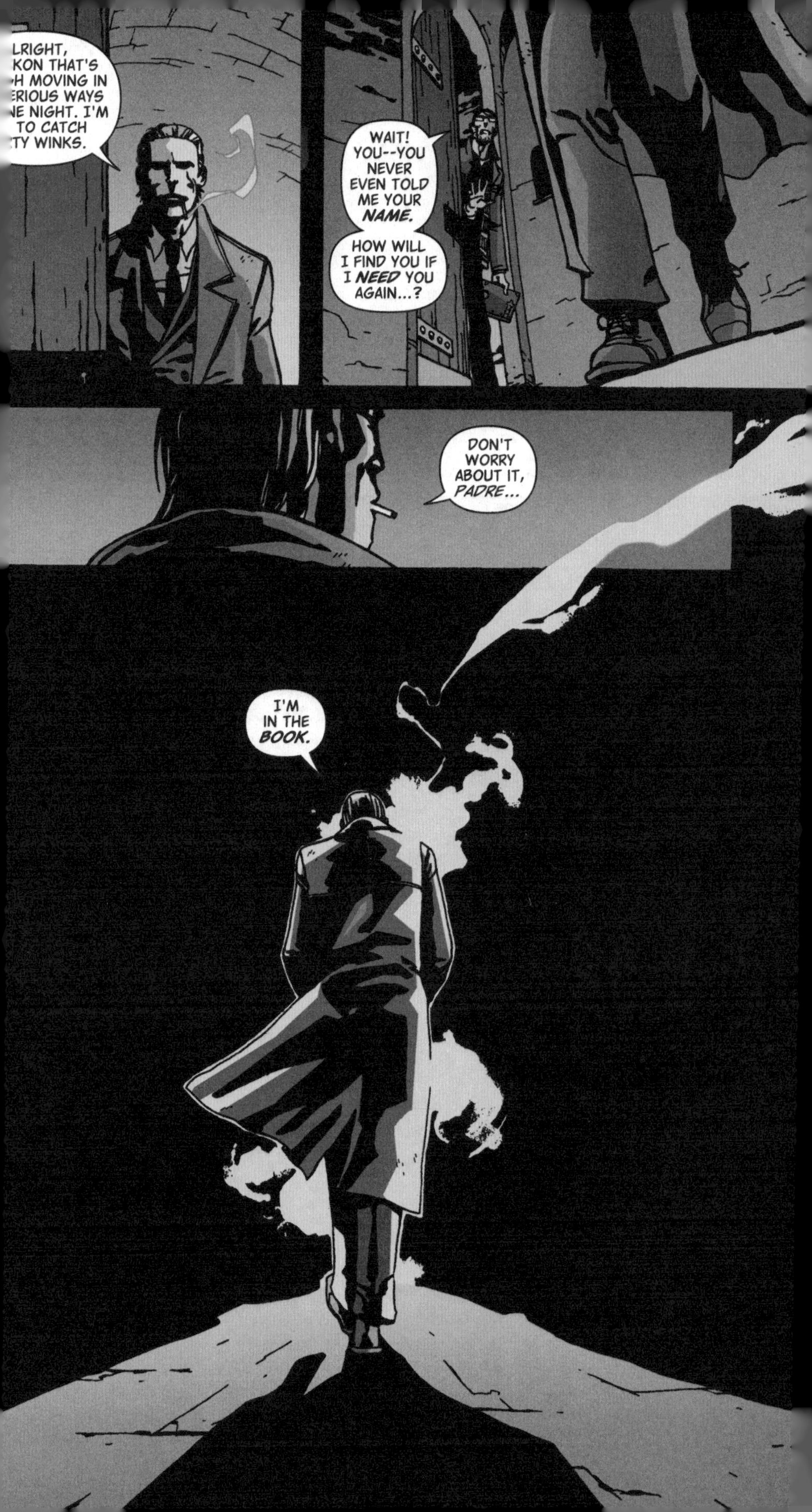
LRIGHT, KON THAT'S H MOVING IN ERIOUS WAYS NE NIGHT. I'M TO CATCH TY WINKS.
WAIT! YOU--YOU NEVER EVEN TOLD ME YOUR NAME.
HOW WILL I FIND YOU IF I NEED YOU AGAIN...?
DON'T WORRY ABOUT IT, PADRE...
I'M IN THE BOOK.

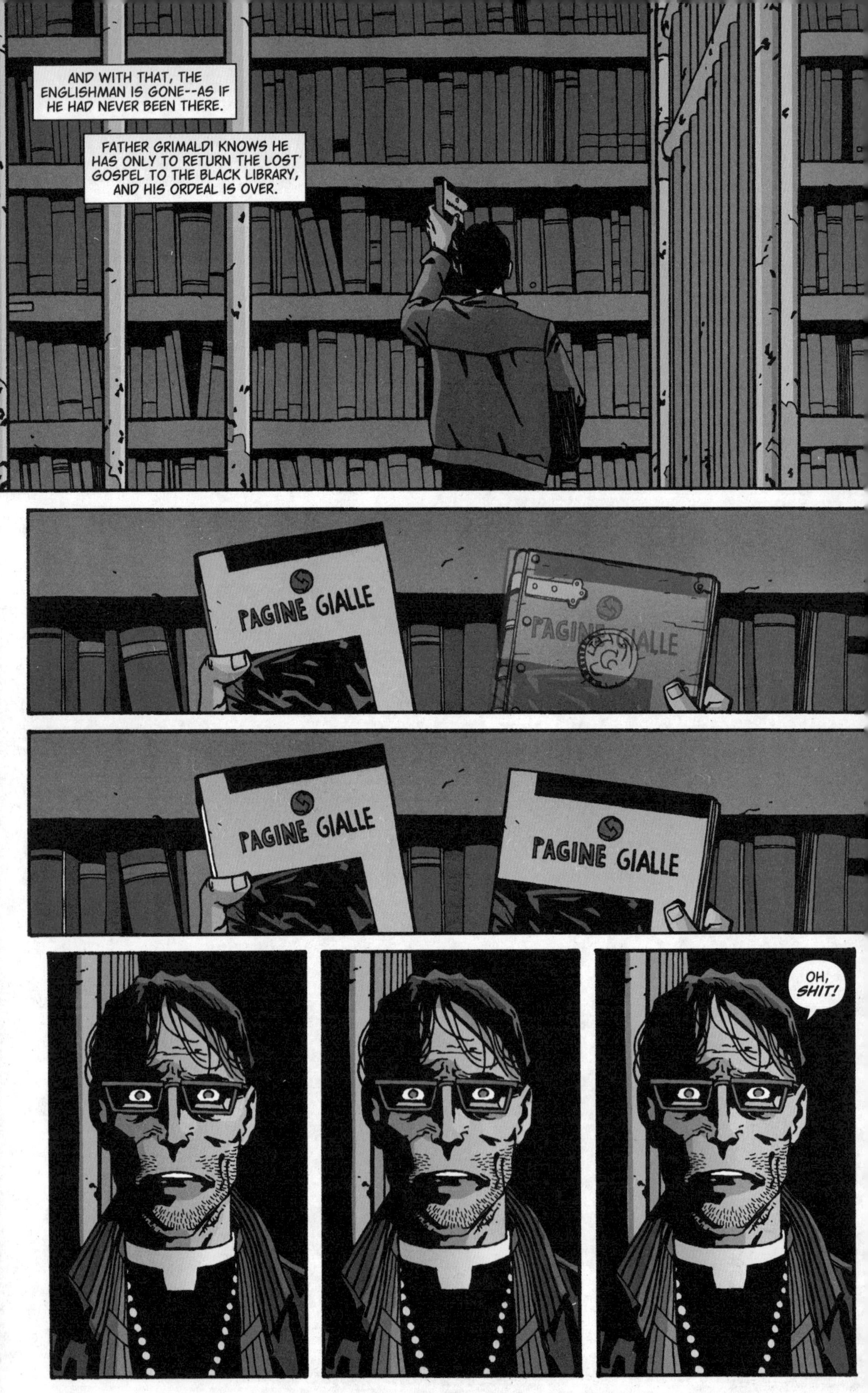
AND WITH THAT, THE ENGLISHMAN IS GONE--AS IF HE HAD NEVER BEEN THERE.
FATHER GRIMALDI KNOWS HE HAS ONLY TO RETURN THE LOST GOSPEL TO THE BLACK LIBRARY, AND HIS ORDEAL IS OVER.
PAGINE GIALLE
PAGINE GIALLE
PAGINE GIALLE
PAGINE GIALLE
OH, SHIT!

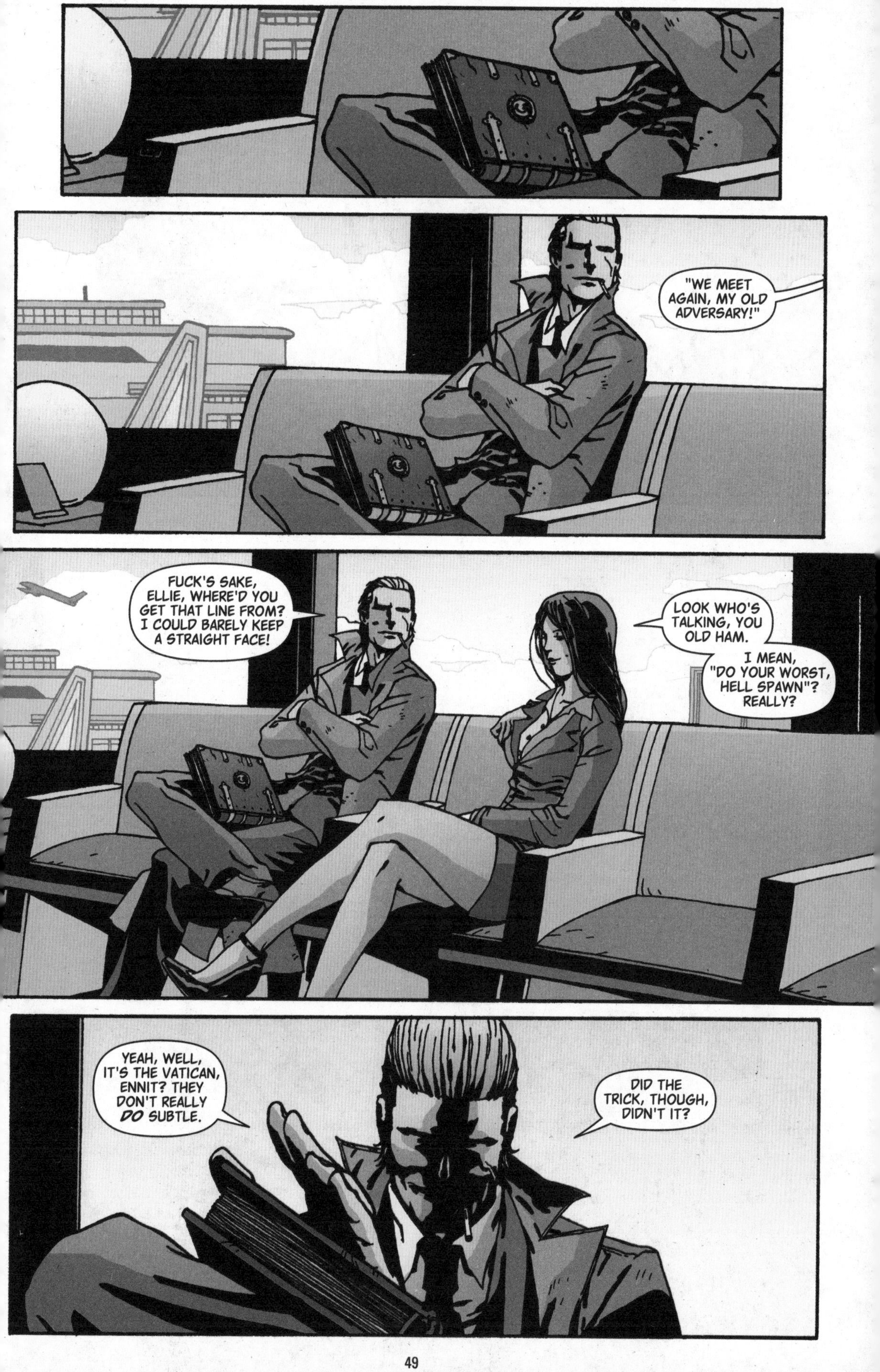
"WE MEET AGAIN, MY OLD ADVERSARY!"
FUCK'S SAKE, ELLIE, WHERE'D YOU GET THAT LINE FROM? I COULD BARELY KEEP A STRAIGHT FACE!
LOOK WHO'S TALKING, YOU OLD HAM.
I MEAN, "DO YOUR WORST, HELL SPAWN"? REALLY?
YEAH, WELL, IT'S THE VATICAN, ENNIT? THEY DON'T REALLY *DO* SUBTLE.
DID THE TRICK, THOUGH, DIDN'T IT?

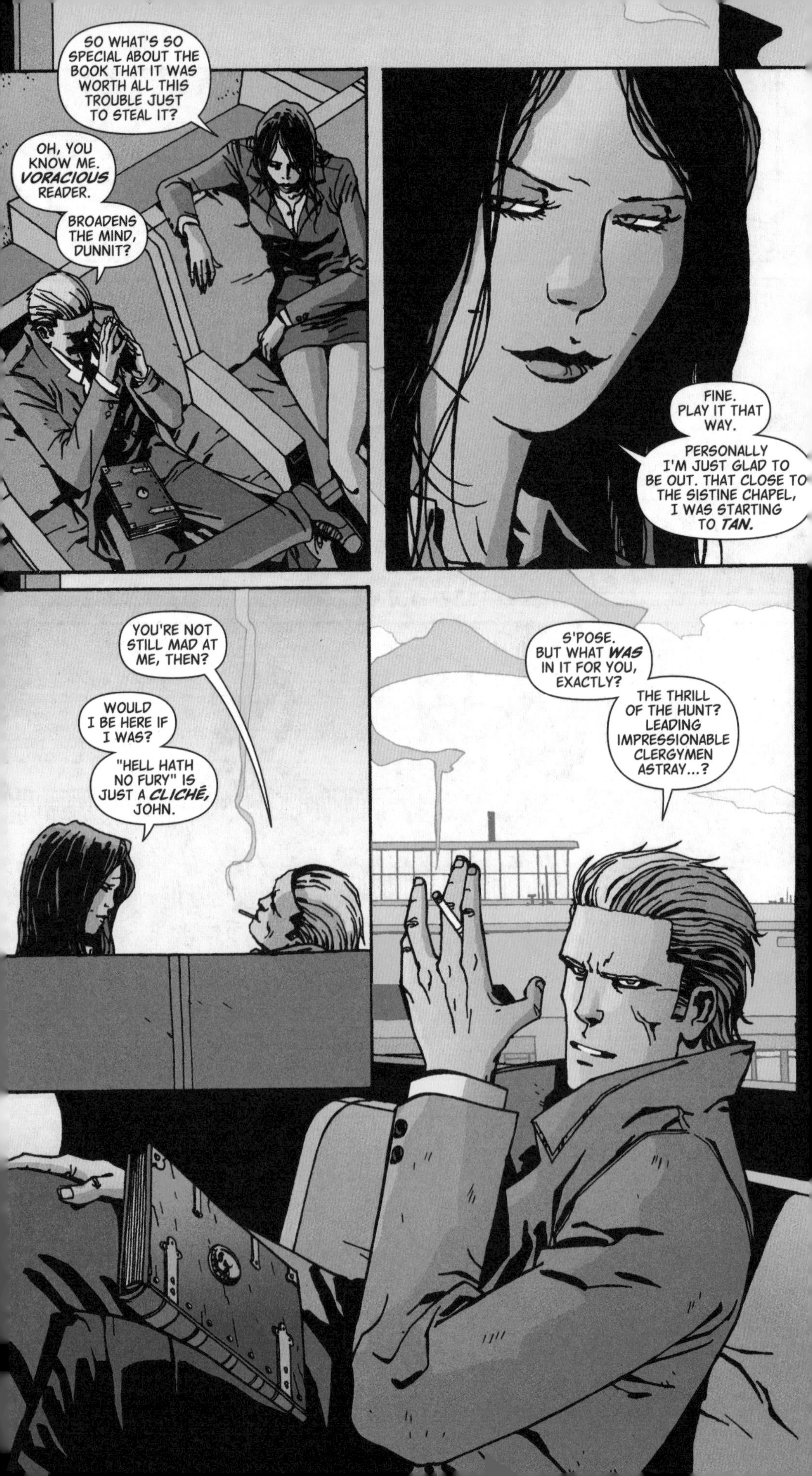
SO WHAT'S SO SPECIAL ABOUT THE BOOK THAT IT WAS WORTH ALL THIS TROUBLE JUST TO STEAL IT?
OH, YOU KNOW ME. VORACIOUS READER.
BROADENS THE MIND, DUNNIT?
FINE. PLAY IT THAT WAY.
PERSONALLY I'M JUST GLAD TO BE OUT. THAT CLOSE TO THE SISTINE CHAPEL, I WAS STARTING TO TAN.
YOU'RE NOT STILL MAD AT ME, THEN?
WOULD I BE HERE IF I WAS?
"HELL HATH NO FURY" IS JUST A CLICHÉ, JOHN.
S'POSE. BUT WHAT WAS IN IT FOR YOU, EXACTLY?
THE THRILL OF THE HUNT? LEADING IMPRESSIONABLE CLERGYMEN ASTRAY...?

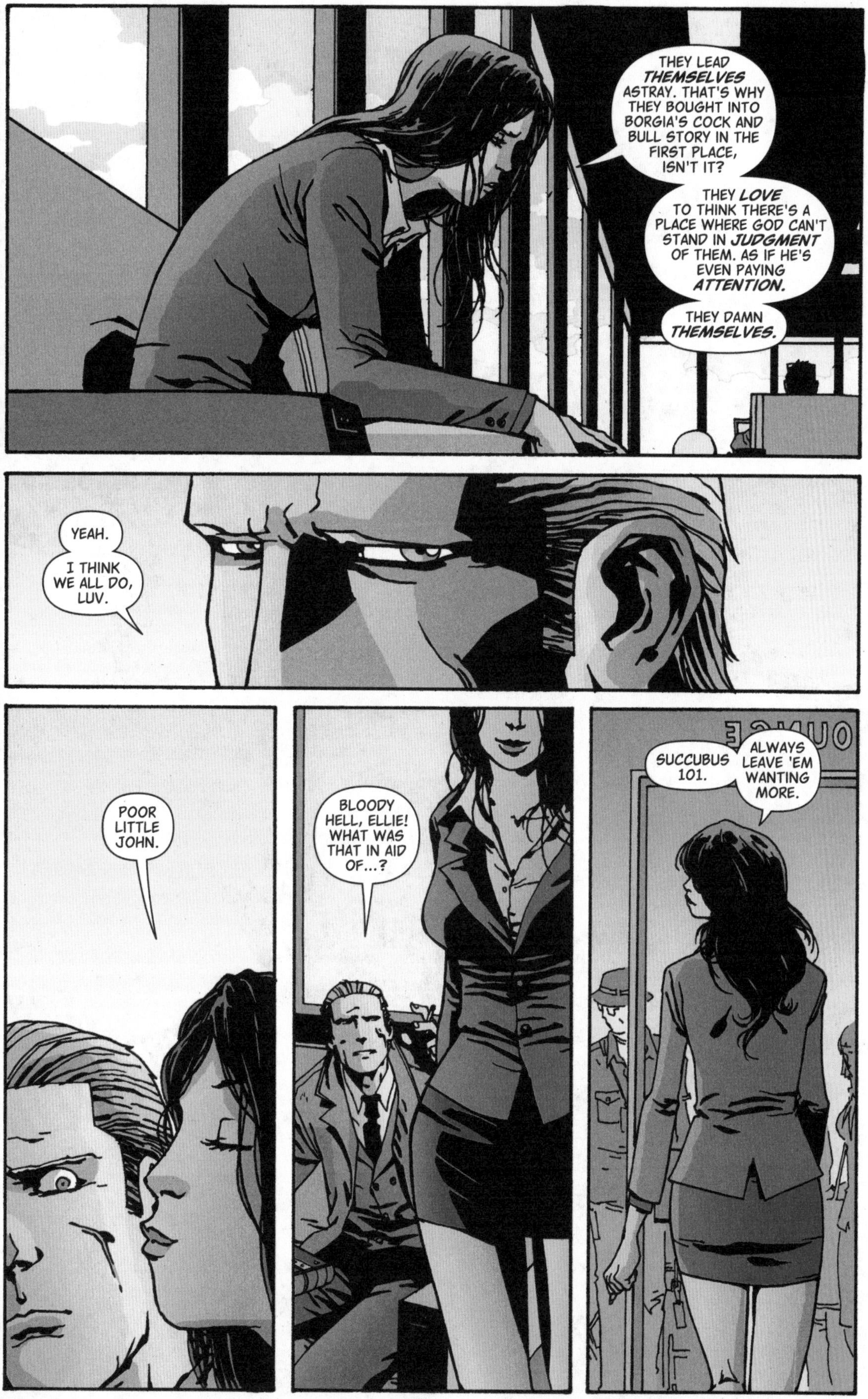
THEY LEAD THEMSELVES ASTRAY. THAT'S WHY THEY BOUGHT INTO BORGIA'S COCK AND BULL STORY IN THE FIRST PLACE, ISN'T IT?
THEY LOVE TO THINK THERE'S A PLACE WHERE GOD CAN'T STAND IN JUDGMENT OF THEM. AS IF HE'S EVEN PAYING ATTENTION.
THEY DAMN THEMSELVES.
YEAH.
I THINK WE ALL DO, LUV.
POOR LITTLE JOHN.
BLOODY HELL, ELLIE! WHAT WAS THAT IN AID OF...?
SUCCUBUS 101.
ALWAYS LEAVE 'EM WANTING MORE.

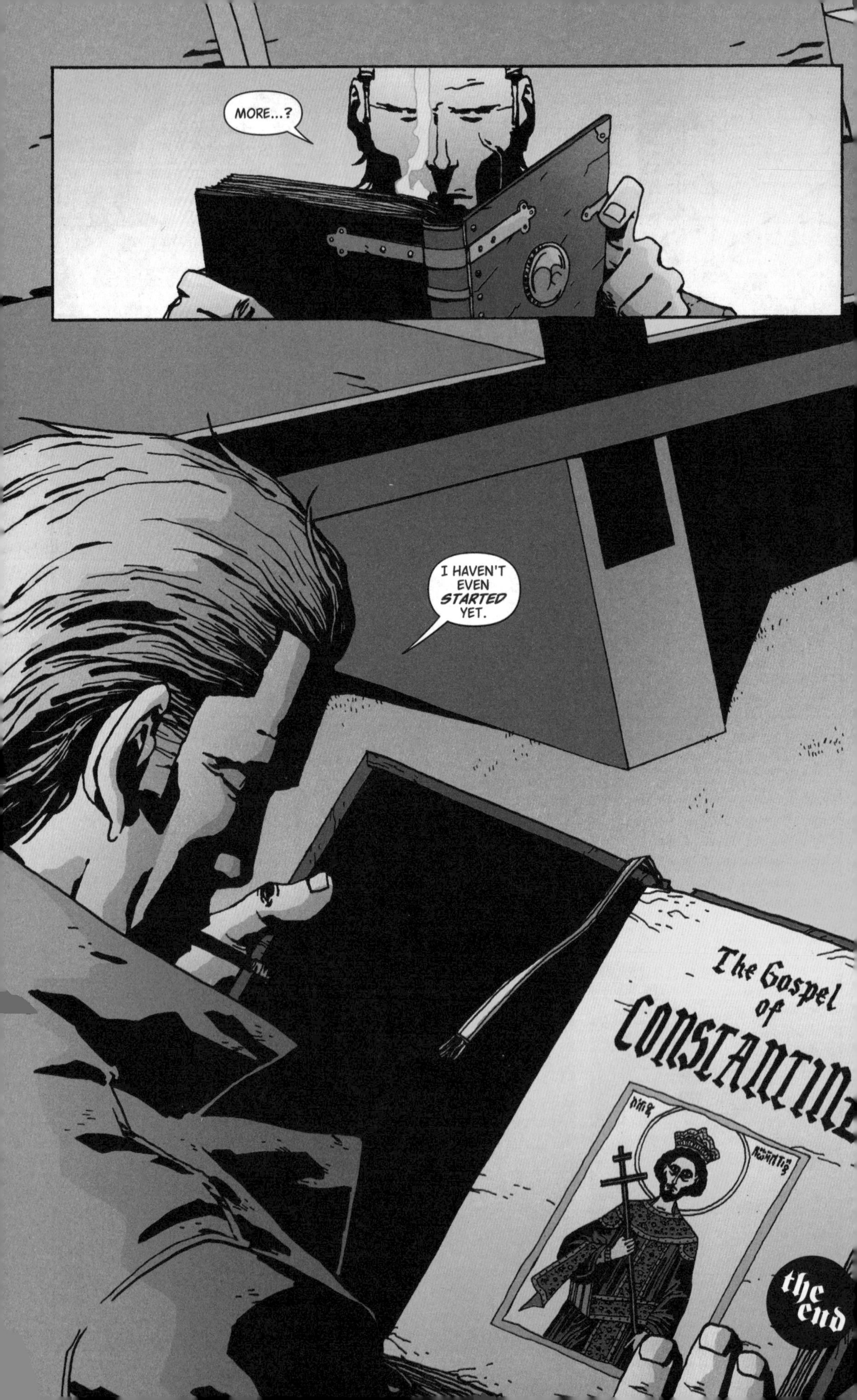
MORE...?
I HAVEN'T EVEN STARTED YET.
The Gospel of CONSTANTINE
the end

The Roots of Coincidence, Part One

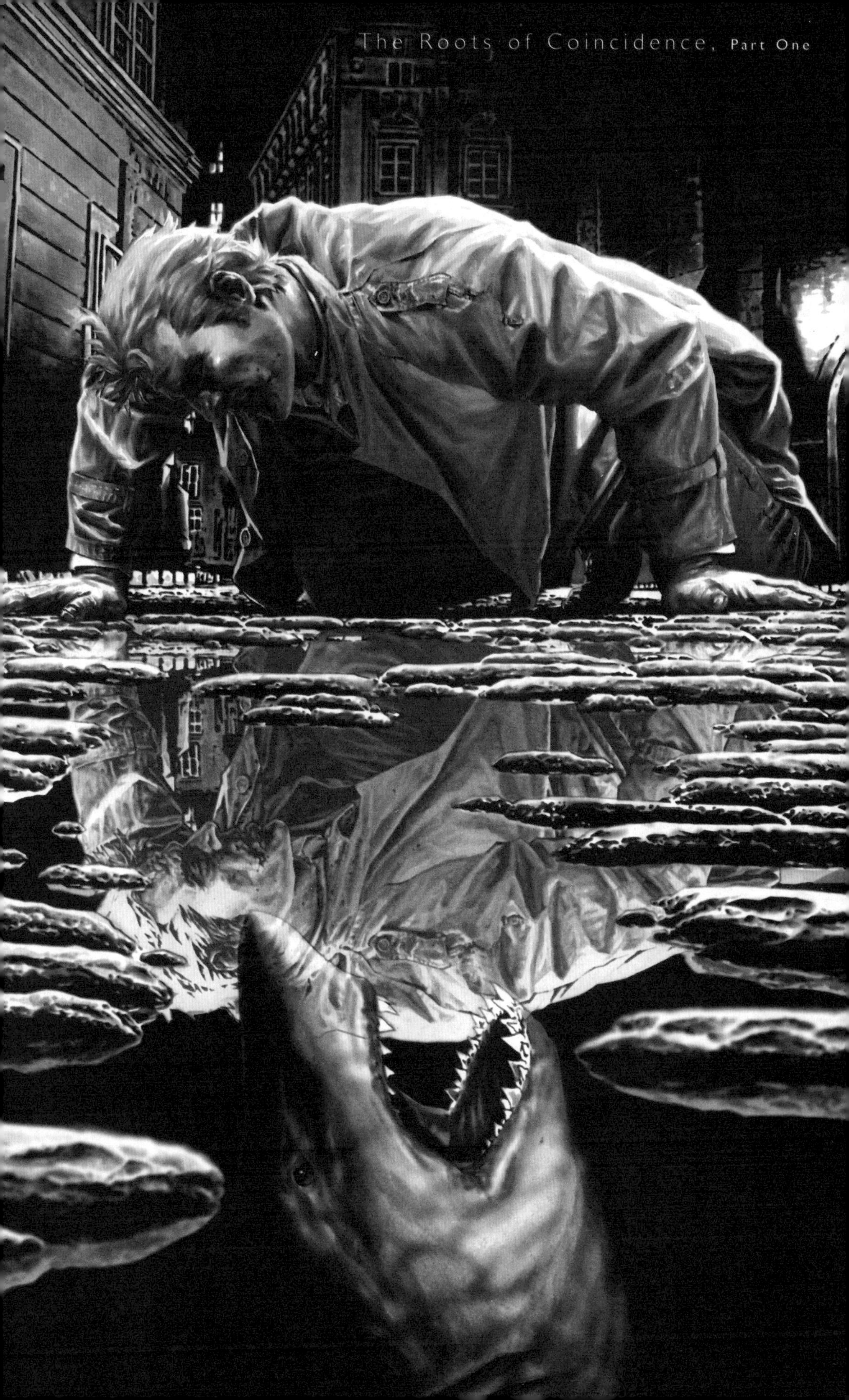

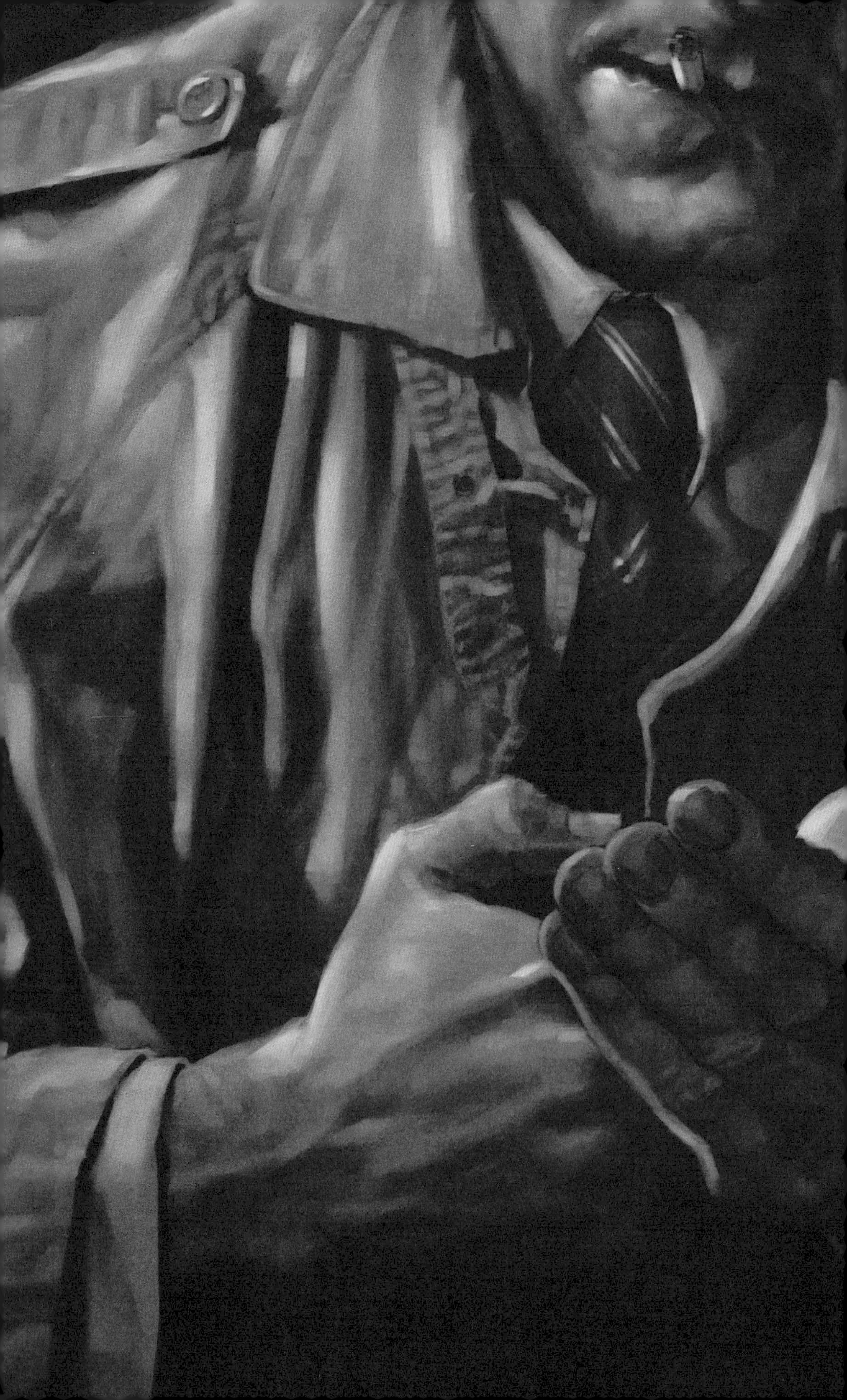

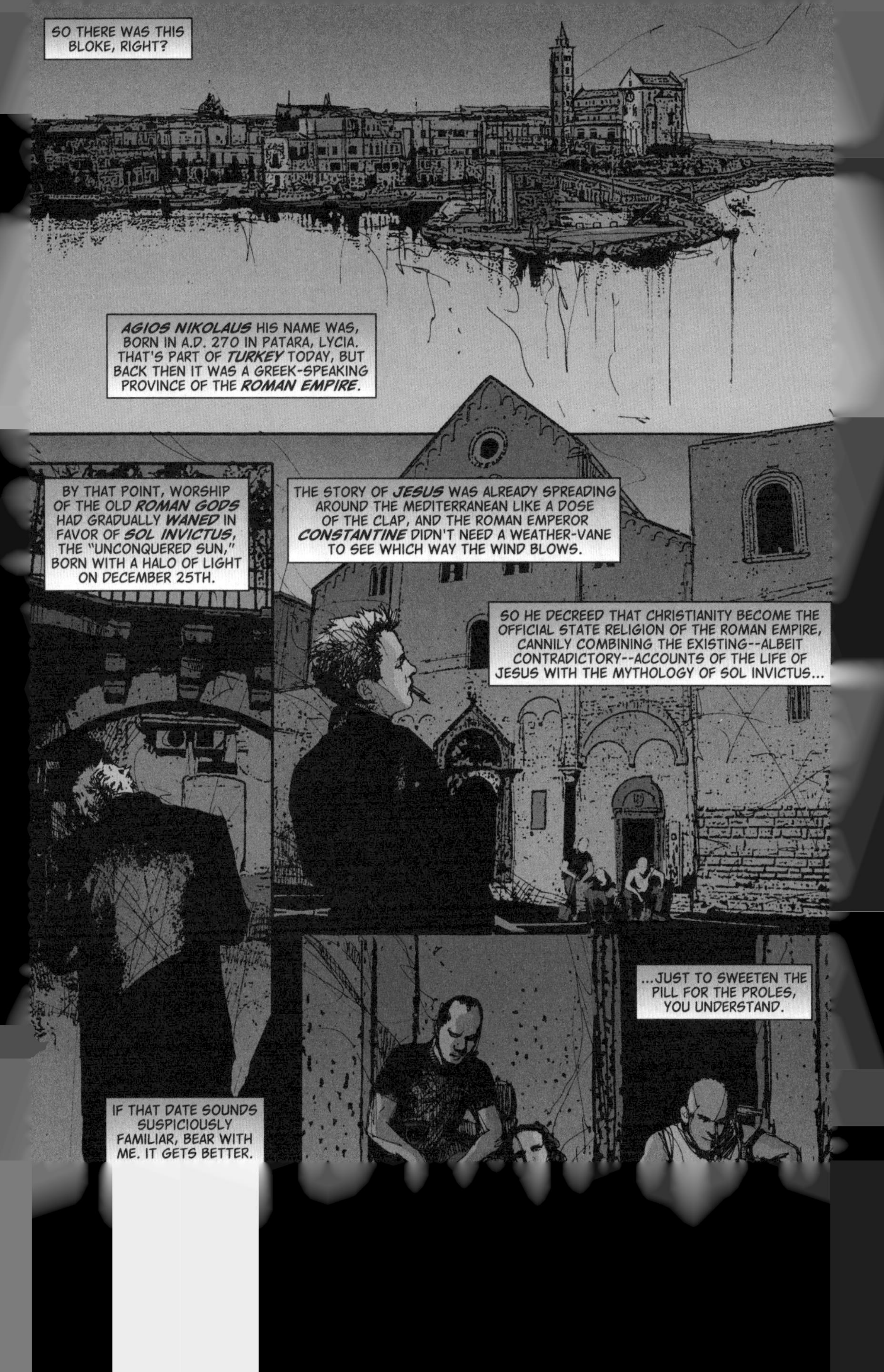
SO THERE WAS THIS BLOKE, RIGHT?
AGIOS NIKOLAUS HIS NAME WAS, BORN IN A.D. 270 IN PATARA, LYCIA. THAT'S PART OF TURKEY TODAY, BUT BACK THEN IT WAS A GREEK-SPEAKING PROVINCE OF THE ROMAN EMPIRE.
BY THAT POINT, WORSHIP OF THE OLD ROMAN GODS HAD GRADUALLY WANED IN FAVOR OF SOL INVICTUS, THE "UNCONQUERED SUN," BORN WITH A HALO OF LIGHT ON DECEMBER 25TH.
IF THAT DATE SOUNDS SUSPICIOUSLY FAMILIAR, BEAR WITH ME. IT GETS BETTER.
THE STORY OF JESUS WAS ALREADY SPREADING AROUND THE MEDITERRANEAN LIKE A DOSE OF THE CLAP, AND THE ROMAN EMPEROR CONSTANTINE DIDN'T NEED A WEATHER-VANE TO SEE WHICH WAY THE WIND BLOWS.
SO HE DECREED THAT CHRISTIANITY BECOME THE OFFICIAL STATE RELIGION OF THE ROMAN EMPIRE, CANNILY COMBINING THE EXISTING--ALBEIT CONTRADICTORY--ACCOUNTS OF THE LIFE OF JESUS WITH THE MYTHOLOGY OF SOL INVICTUS...
...JUST TO SWEETEN THE PILL FOR THE PROLES, YOU UNDERSTAND.

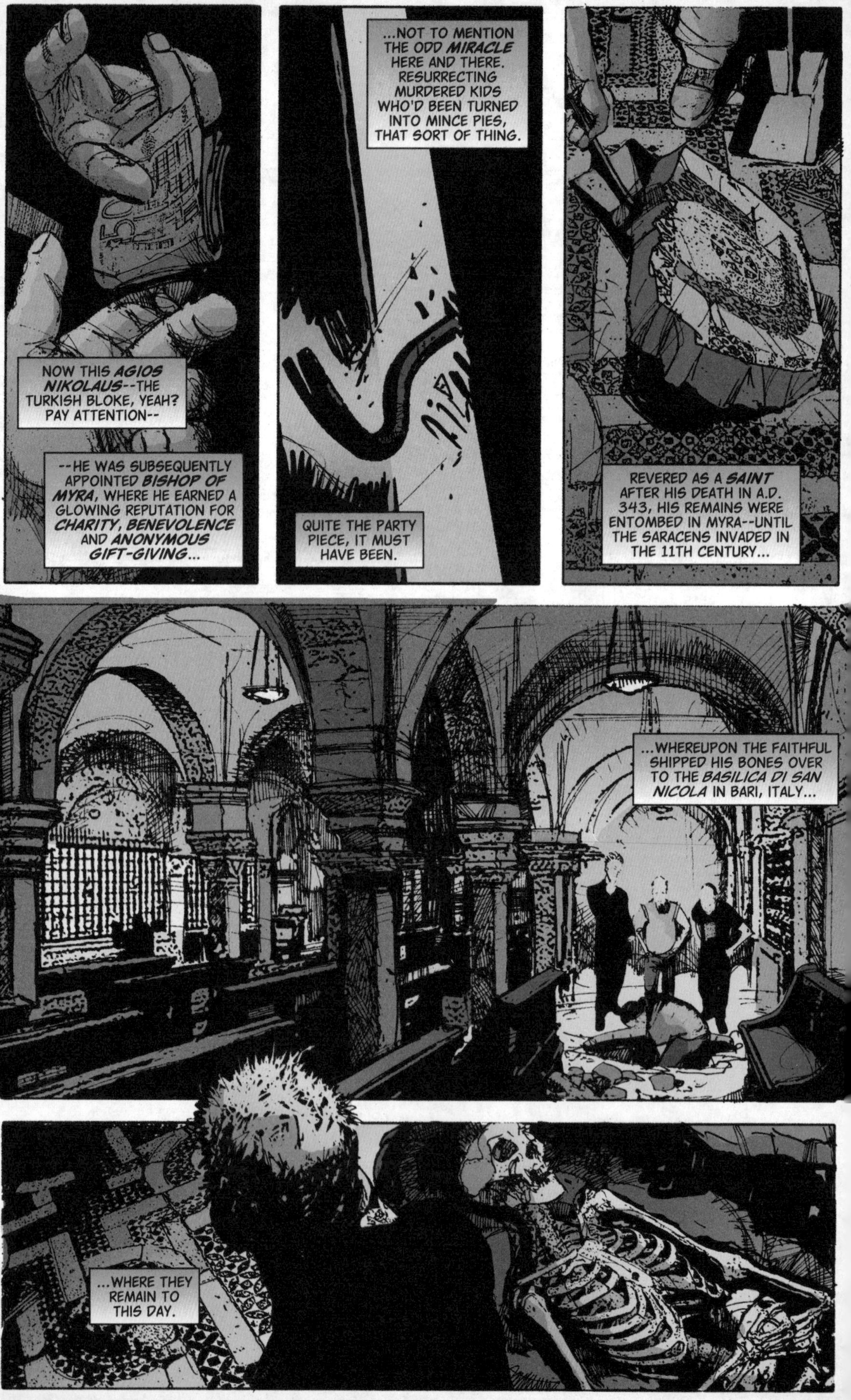
NOW THIS *AGIOS NIKOLAUS*--THE TURKISH BLOKE, YEAH? PAY ATTENTION--
--HE WAS SUBSEQUENTLY APPOINTED *BISHOP OF MYRA*, WHERE HE EARNED A GLOWING REPUTATION FOR *CHARITY, BENEVOLENCE* AND *ANONYMOUS GIFT-GIVING*...
...NOT TO MENTION THE ODD *MIRACLE* HERE AND THERE. RESURRECTING MURDERED KIDS WHO'D BEEN TURNED INTO MINCE PIES, THAT SORT OF THING.
QUITE THE PARTY PIECE, IT MUST HAVE BEEN.
REVERED AS A *SAINT* AFTER HIS DEATH IN A.D. 343, HIS REMAINS WERE ENTOMBED IN MYRA--UNTIL THE SARACENS INVADED IN THE 11TH CENTURY...
...WHEREUPON THE FAITHFUL SHIPPED HIS BONES OVER TO THE *BASILICA DI SAN NICOLA* IN BARI, ITALY...
...WHERE THEY REMAIN TO THIS DAY.

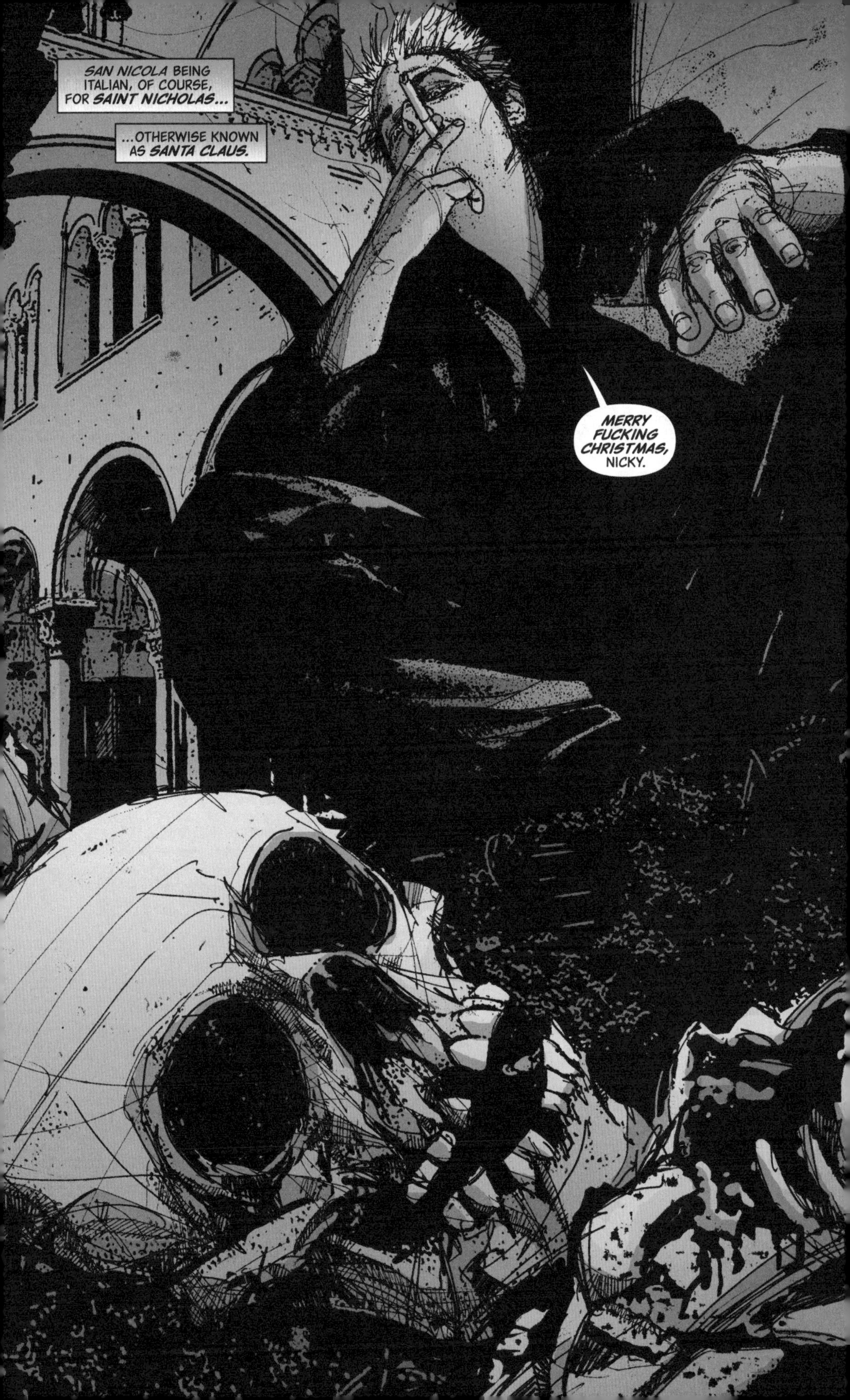
SAN NICOLA BEING ITALIAN, OF COURSE, FOR SAINT NICHOLAS...
...OTHERWISE KNOWN AS SANTA CLAUS.
MERRY FUCKING CHRISTMAS, NICKY.

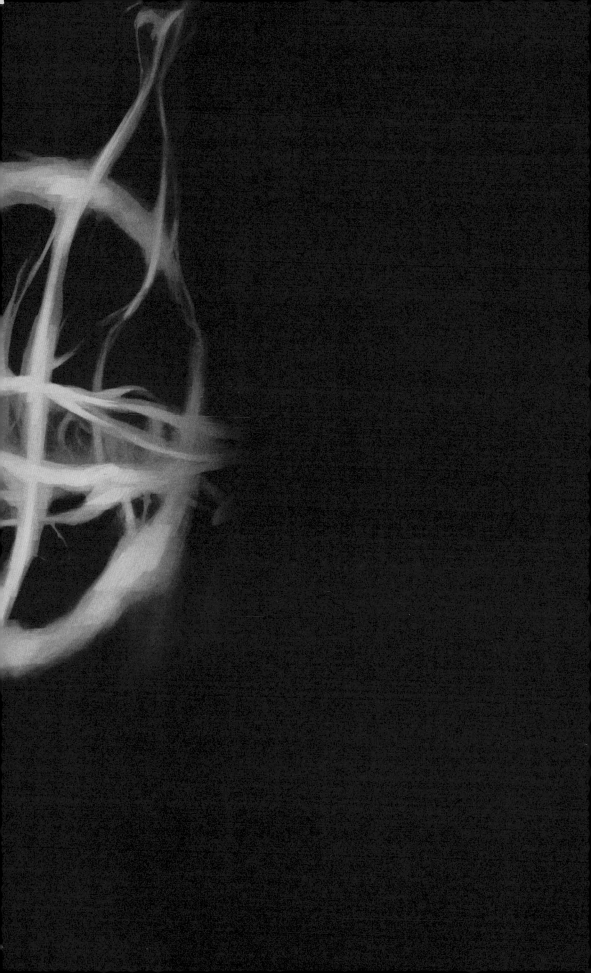

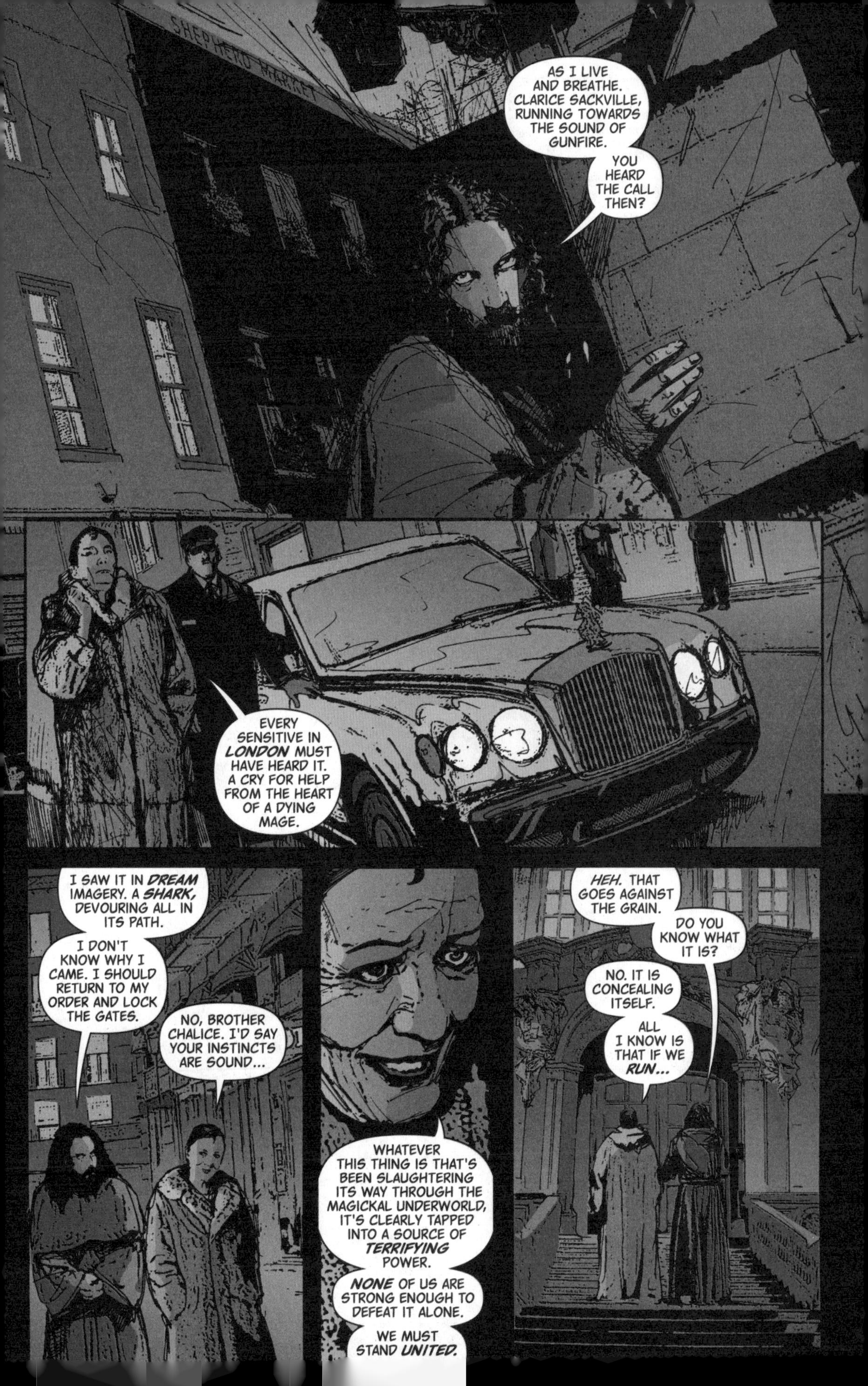
SHEPHERD MARKET
AS I LIVE AND BREATHE. CLARICE SACKVILLE, RUNNING TOWARDS THE SOUND OF GUNFIRE.
YOU HEARD THE CALL THEN?
EVERY SENSITIVE IN LONDON MUST HAVE HEARD IT. A CRY FOR HELP FROM THE HEART OF A DYING MAGE.
I SAW IT IN DREAM IMAGERY. A SHARK, DEVOURING ALL IN ITS PATH.
I DON'T KNOW WHY I CAME. I SHOULD RETURN TO MY ORDER AND LOCK THE GATES.
NO, BROTHER CHALICE. I'D SAY YOUR INSTINCTS ARE SOUND...
WHATEVER THIS THING IS THAT'S BEEN SLAUGHTERING ITS WAY THROUGH THE MAGICKAL UNDERWORLD, IT'S CLEARLY TAPPED INTO A SOURCE OF TERRIFYING POWER.
NONE OF US ARE STRONG ENOUGH TO DEFEAT IT ALONE.
WE MUST STAND UNITED.
HEH. THAT GOES AGAINST THE GRAIN.
DO YOU KNOW WHAT IT IS?
NO. IT IS CONCEALING ITSELF.
ALL I KNOW IS THAT IF WE RUN...

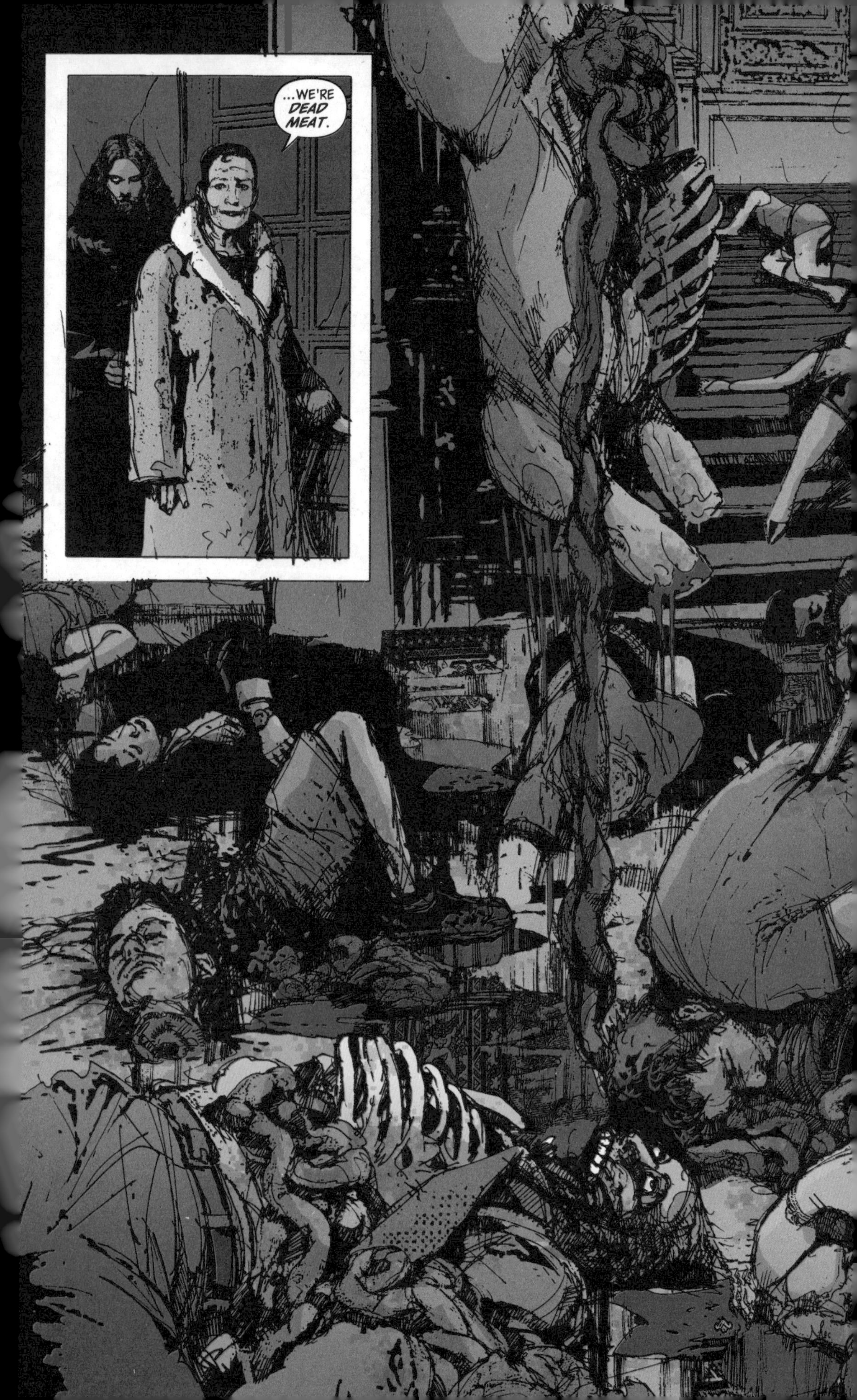
...WE'RE DEAD MEAT.

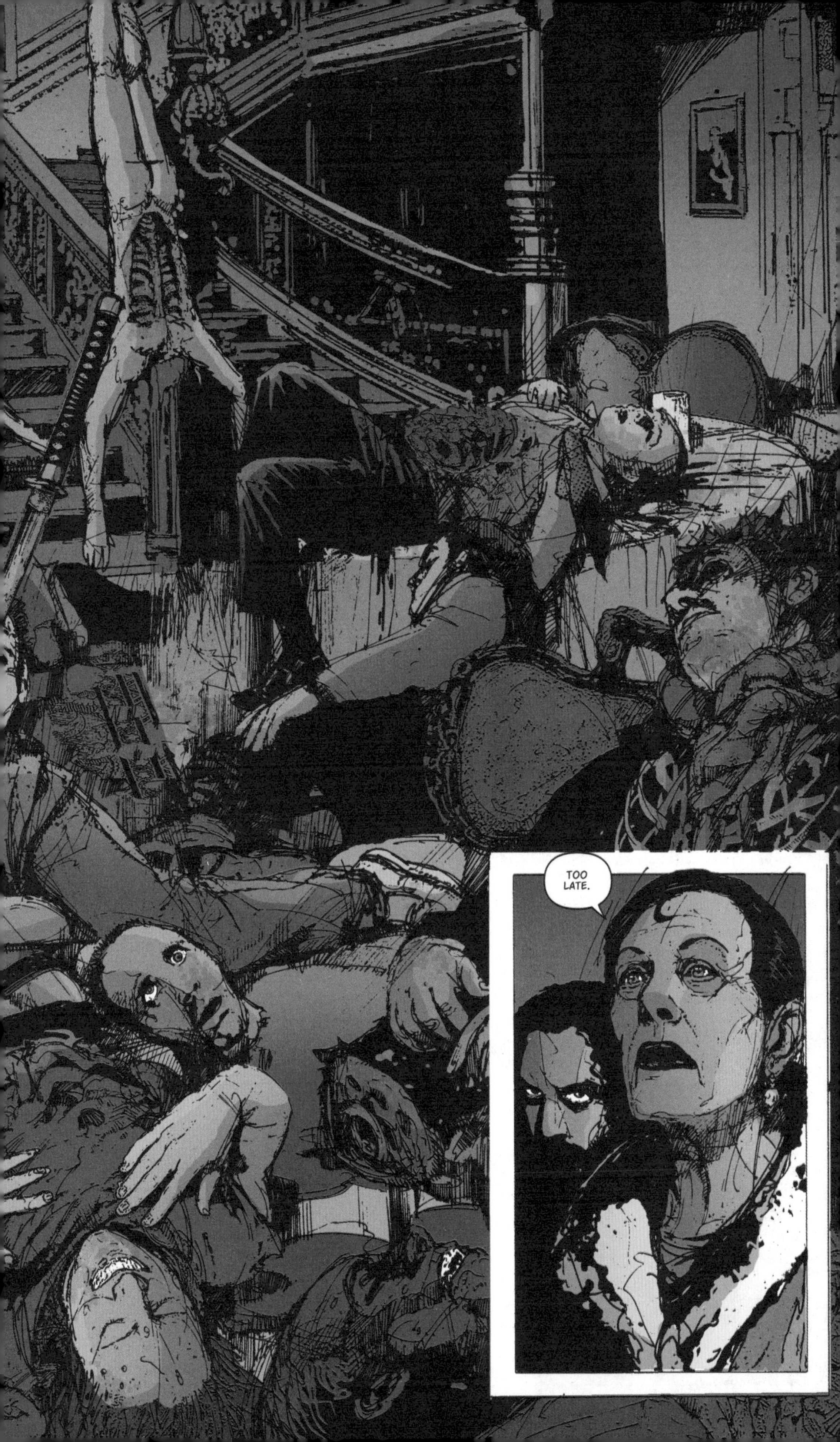
TOO LATE.

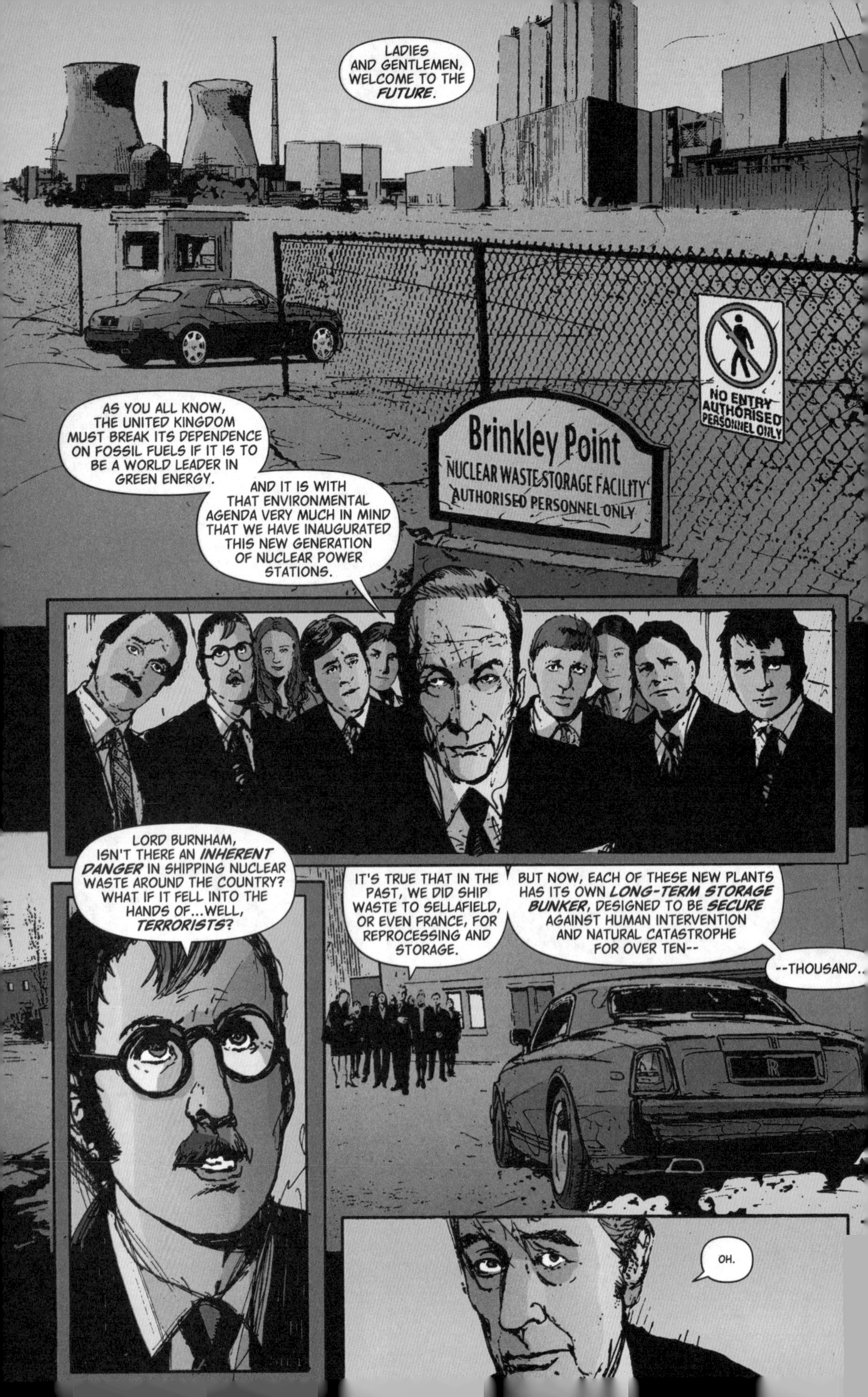
LADIES AND GENTLEMEN, WELCOME TO THE FUTURE.
NO ENTRY AUTHORISED PERSONNEL ONLY
Brinkley Point
NUCLEAR WASTE STORAGE FACILITY
AUTHORISED PERSONNEL ONLY
AS YOU ALL KNOW, THE UNITED KINGDOM MUST BREAK ITS DEPENDENCE ON FOSSIL FUELS IF IT IS TO BE A WORLD LEADER IN GREEN ENERGY.
AND IT IS WITH THAT ENVIRONMENTAL AGENDA VERY MUCH IN MIND THAT WE HAVE INAUGURATED THIS NEW GENERATION OF NUCLEAR POWER STATIONS.
LORD BURNHAM, ISN'T THERE AN INHERENT DANGER IN SHIPPING NUCLEAR WASTE AROUND THE COUNTRY? WHAT IF IT FELL INTO THE HANDS OF...WELL, TERRORISTS?
IT'S TRUE THAT IN THE PAST, WE DID SHIP WASTE TO SELLAFIELD, OR EVEN FRANCE, FOR REPROCESSING AND STORAGE.
BUT NOW, EACH OF THESE NEW PLANTS HAS ITS OWN LONG-TERM STORAGE BUNKER, DESIGNED TO BE SECURE AGAINST HUMAN INTERVENTION AND NATURAL CATASTROPHE FOR OVER TEN--
--THOUSAND..
OH.

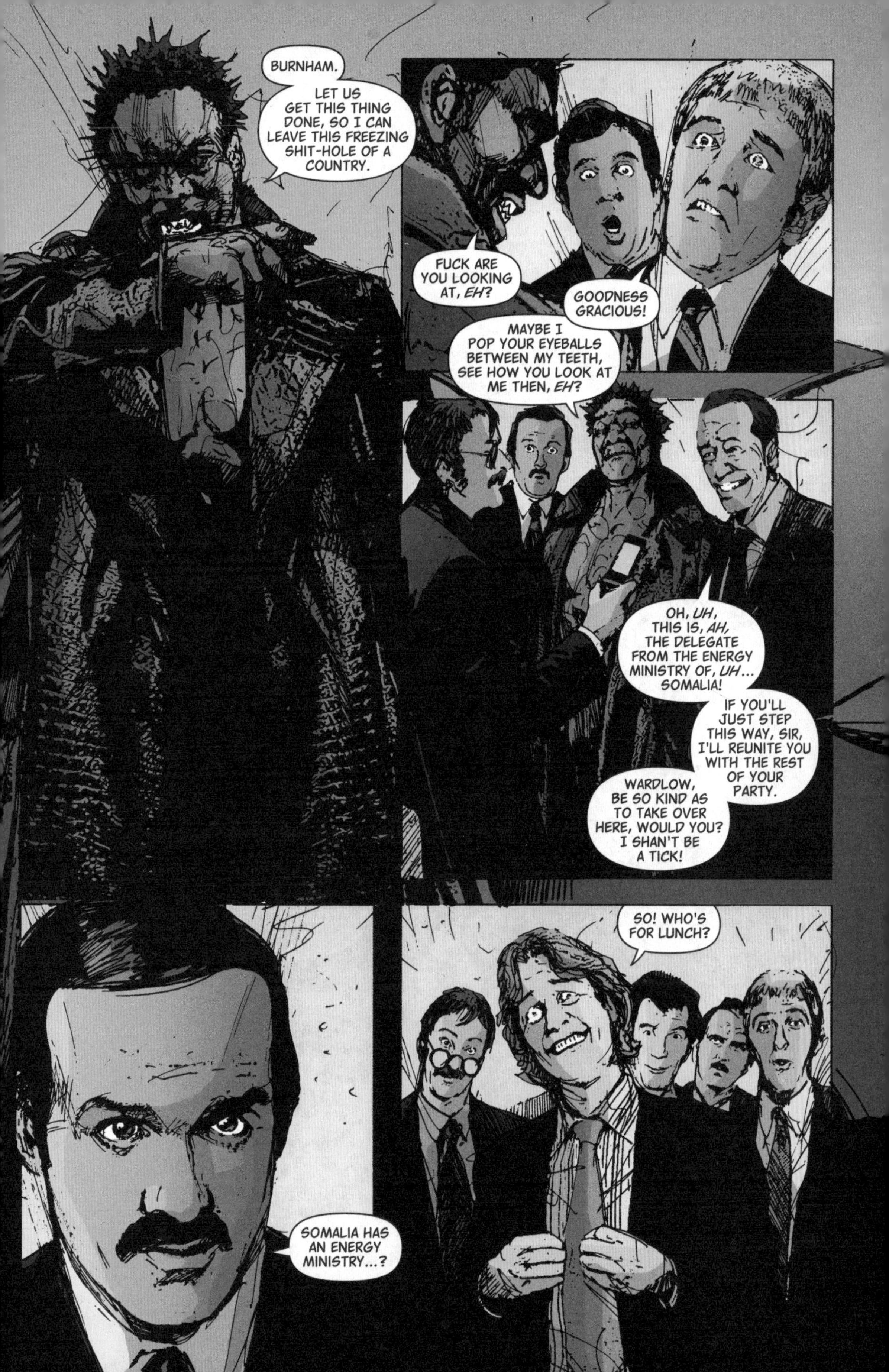
BURNHAM.
LET US GET THIS THING DONE, SO I CAN LEAVE THIS FREEZING SHIT-HOLE OF A COUNTRY.
FUCK ARE YOU LOOKING AT, *EH*?
GOODNESS GRACIOUS!
MAYBE I POP YOUR EYEBALLS BETWEEN MY TEETH, SEE HOW YOU LOOK AT ME THEN, *EH*?
OH, *UH*, THIS IS, *AH*, THE DELEGATE FROM THE ENERGY MINISTRY OF, *UH*... SOMALIA!
IF YOU'LL JUST STEP THIS WAY, SIR, I'LL REUNITE YOU WITH THE REST OF YOUR PARTY.
WARDLOW, BE SO KIND AS TO TAKE OVER HERE, WOULD YOU? I SHAN'T BE A TICK!
SOMALIA HAS AN ENERGY MINISTRY...?
SO! WHO'S FOR LUNCH?

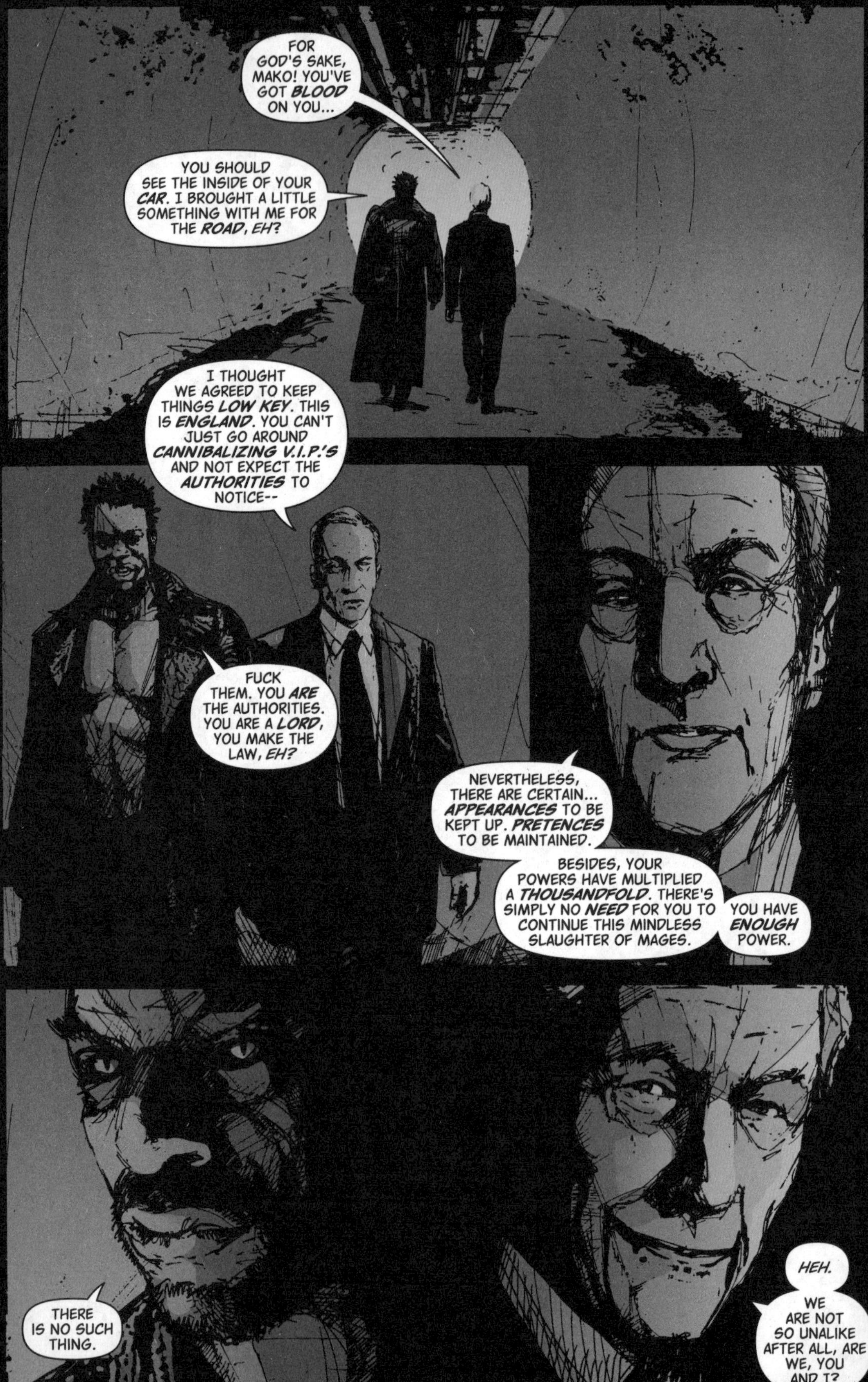
FOR GOD'S SAKE, MAKO! YOU'VE GOT BLOOD ON YOU...
YOU SHOULD SEE THE INSIDE OF YOUR CAR. I BROUGHT A LITTLE SOMETHING WITH ME FOR THE ROAD, EH?
I THOUGHT WE AGREED TO KEEP THINGS LOW KEY. THIS IS ENGLAND. YOU CAN'T JUST GO AROUND CANNIBALIZING V.I.P.'S AND NOT EXPECT THE AUTHORITIES TO NOTICE--
FUCK THEM. YOU ARE THE AUTHORITIES. YOU ARE A LORD, YOU MAKE THE LAW, EH?
NEVERTHELESS, THERE ARE CERTAIN... APPEARANCES TO BE KEPT UP. PRETENCES TO BE MAINTAINED.
BESIDES, YOUR POWERS HAVE MULTIPLIED A THOUSANDFOLD. THERE'S SIMPLY NO NEED FOR YOU TO CONTINUE THIS MINDLESS SLAUGHTER OF MAGES.
YOU HAVE ENOUGH POWER.
THERE IS NO SUCH THING.
HEH.
WE ARE NOT SO UNALIKE AFTER ALL, ARE WE, YOU AND I?

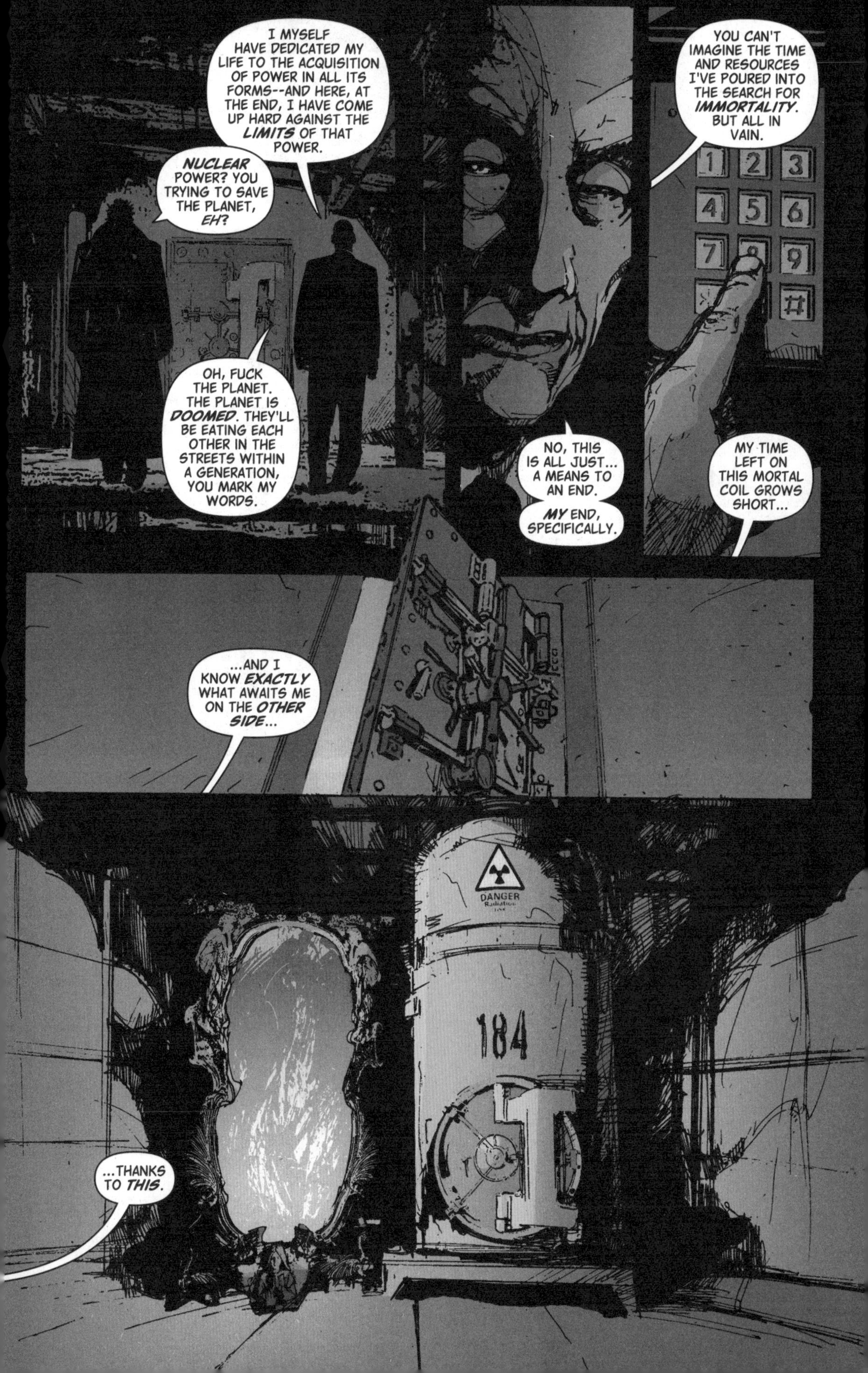
I MYSELF HAVE DEDICATED MY LIFE TO THE ACQUISITION OF POWER IN ALL ITS FORMS--AND HERE, AT THE END, I HAVE COME UP HARD AGAINST THE LIMITS OF THAT POWER.
NUCLEAR POWER? YOU TRYING TO SAVE THE PLANET, EH?
OH, FUCK THE PLANET. THE PLANET IS DOOMED. THEY'LL BE EATING EACH OTHER IN THE STREETS WITHIN A GENERATION, YOU MARK MY WORDS.
NO, THIS IS ALL JUST... A MEANS TO AN END.
MY END, SPECIFICALLY.
YOU CAN'T IMAGINE THE TIME AND RESOURCES I'VE POURED INTO THE SEARCH FOR IMMORTALITY. BUT ALL IN VAIN.
1 2 3
4 5 6
7 8 9
#
MY TIME LEFT ON THIS MORTAL COIL GROWS SHORT...
...AND I KNOW EXACTLY WHAT AWAITS ME ON THE OTHER SIDE...
DANGER
184
...THANKS TO THIS.

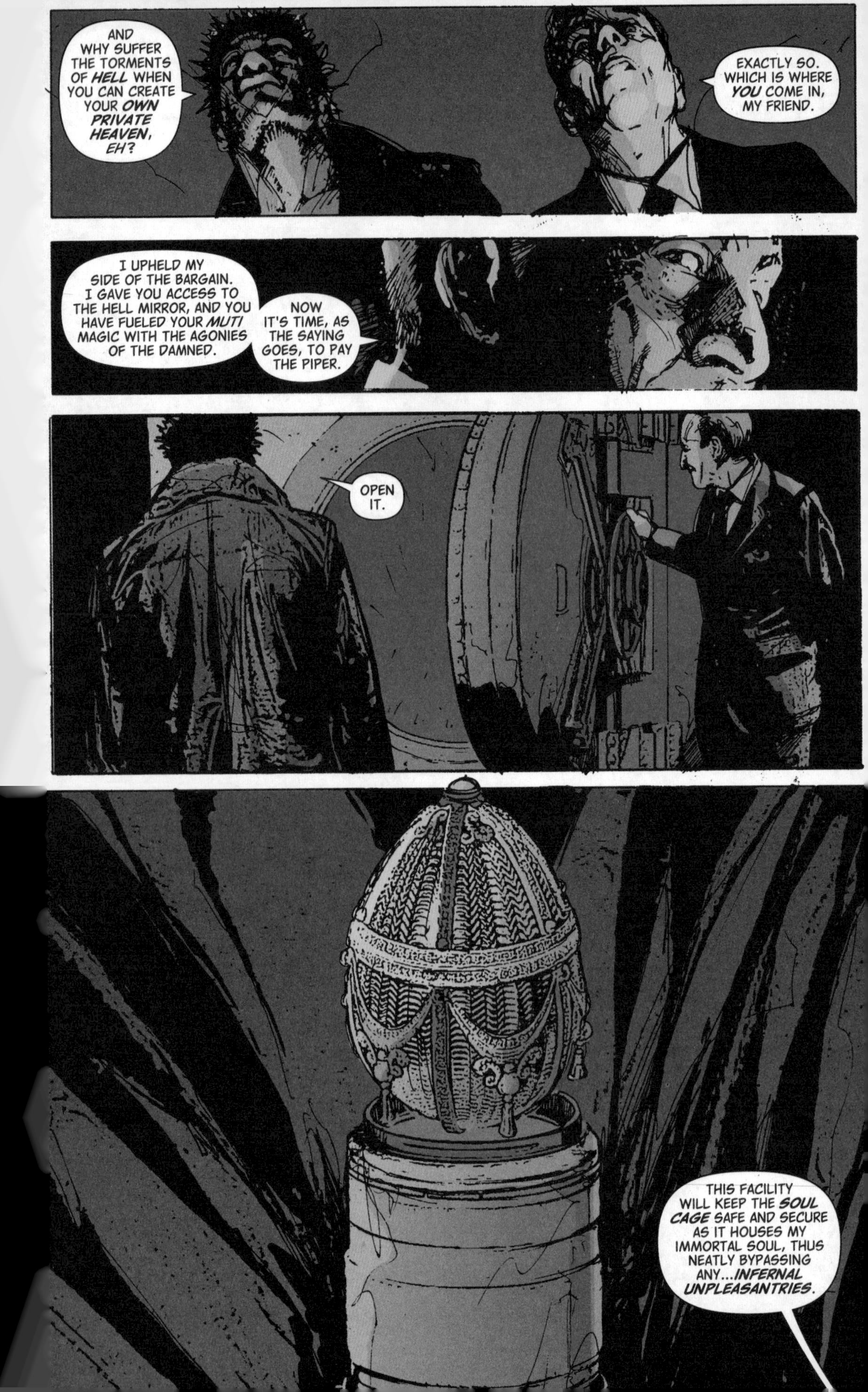
AND WHY SUFFER THE TORMENTS OF HELL WHEN YOU CAN CREATE YOUR OWN PRIVATE HEAVEN, EH?
EXACTLY SO. WHICH IS WHERE YOU COME IN, MY FRIEND.
I UPHELD MY SIDE OF THE BARGAIN. I GAVE YOU ACCESS TO THE HELL MIRROR, AND YOU HAVE FUELED YOUR MUTI MAGIC WITH THE AGONIES OF THE DAMNED.
NOW IT'S TIME, AS THE SAYING GOES, TO PAY THE PIPER.
OPEN IT.
THIS FACILITY WILL KEEP THE SOUL CAGE SAFE AND SECURE AS IT HOUSES MY IMMORTAL SOUL, THUS NEATLY BYPASSING ANY...INFERNAL UNPLEASANTRIES.

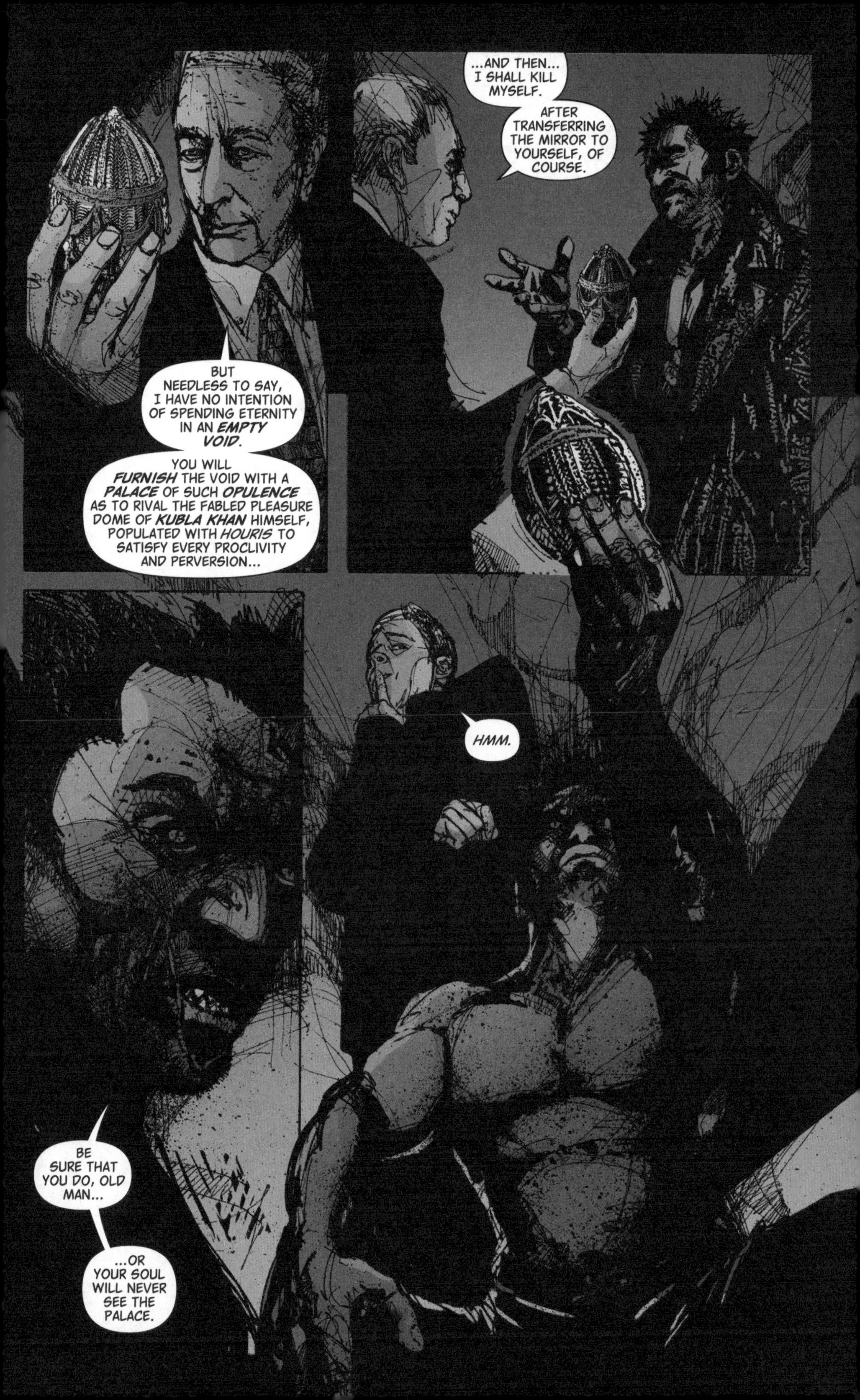
BUT NEEDLESS TO SAY, I HAVE NO INTENTION OF SPENDING ETERNITY IN AN *EMPTY VOID*.
YOU WILL *FURNISH* THE VOID WITH A *PALACE* OF SUCH *OPULENCE* AS TO RIVAL THE FABLED PLEASURE DOME OF *KUBLA KHAN* HIMSELF, POPULATED WITH *HOURIS* TO SATISFY EVERY PROCLIVITY AND PERVERSION...
...AND THEN... I SHALL KILL MYSELF.
AFTER TRANSFERRING THE MIRROR TO YOURSELF, OF COURSE.
HMM.
BE SURE THAT YOU DO, OLD MAN...
...OR YOUR SOUL WILL NEVER SEE THE PALACE.

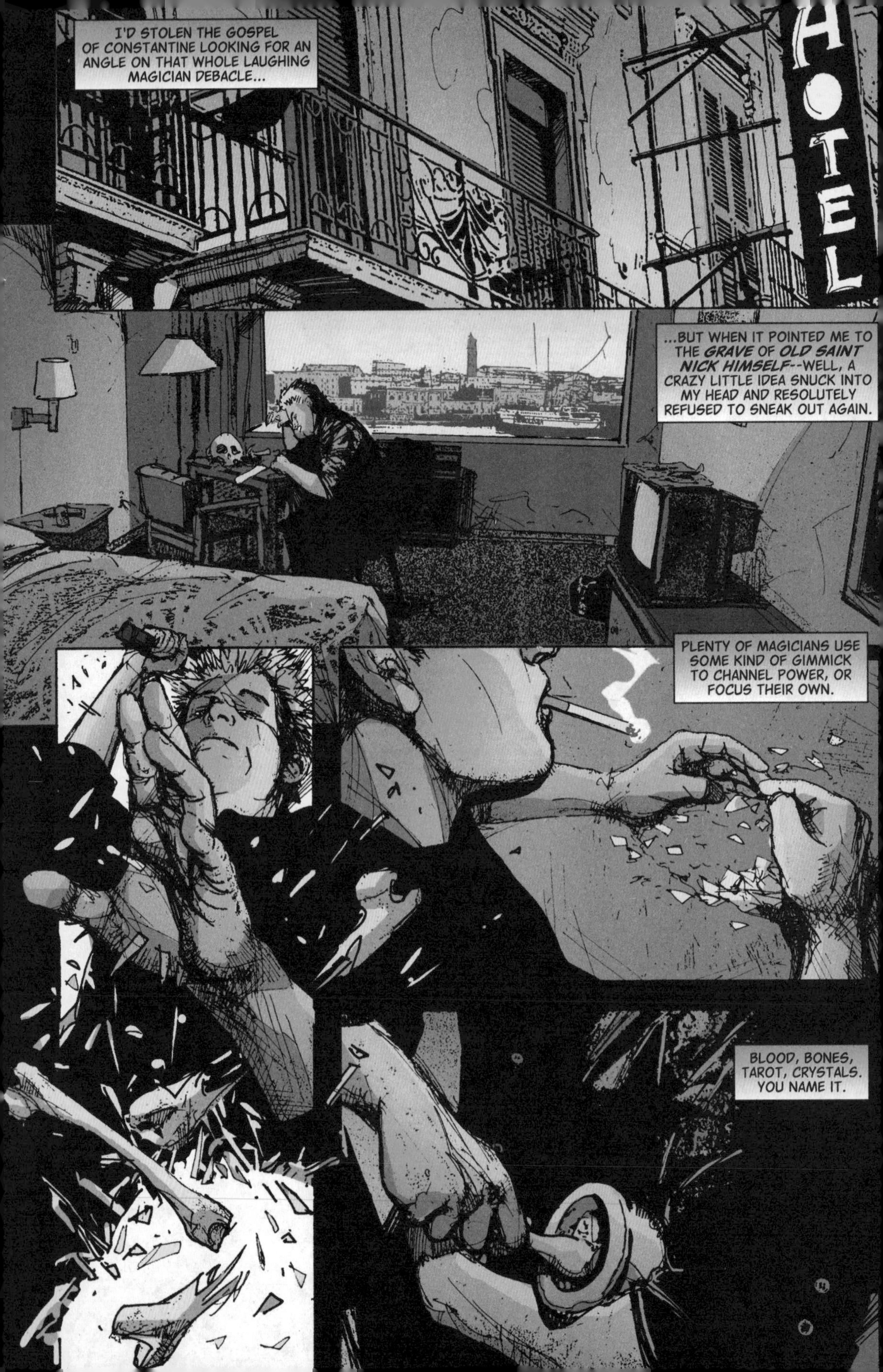
I'D STOLEN THE GOSPEL OF CONSTANTINE LOOKING FOR AN ANGLE ON THAT WHOLE LAUGHING MAGICIAN DEBACLE...
HOTEL
...BUT WHEN IT POINTED ME TO THE *GRAVE* OF *OLD SAINT NICK HIMSELF*--WELL, A CRAZY LITTLE IDEA SNUCK INTO MY HEAD AND RESOLUTELY REFUSED TO SNEAK OUT AGAIN.
PLENTY OF MAGICIANS USE SOME KIND OF GIMMICK TO CHANNEL POWER, OR FOCUS THEIR OWN.
BLOOD, BONES, TAROT, CRYSTALS. YOU NAME IT.

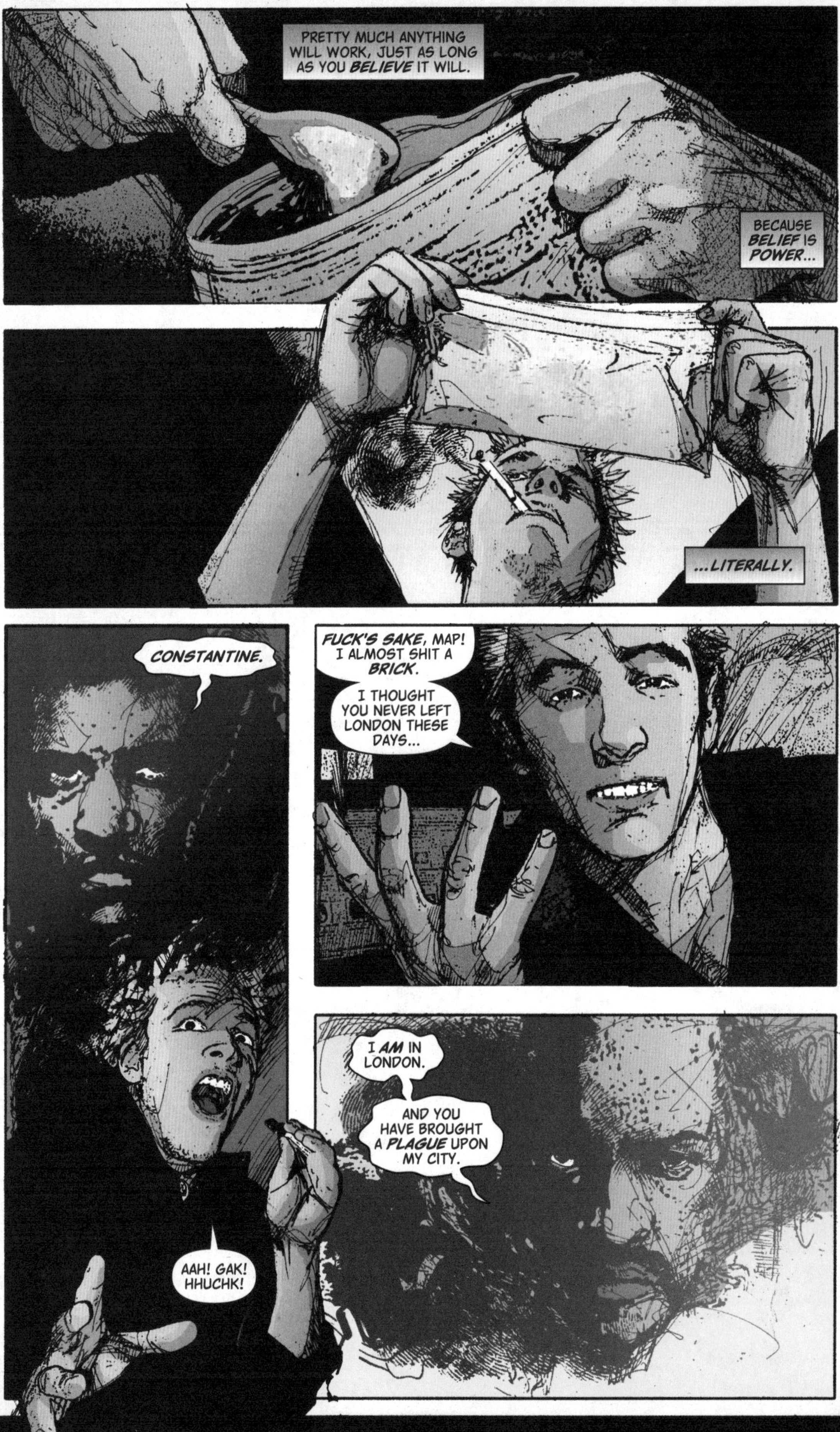

PRETTY MUCH ANYTHING WILL WORK, JUST AS LONG AS YOU BELIEVE IT WILL.
BECAUSE BELIEF IS POWER...
...LITERALLY.
CONSTANTINE.
FUCK'S SAKE, MAP! I ALMOST SHIT A BRICK.
I THOUGHT YOU NEVER LEFT LONDON THESE DAYS...
AAH! GAK! HHUCHK!
I AM IN LONDON.
AND YOU HAVE BROUGHT A PLAGUE UPON MY CITY.

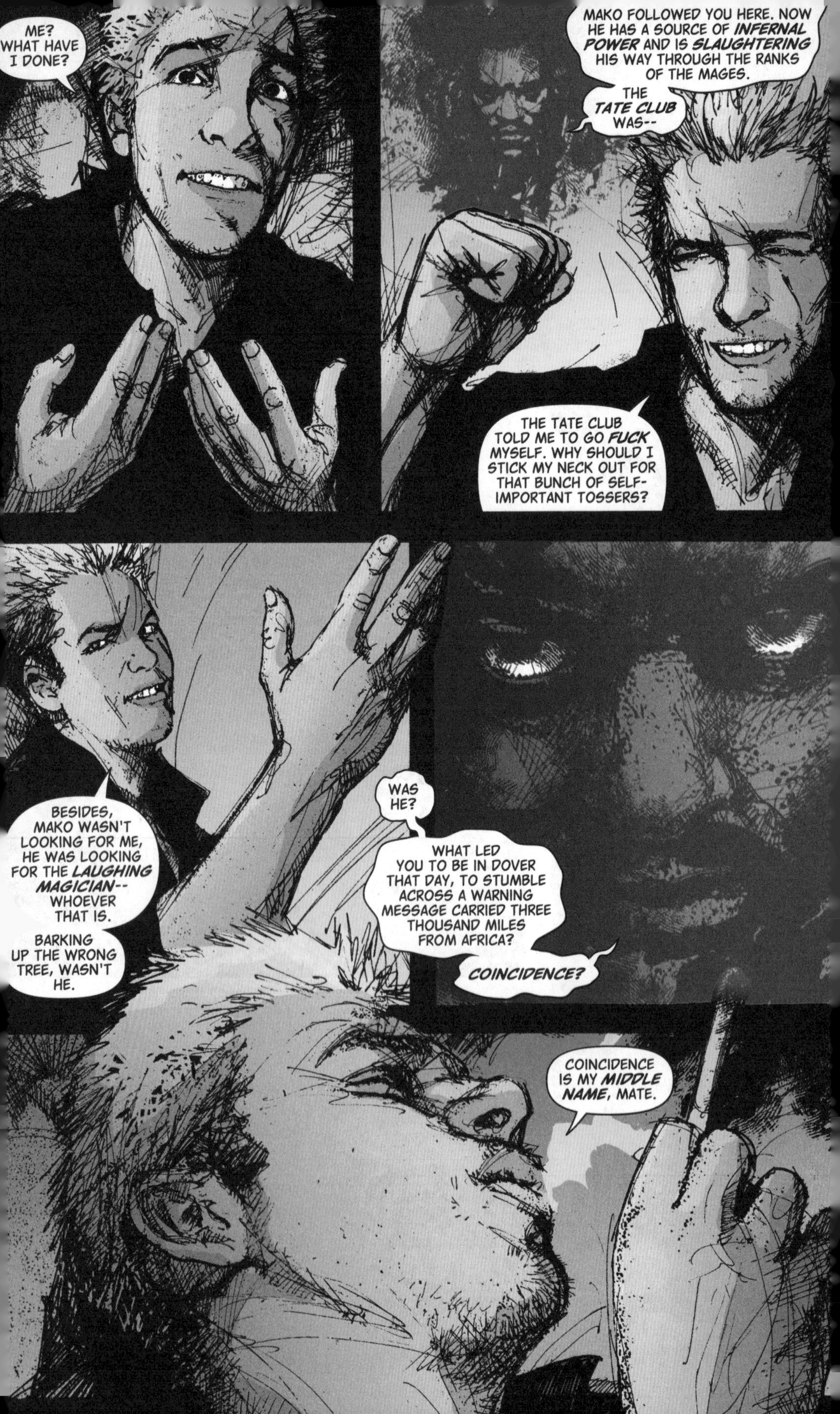
ME? WHAT HAVE I DONE?
MAKO FOLLOWED YOU HERE. NOW HE HAS A SOURCE OF INFERNAL POWER AND IS SLAUGHTERING HIS WAY THROUGH THE RANKS OF THE MAGES.
THE TATE CLUB WAS--
THE TATE CLUB TOLD ME TO GO FUCK MYSELF. WHY SHOULD I STICK MY NECK OUT FOR THAT BUNCH OF SELF-IMPORTANT TOSSERS?
BESIDES, MAKO WASN'T LOOKING FOR ME, HE WAS LOOKING FOR THE LAUGHING MAGICIAN-- WHOEVER THAT IS.
BARKING UP THE WRONG TREE, WASN'T HE.
WAS HE?
WHAT LED YOU TO BE IN DOVER THAT DAY, TO STUMBLE ACROSS A WARNING MESSAGE CARRIED THREE THOUSAND MILES FROM AFRICA?
COINCIDENCE?
COINCIDENCE IS MY MIDDLE NAME, MATE.

SO IT WOULD SEEM. YOU WALK THE *SYNCHRONICITY HIGHWAY*, DANCING BETWEEN THE RAINDROPS-- APPEARING WHERE YOU ARE NEEDED, ALWAYS IN THE RIGHT PLACE AT THE RIGHT TIME...

BUT HAS IT NEVER OCCURRED TO YOU TO QUESTION *WHY?*

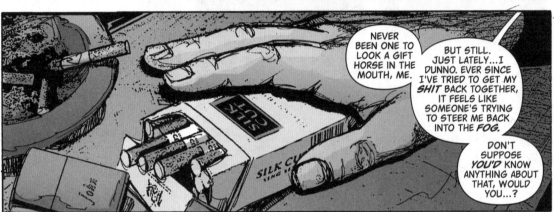

NEVER BEEN ONE TO LOOK A GIFT HORSE IN THE MOUTH, ME.

BUT STILL. JUST LATELY...I DUNNO. EVER SINCE I'VE TRIED TO GET MY *SHIT* BACK TOGETHER, IT FEELS LIKE SOMEONE'S TRYING TO STEER ME BACK INTO THE *FOG.*

DON'T SUPPOSE *YOU'D* KNOW ANYTHING ABOUT THAT, WOULD YOU...?

I CANNOT SEE. THERE IS A SHADOW ABOUT YOU.

YEAH, I KNOW-- AND THAT'S SOMETHING *ELSE* THAT BOTHERS ME.

BUT I'M ABOUT TO TAP INTO A POWER SOURCE OF ME *OWN*--AND *THEN* I'LL BE ABLE TO SEE HOW I *REALLY* FIT INTO THE GRAND SCHEME OF THINGS.

YOU ARE PLAYING WITH *FIRE*, CONSTANTINE.

YEAH, WELL. I NEEDED A *LIGHT.*

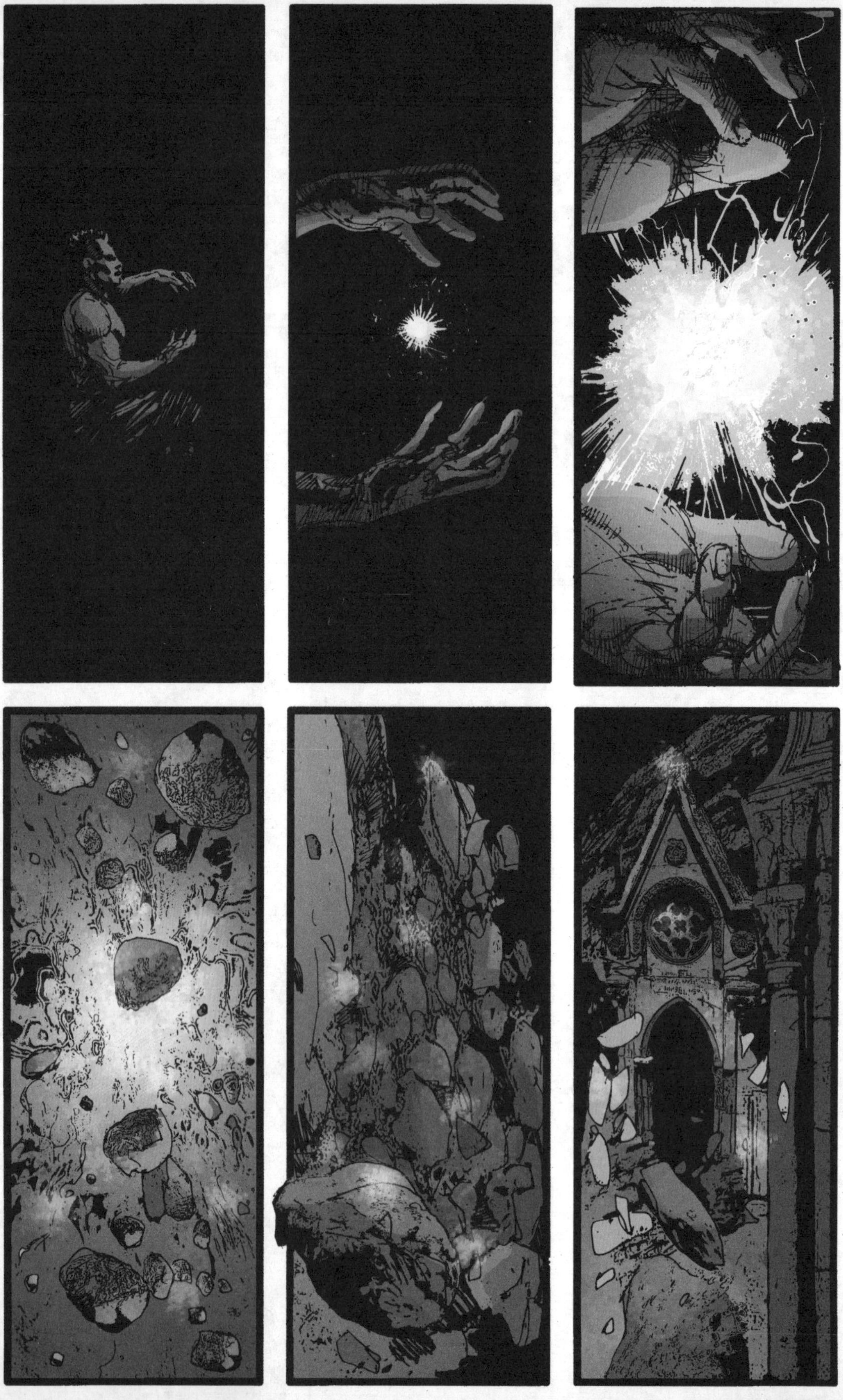

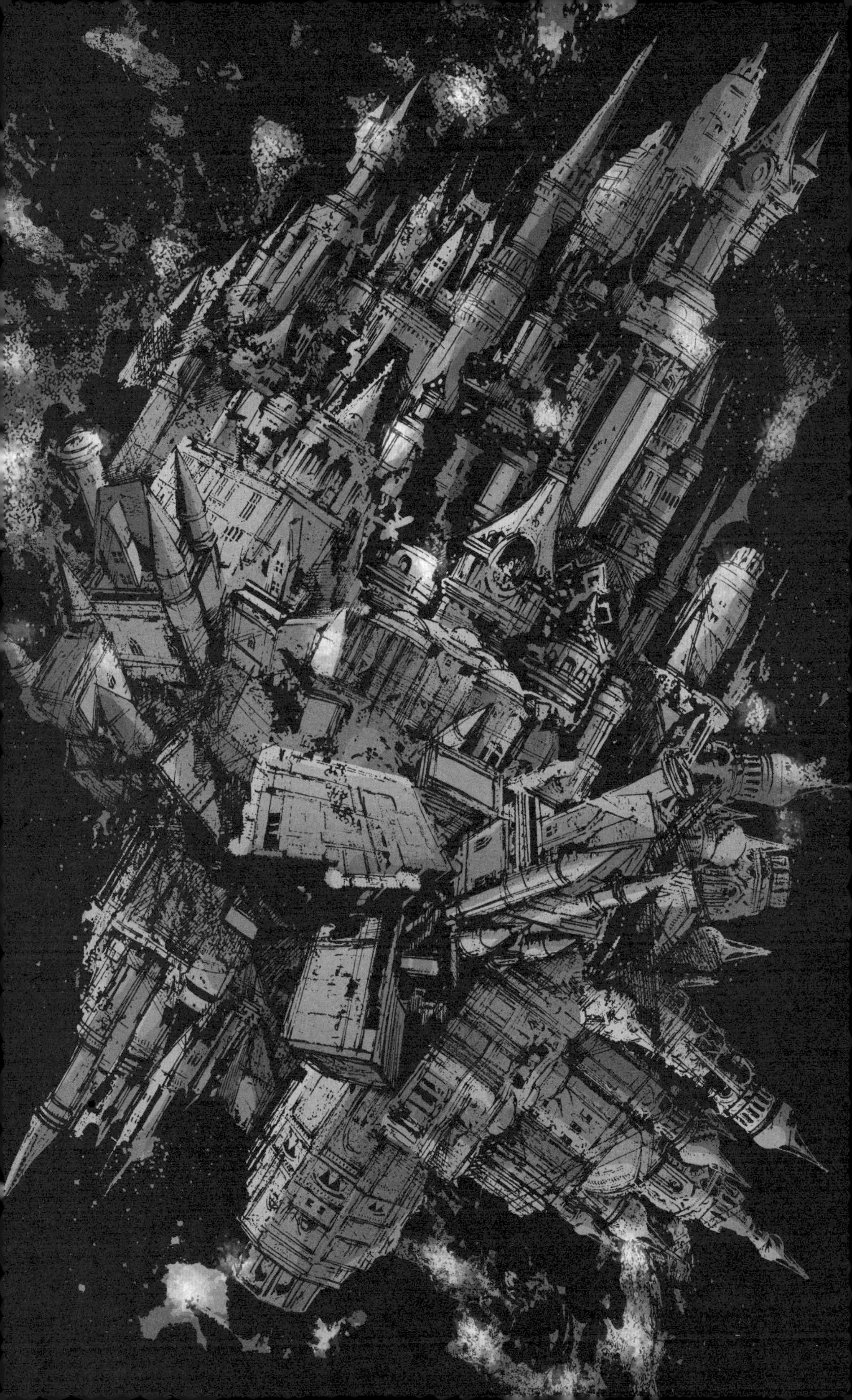

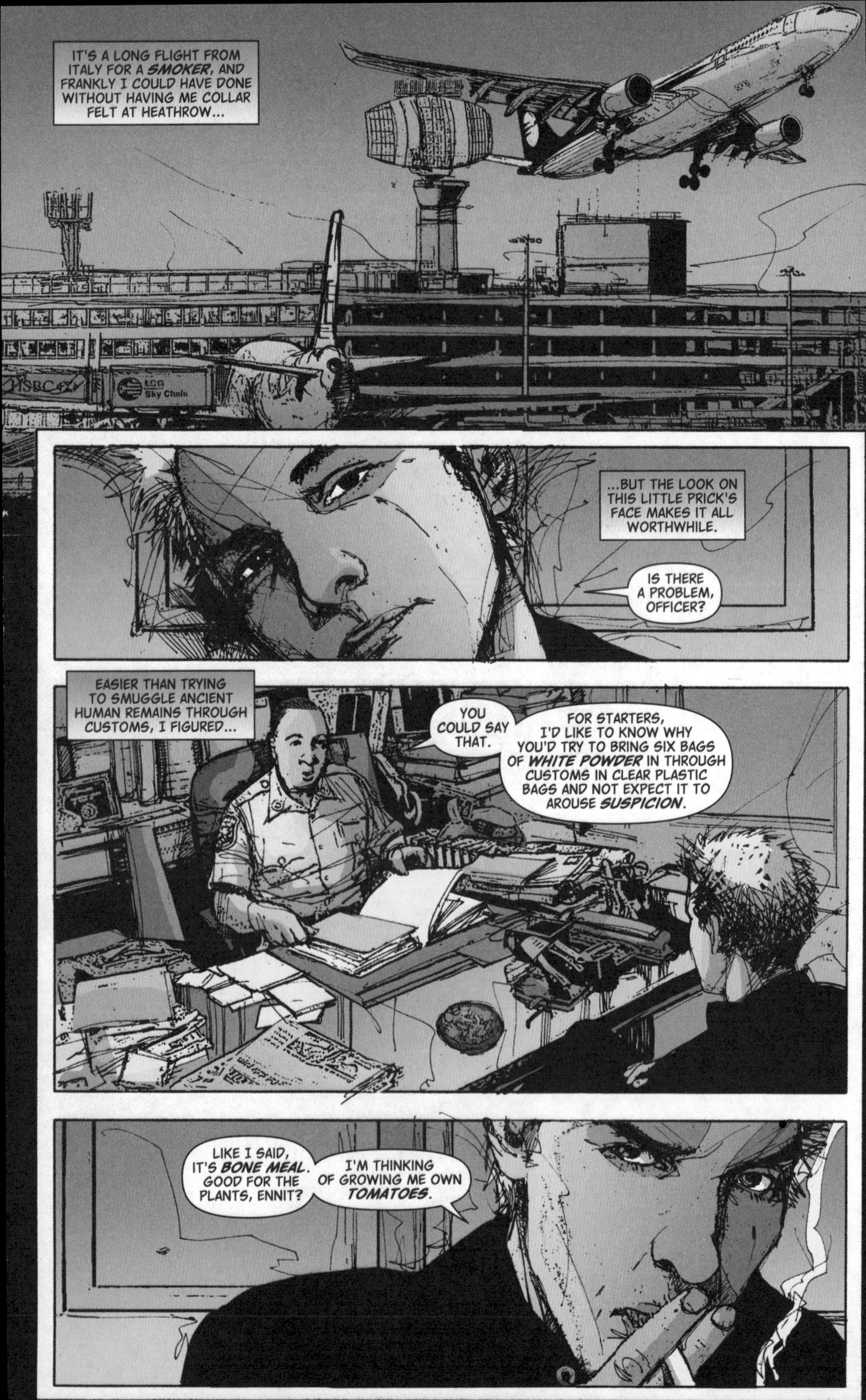
IT'S A LONG FLIGHT FROM ITALY FOR A SMOKER, AND FRANKLY I COULD HAVE DONE WITHOUT HAVING ME COLLAR FELT AT HEATHROW...
HSBC
Sky Chain
...BUT THE LOOK ON THIS LITTLE PRICK'S FACE MAKES IT ALL WORTHWHILE.
IS THERE A PROBLEM, OFFICER?
EASIER THAN TRYING TO SMUGGLE ANCIENT HUMAN REMAINS THROUGH CUSTOMS, I FIGURED...
YOU COULD SAY THAT.
FOR STARTERS, I'D LIKE TO KNOW WHY YOU'D TRY TO BRING SIX BAGS OF WHITE POWDER IN THROUGH CUSTOMS IN CLEAR PLASTIC BAGS AND NOT EXPECT IT TO AROUSE SUSPICION.
LIKE I SAID, IT'S BONE MEAL. GOOD FOR THE PLANTS, ENNIT?
I'M THINKING OF GROWING ME OWN TOMATOES.

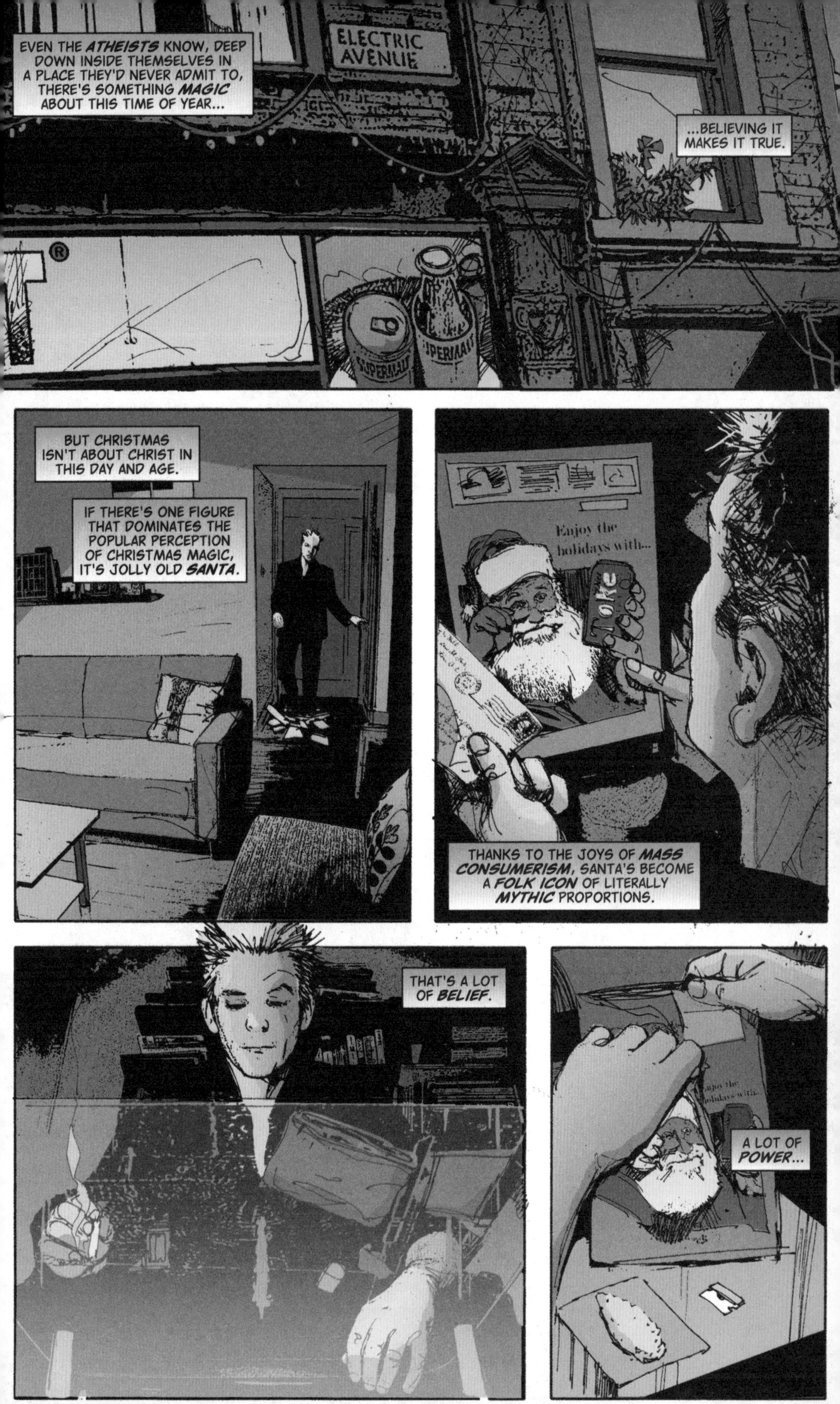
ELECTRIC AVENUE
EVEN THE *ATHEISTS* KNOW, DEEP DOWN INSIDE THEMSELVES IN A PLACE THEY'D NEVER ADMIT TO, THERE'S SOMETHING *MAGIC* ABOUT THIS TIME OF YEAR...
...BELIEVING IT MAKES IT TRUE.
BUT CHRISTMAS ISN'T ABOUT CHRIST IN THIS DAY AND AGE.
IF THERE'S ONE FIGURE THAT DOMINATES THE POPULAR PERCEPTION OF CHRISTMAS MAGIC, IT'S JOLLY OLD *SANTA*.
Enjoy the holidays with...
THANKS TO THE JOYS OF *MASS CONSUMERISM*, SANTA'S BECOME A *FOLK ICON* OF LITERALLY *MYTHIC* PROPORTIONS.
THAT'S A LOT OF *BELIEF*.
A LOT OF *POWER*...

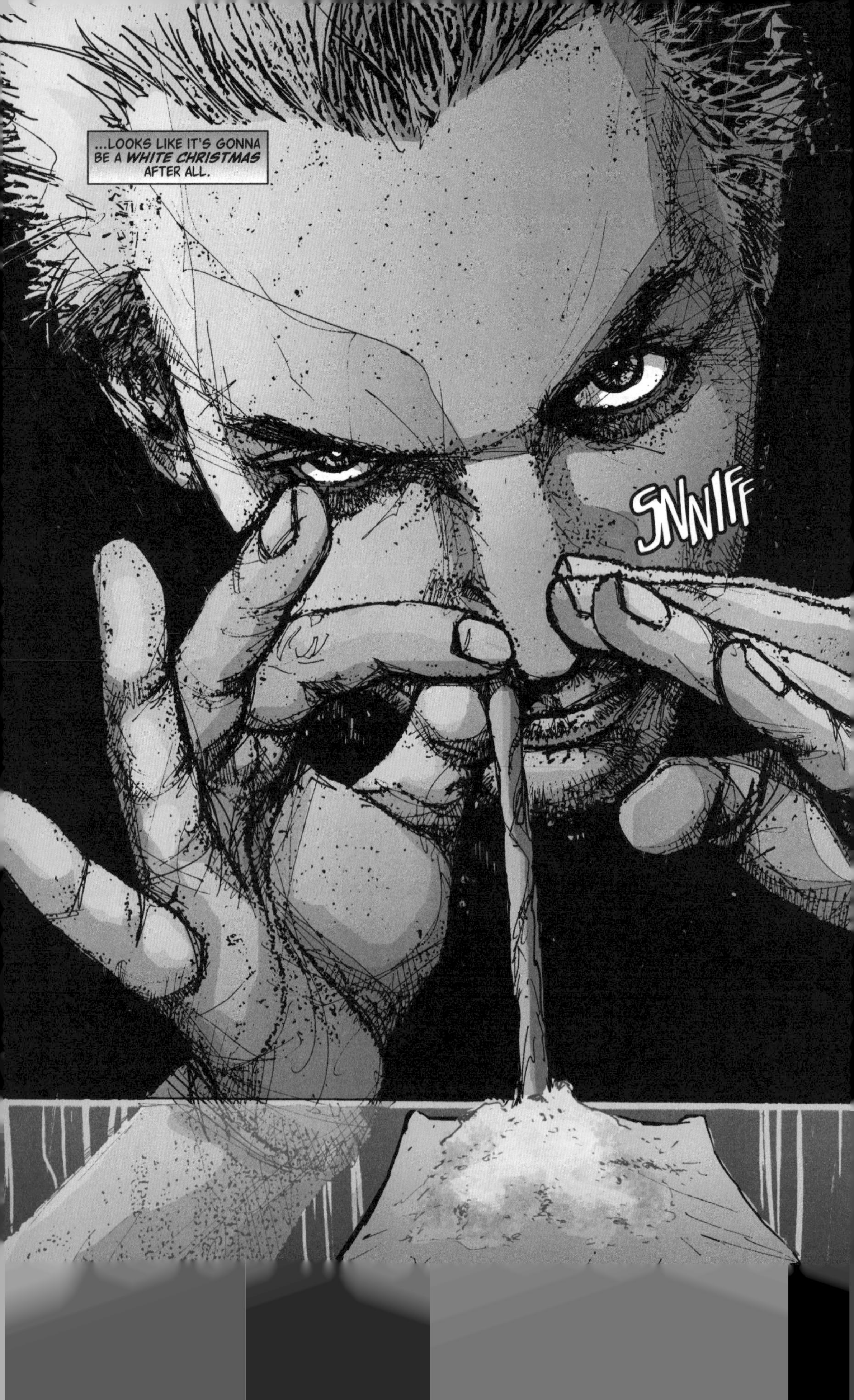
...LOOKS LIKE IT'S GONNA BE A WHITE CHRISTMAS AFTER ALL.
SNNIFF

AND JUST LIKE THAT, I'M PLUGGED INTO THE MAIN SOURCE.

ELECTRIC WITH ENERGY. LIT UP LIKE BLOODY *OXFORD STREET* ON *CHRISTMAS EVE*...

IT'S ALMOST TOO MUCH. OVERWHELMING, A TIDAL WAVE OF *RAW POWER* THREATENING TO *ENGULF* ME...

BUT IT'S NOT MY FIRST WHITE-KNUCKLE HEAD TRIP. I CAN RIDE IT OUT. HANG ON TIGHT AND GO WITH THE FLOW.

AND EVENTUALLY THE TIDAL WAVE SETTLES AND I'M *FLOATING* FACE-UP IN A SEA OF ENERGY. PURE, UNREFINED *BELIEF.*

IT'S *INTOXICATING.* I COULD GET *USED* TO THIS...

NO. *FOCUS,* JOHN...

YOU CAN'T *SEE* ME, CAN YOU, MAKO...?

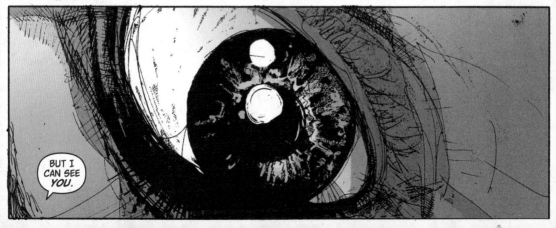

BUT I CAN SEE *YOU.*

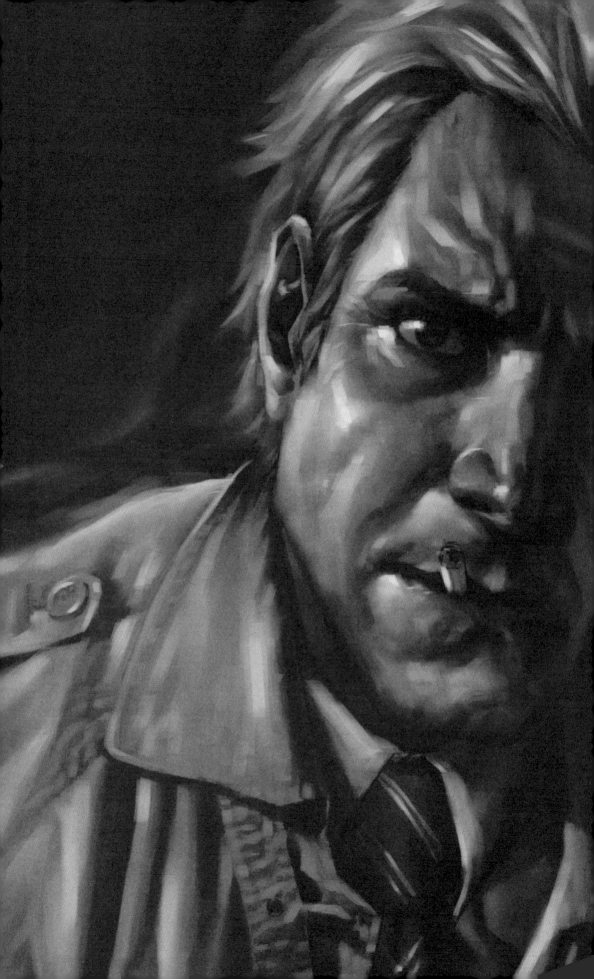

The Roots of Coincidence, Part Two

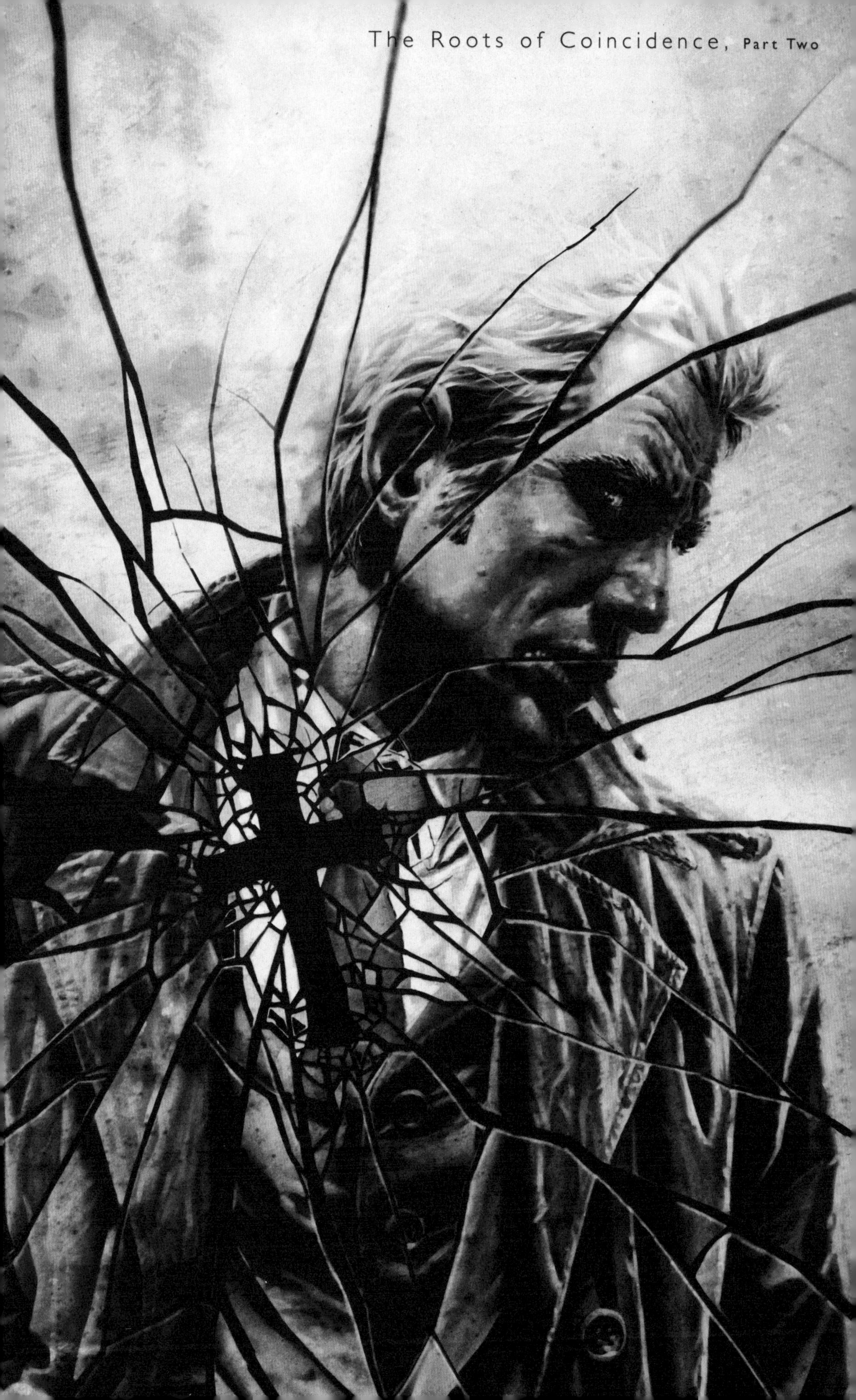

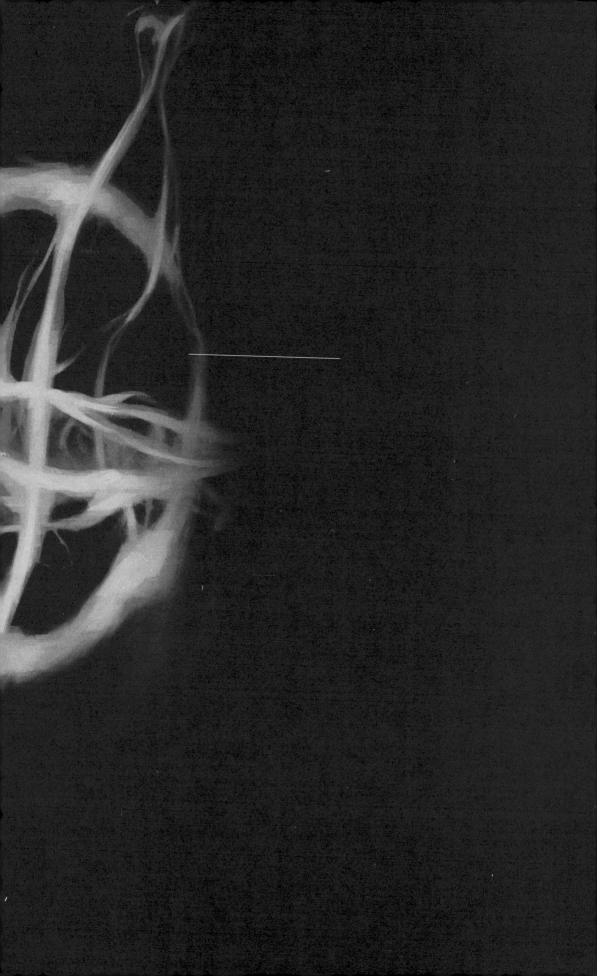

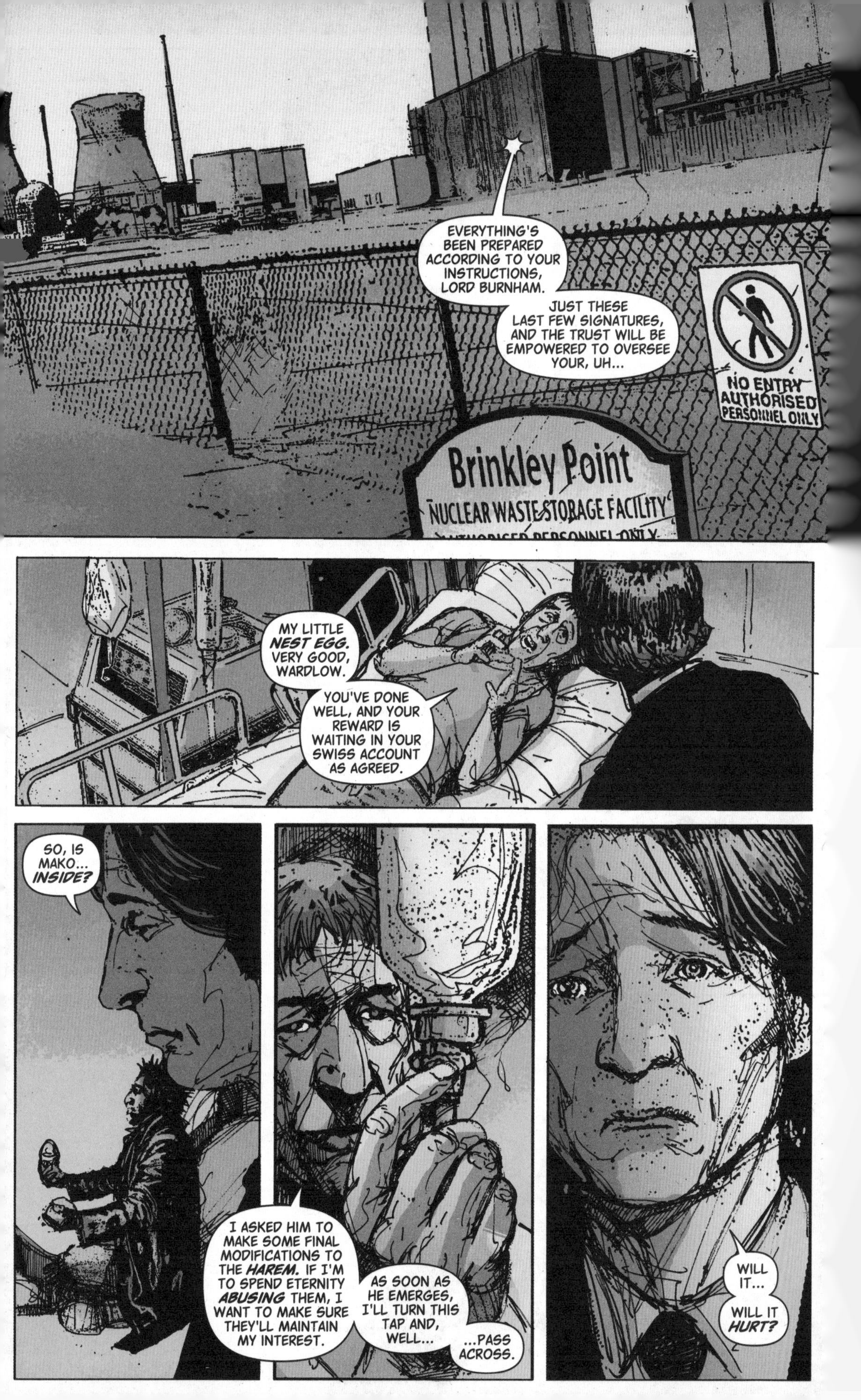
EVERYTHING'S BEEN PREPARED ACCORDING TO YOUR INSTRUCTIONS, LORD BURNHAM.
JUST THESE LAST FEW SIGNATURES, AND THE TRUST WILL BE EMPOWERED TO OVERSEE YOUR, UH...
NO ENTRY AUTHORISED PERSONNEL ONLY
Brinkley Point
NUCLEAR WASTE STORAGE FACILITY
MY LITTLE NEST EGG. VERY GOOD, WARDLOW.
YOU'VE DONE WELL, AND YOUR REWARD IS WAITING IN YOUR SWISS ACCOUNT AS AGREED.
SO, IS MAKO... INSIDE?
I ASKED HIM TO MAKE SOME FINAL MODIFICATIONS TO THE HAREM. IF I'M TO SPEND ETERNITY ABUSING THEM, I WANT TO MAKE SURE THEY'LL MAINTAIN MY INTEREST.
AS SOON AS HE EMERGES, I'LL TURN THIS TAP AND, WELL...
...PASS ACROSS.
WILL IT...
WILL IT HURT?

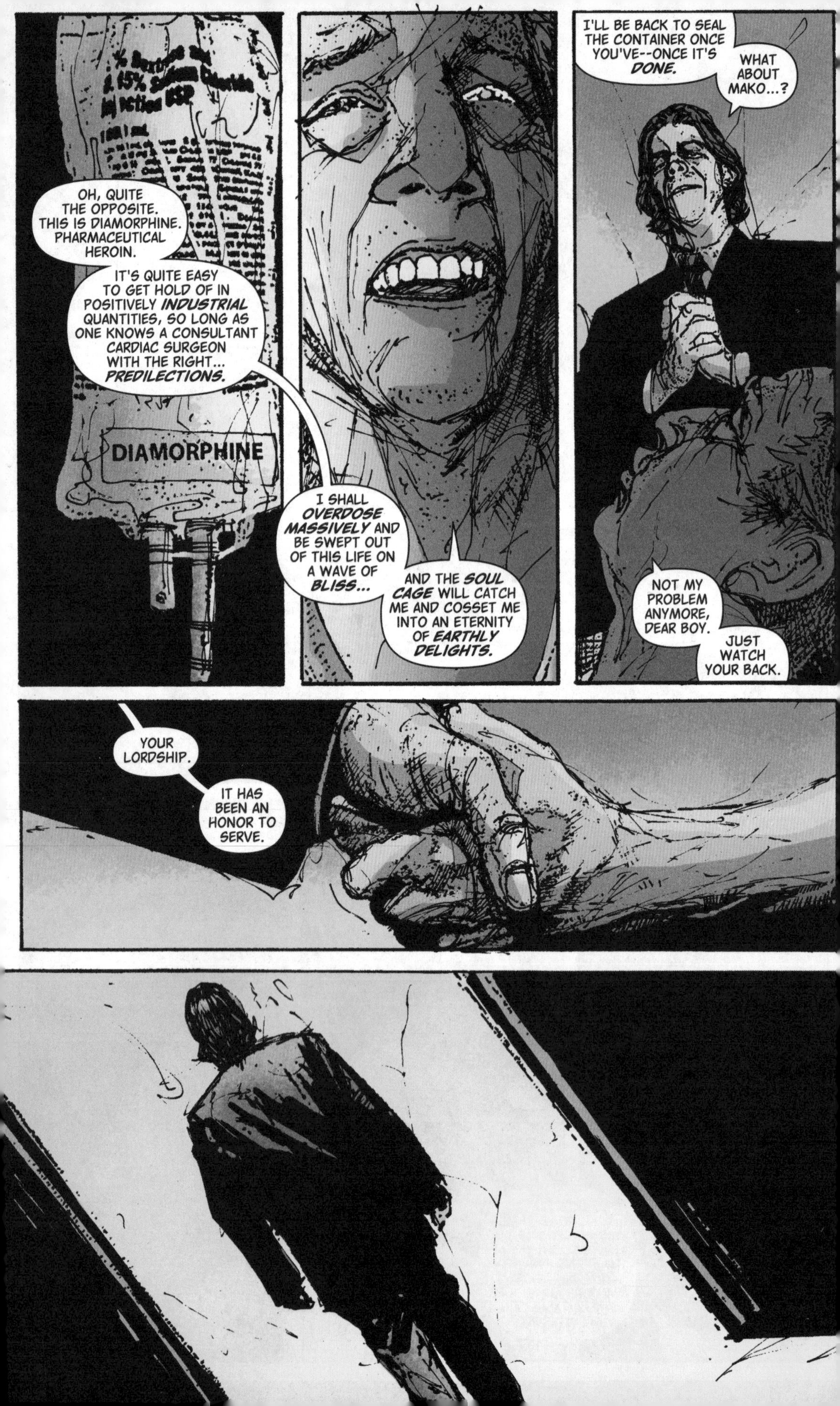
DIAMORPHINE
OH, QUITE THE OPPOSITE. THIS IS DIAMORPHINE. PHARMACEUTICAL HEROIN.
IT'S QUITE EASY TO GET HOLD OF IN POSITIVELY INDUSTRIAL QUANTITIES, SO LONG AS ONE KNOWS A CONSULTANT CARDIAC SURGEON WITH THE RIGHT... PREDILECTIONS.
I SHALL OVERDOSE MASSIVELY AND BE SWEPT OUT OF THIS LIFE ON A WAVE OF BLISS...
AND THE SOUL CAGE WILL CATCH ME AND COSSET ME INTO AN ETERNITY OF EARTHLY DELIGHTS.
I'LL BE BACK TO SEAL THE CONTAINER ONCE YOU'VE--ONCE IT'S DONE.
WHAT ABOUT MAKO...?
NOT MY PROBLEM ANYMORE, DEAR BOY.
JUST WATCH YOUR BACK.
YOUR LORDSHIP.
IT HAS BEEN AN HONOR TO SERVE.

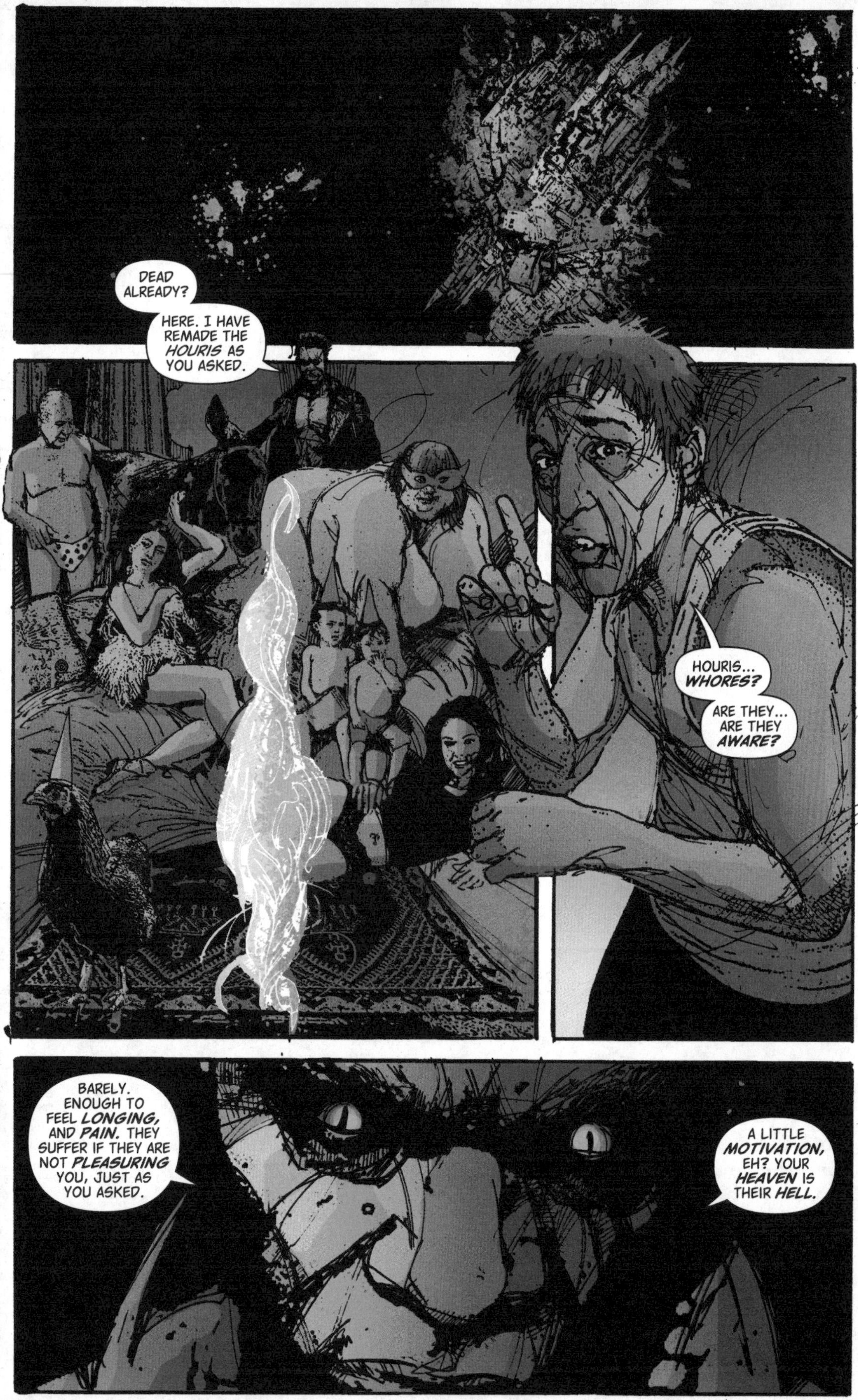
DEAD ALREADY?
HERE. I HAVE REMADE THE *HOURIS* AS YOU ASKED.
HOURIS... ***WHORES?***
ARE THEY... ARE THEY ***AWARE?***
BARELY. ENOUGH TO FEEL ***LONGING,*** AND ***PAIN.*** THEY SUFFER IF THEY ARE NOT ***PLEASURING*** YOU, JUST AS YOU ASKED.
A LITTLE ***MOTIVATION,*** EH? YOUR ***HEAVEN*** IS THEIR ***HELL.***

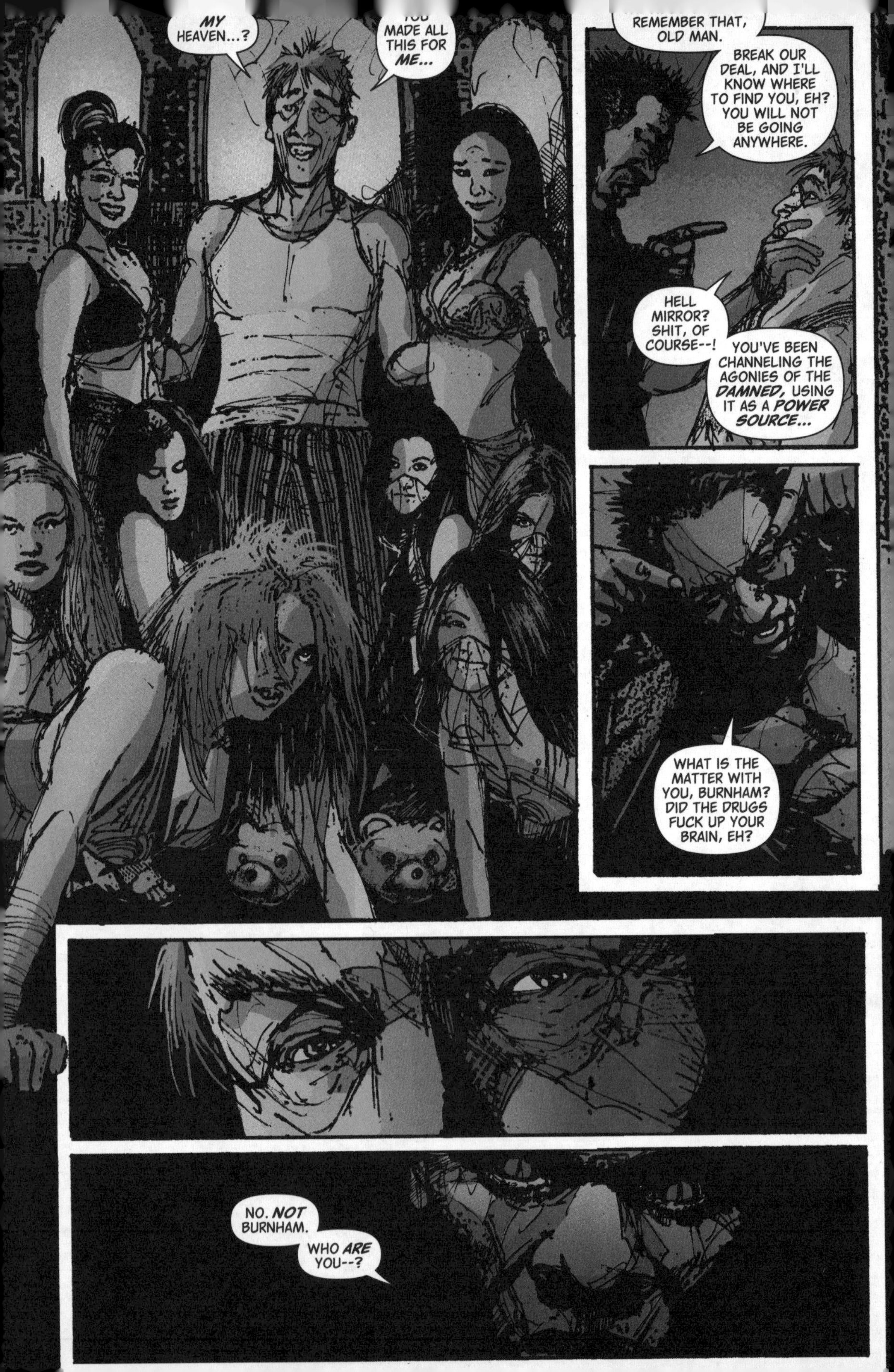
MY HEAVEN...?
MADE ALL THIS FOR ME...
REMEMBER THAT, OLD MAN.
BREAK OUR DEAL, AND I'LL KNOW WHERE TO FIND YOU, EH? YOU WILL NOT BE GOING ANYWHERE.
HELL MIRROR? SHIT, OF COURSE--!
YOU'VE BEEN CHANNELING THE AGONIES OF THE DAMNED, USING IT AS A POWER SOURCE...
WHAT IS THE MATTER WITH YOU, BURNHAM? DID THE DRUGS FUCK UP YOUR BRAIN, EH?
NO. NOT BURNHAM.
WHO ARE YOU--?

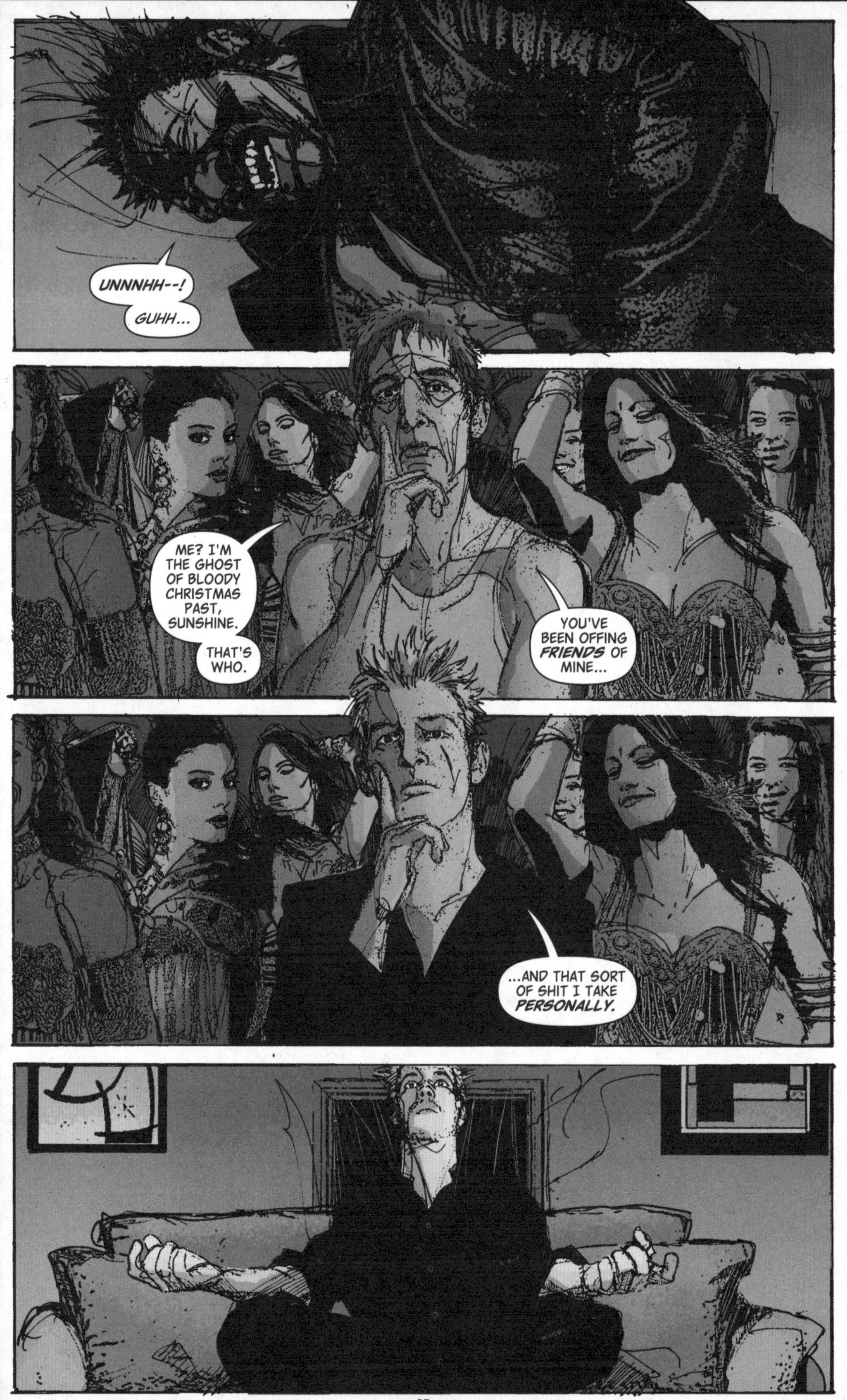
UNNNHH--!
GUHH...
ME? I'M THE GHOST OF BLOODY CHRISTMAS PAST, SUNSHINE.
THAT'S WHO.
YOU'VE BEEN OFFING FRIENDS OF MINE...
...AND THAT SORT OF SHIT I TAKE PERSONALLY.

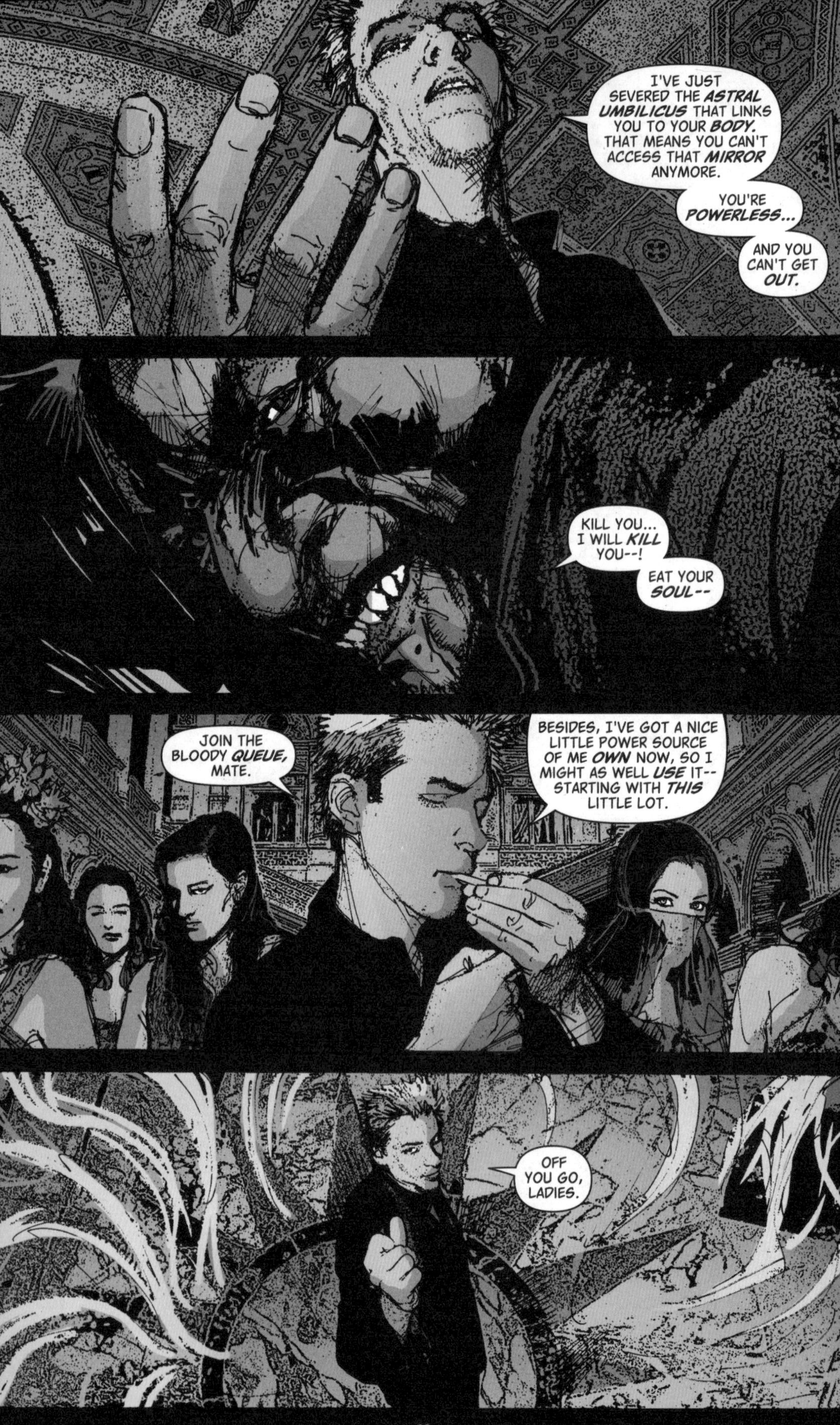
I'VE JUST SEVERED THE ASTRAL UMBILICUS THAT LINKS YOU TO YOUR BODY. THAT MEANS YOU CAN'T ACCESS THAT MIRROR ANYMORE.
YOU'RE POWERLESS...
AND YOU CAN'T GET OUT.
KILL YOU... I WILL KILL YOU--!
EAT YOUR SOUL--
JOIN THE BLOODY QUEUE, MATE.
BESIDES, I'VE GOT A NICE LITTLE POWER SOURCE OF ME OWN NOW, SO I MIGHT AS WELL USE IT-- STARTING WITH THIS LITTLE LOT.
OFF YOU GO, LADIES.

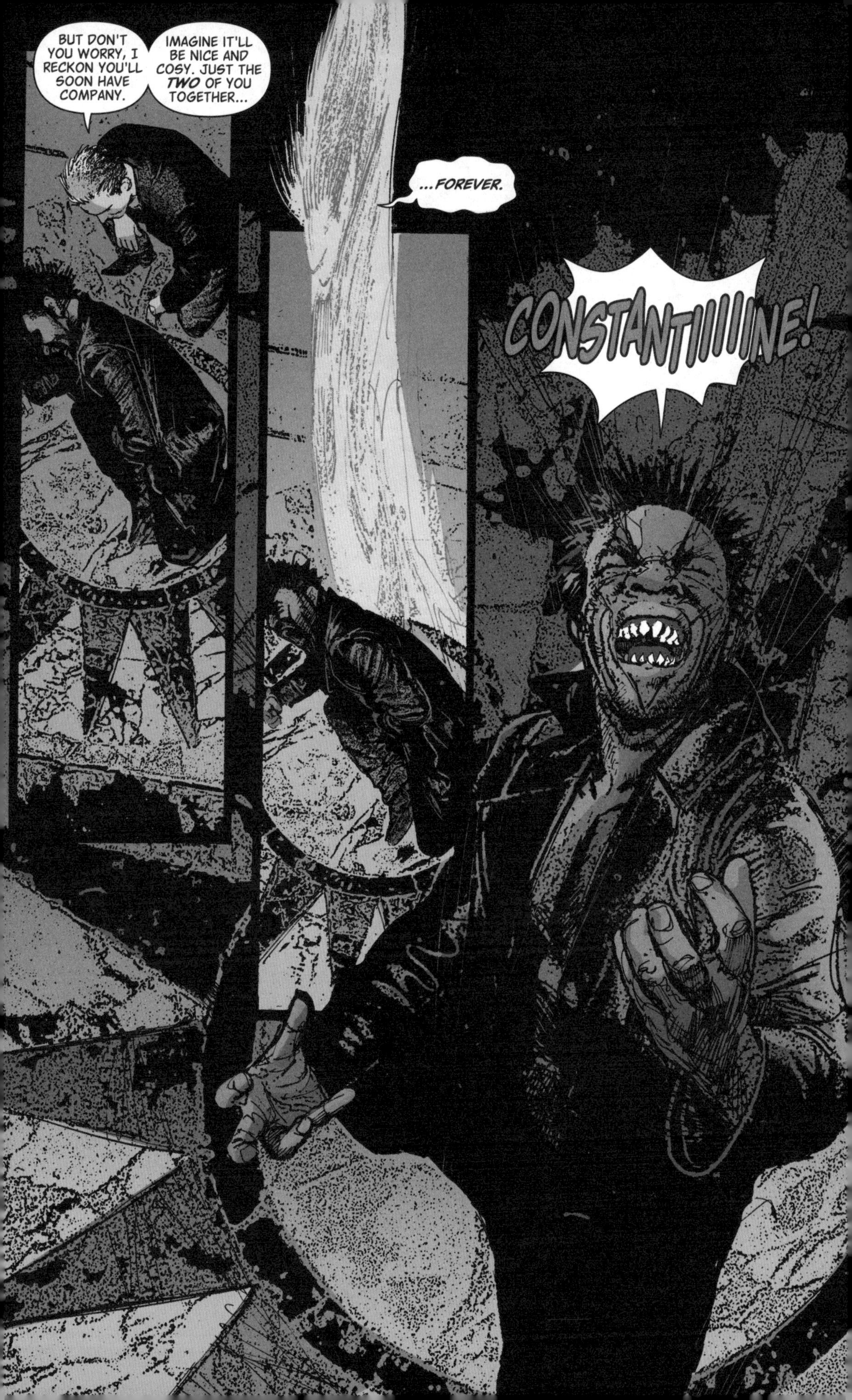
BUT DON'T YOU WORRY, I RECKON YOU'LL SOON HAVE COMPANY.
IMAGINE IT'LL BE NICE AND COSY. JUST THE *TWO* OF YOU TOGETHER...
...FOREVER.
CONSTANTIIIIIINE!

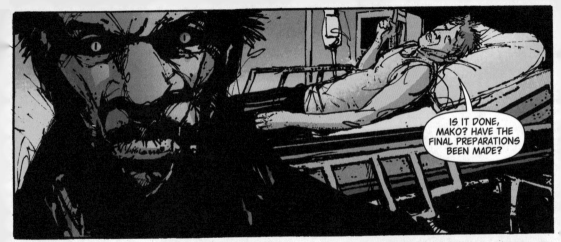

IS IT DONE, MAKO? HAVE THE FINAL PREPARATIONS BEEN MADE?

...READY WHEN YOU ARE.

THEN IT'S TIME.

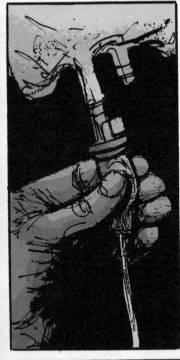

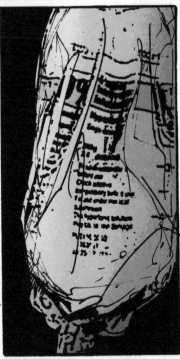

AAAAAHHH...

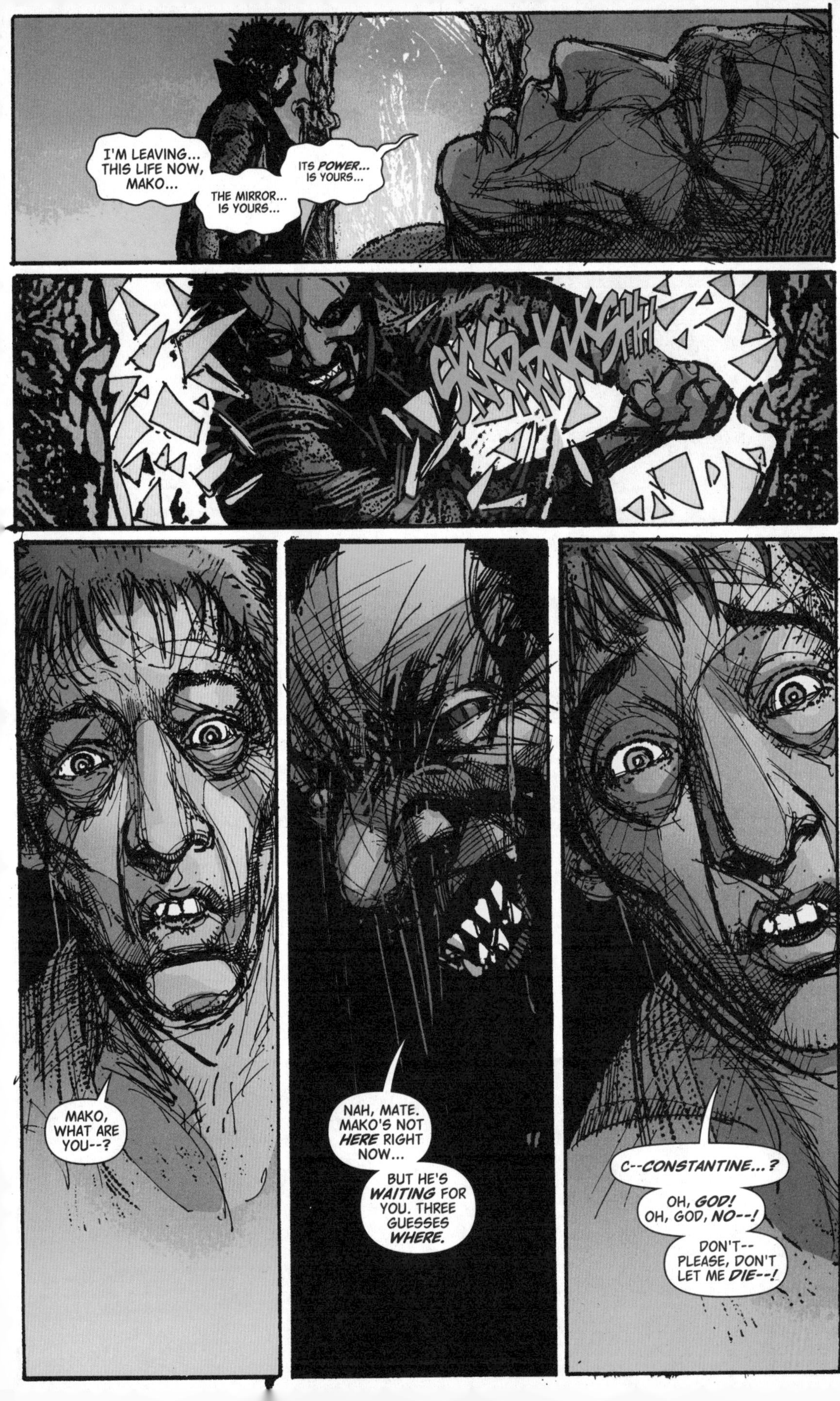
I'M LEAVING... THIS LIFE NOW, MAKO...
THE MIRROR... IS YOURS...
ITS *POWER*... IS YOURS...
SKRRKKSHH
MAKO, WHAT ARE YOU--?
NAH, MATE. MAKO'S NOT *HERE* RIGHT NOW...
BUT HE'S *WAITING* FOR YOU. THREE GUESSES *WHERE.*
C--*CONSTANTINE...?*
OH, *GOD!* OH, GOD, *NO--!*
DON'T-- PLEASE, DON'T LET ME *DIE--!*

THE *SYRINGE!* NEED... *ADRENALINE--*

P-PLEASE...

YOU WERE IN MAKO'S *MIND.* I CAN SEE IT *ALL* NOW. ALL THE *ANGLES...*

ALL THE *LITTLE PEOPLE* YOU'VE FUCKED OVER--ALL THE *INNOCENT LIVES* YOU'VE DESTROYED-- IN YOUR SCRAMBLE FOR MONEY AND POWER AND NASTY KICKS WITHOUT CONSEQUENCES.

WELL *I'M* THE FUCKING CONSEQUENCES, SUNSHINE.

AND I'M THINKING *MAKO* WON'T BE TOO CHUFFED THAT YOU GOT HIM TRAPPED IN THAT *SOUL CAGE* FOR THE REST OF ETERNITY.

YOUR PRIVATE HEAVEN JUST TURNED INTO A PRIVATE *HELL,* MATE-- AND *MAKO'S* THE *DEVIL.*

GIVE HIM MY BEST WHEN YOU GET THERE, WON'T YOU?

A-ANYTHING... I'LL GIVE YOU ANYTHING...

I CAN MAKE YOU RICH...

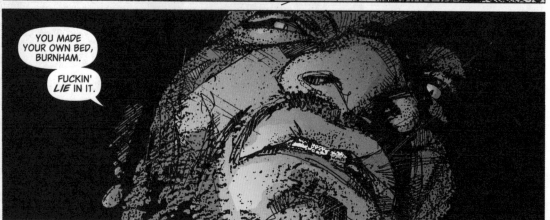

YOU MADE YOUR OWN BED, BURNHAM.

FUCKIN' *LIE* IN IT.

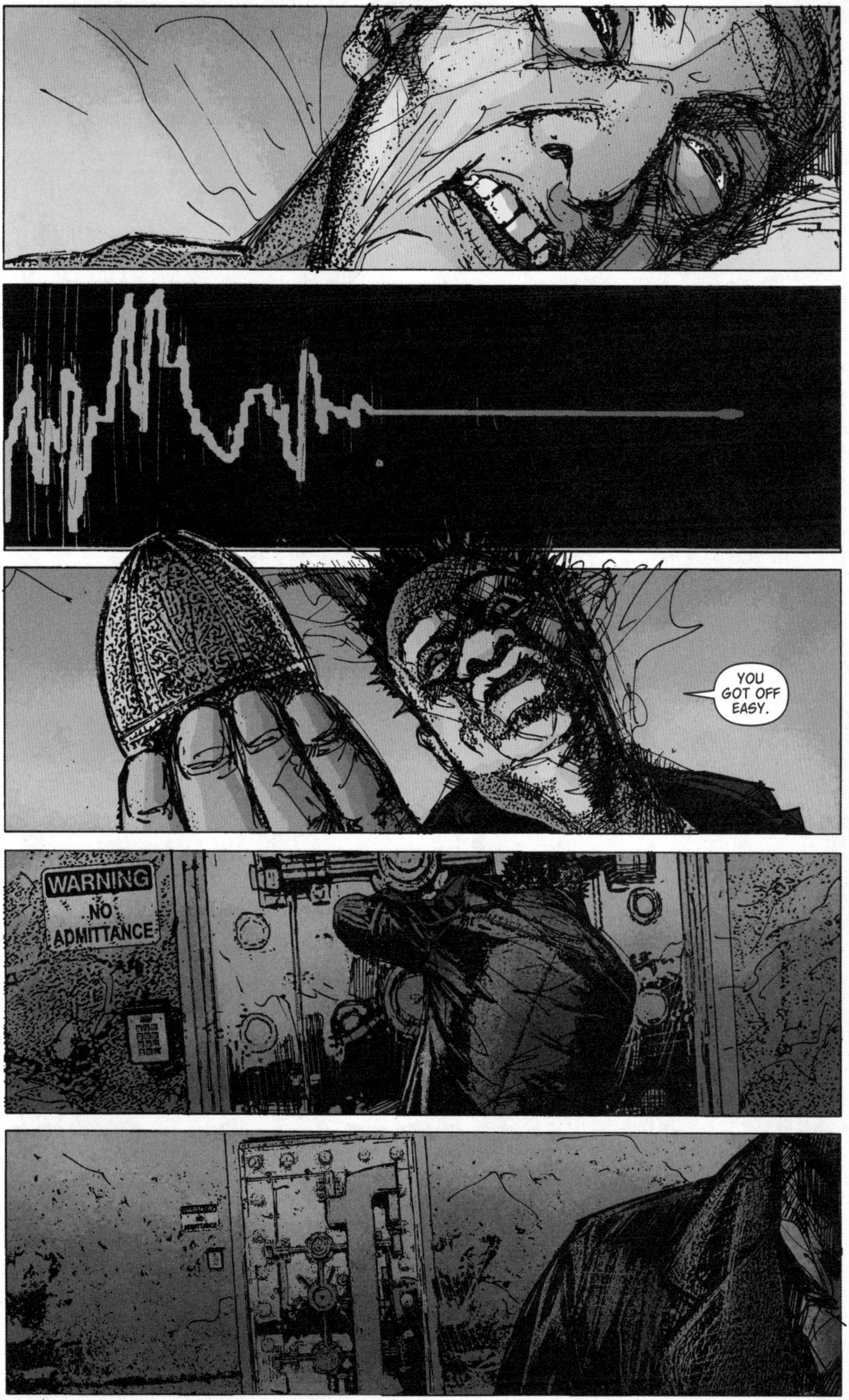
YOU GOT OFF EASY.
WARNING
NO
ADMITTANCE

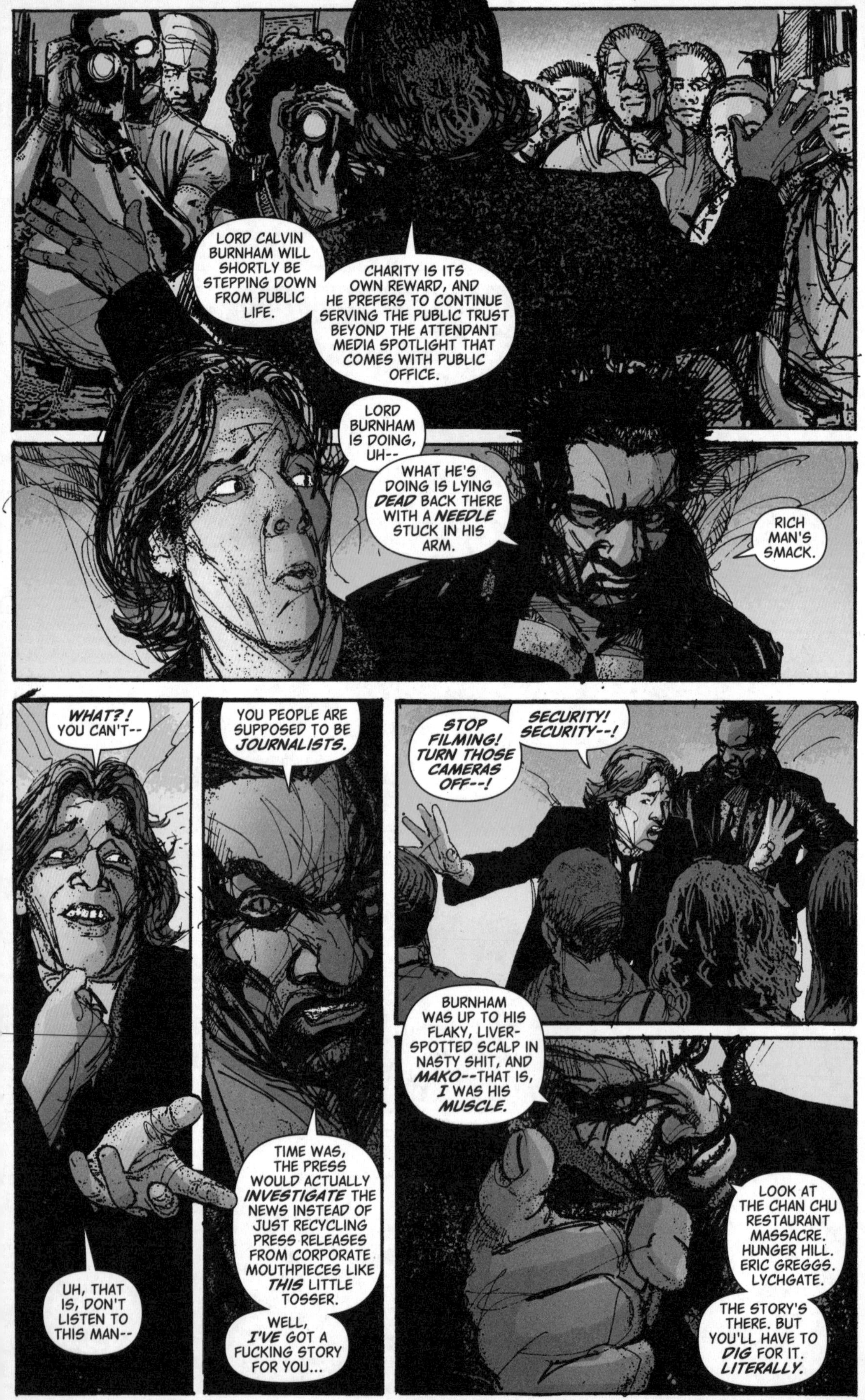
LORD CALVIN BURNHAM WILL SHORTLY BE STEPPING DOWN FROM PUBLIC LIFE.
CHARITY IS ITS OWN REWARD, AND HE PREFERS TO CONTINUE SERVING THE PUBLIC TRUST BEYOND THE ATTENDANT MEDIA SPOTLIGHT THAT COMES WITH PUBLIC OFFICE.
LORD BURNHAM IS DOING, UH--
WHAT HE'S DOING IS LYING DEAD BACK THERE WITH A NEEDLE STUCK IN HIS ARM.
RICH MAN'S SMACK.
WHAT?! YOU CAN'T--
UH, THAT IS, DON'T LISTEN TO THIS MAN--
YOU PEOPLE ARE SUPPOSED TO BE JOURNALISTS.
TIME WAS, THE PRESS WOULD ACTUALLY INVESTIGATE THE NEWS INSTEAD OF JUST RECYCLING PRESS RELEASES FROM CORPORATE MOUTHPIECES LIKE THIS LITTLE TOSSER.
WELL, I'VE GOT A FUCKING STORY FOR YOU...
STOP FILMING! TURN THOSE CAMERAS OFF--!
SECURITY! SECURITY--!
BURNHAM WAS UP TO HIS FLAKY, LIVER-SPOTTED SCALP IN NASTY SHIT, AND MAKO--THAT IS, I WAS HIS MUSCLE.
LOOK AT THE CHAN CHU RESTAURANT MASSACRE. HUNGER HILL. ERIC GREGGS. LYCHGATE.
THE STORY'S THERE. BUT YOU'LL HAVE TO DIG FOR IT. LITERALLY.

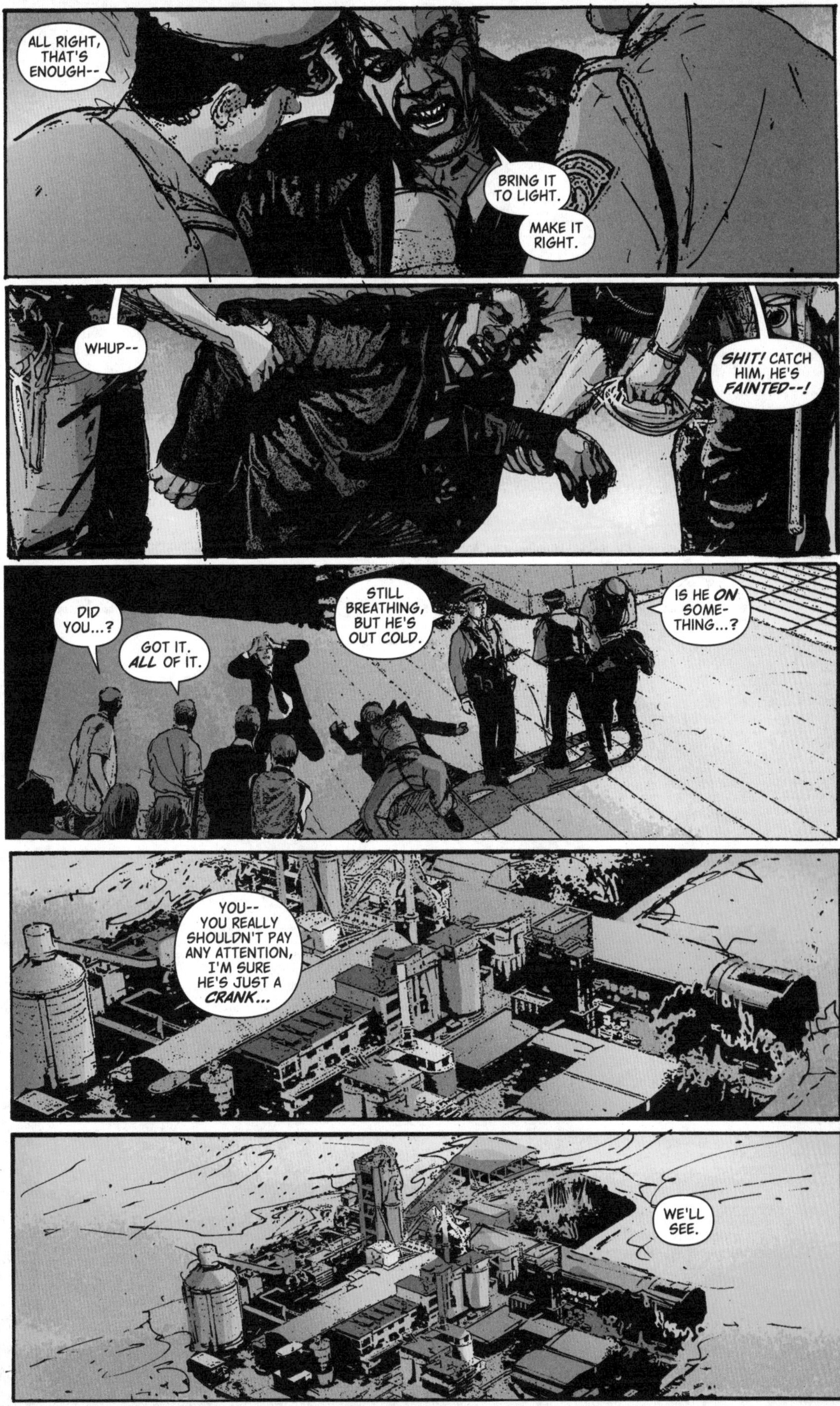
ALL RIGHT, THAT'S ENOUGH--
BRING IT TO LIGHT.
MAKE IT RIGHT.
WHUP--
SHIT! CATCH HIM, HE'S FAINTED--!
DID YOU...?
GOT IT. ALL OF IT.
STILL BREATHING, BUT HE'S OUT COLD.
IS HE ON SOME-THING...?
YOU-- YOU REALLY SHOULDN'T PAY ANY ATTENTION, I'M SURE HE'S JUST A CRANK...
WE'LL SEE.

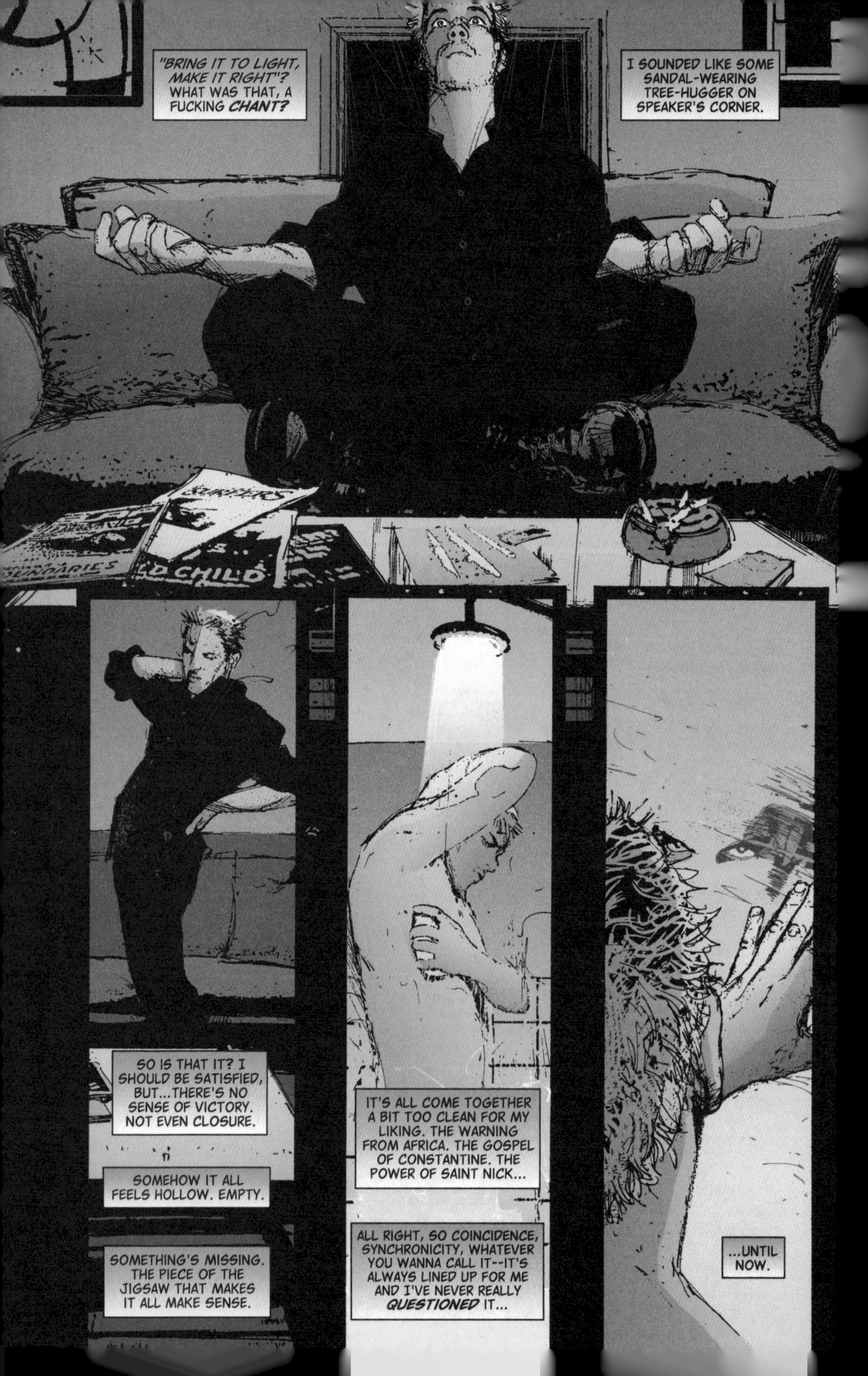
"BRING IT TO LIGHT, MAKE IT RIGHT"? WHAT WAS THAT, A FUCKING CHANT?
I SOUNDED LIKE SOME SANDAL-WEARING TREE-HUGGER ON SPEAKER'S CORNER.
SO IS THAT IT? I SHOULD BE SATISFIED, BUT...THERE'S NO SENSE OF VICTORY. NOT EVEN CLOSURE.
SOMEHOW IT ALL FEELS HOLLOW. EMPTY.
SOMETHING'S MISSING. THE PIECE OF THE JIGSAW THAT MAKES IT ALL MAKE SENSE.
IT'S ALL COME TOGETHER A BIT TOO CLEAN FOR MY LIKING. THE WARNING FROM AFRICA. THE GOSPEL OF CONSTANTINE. THE POWER OF SAINT NICK...
ALL RIGHT, SO COINCIDENCE, SYNCHRONICITY, WHATEVER YOU WANNA CALL IT--IT'S ALWAYS LINED UP FOR ME AND I'VE NEVER REALLY QUESTIONED IT...
...UNTIL NOW.

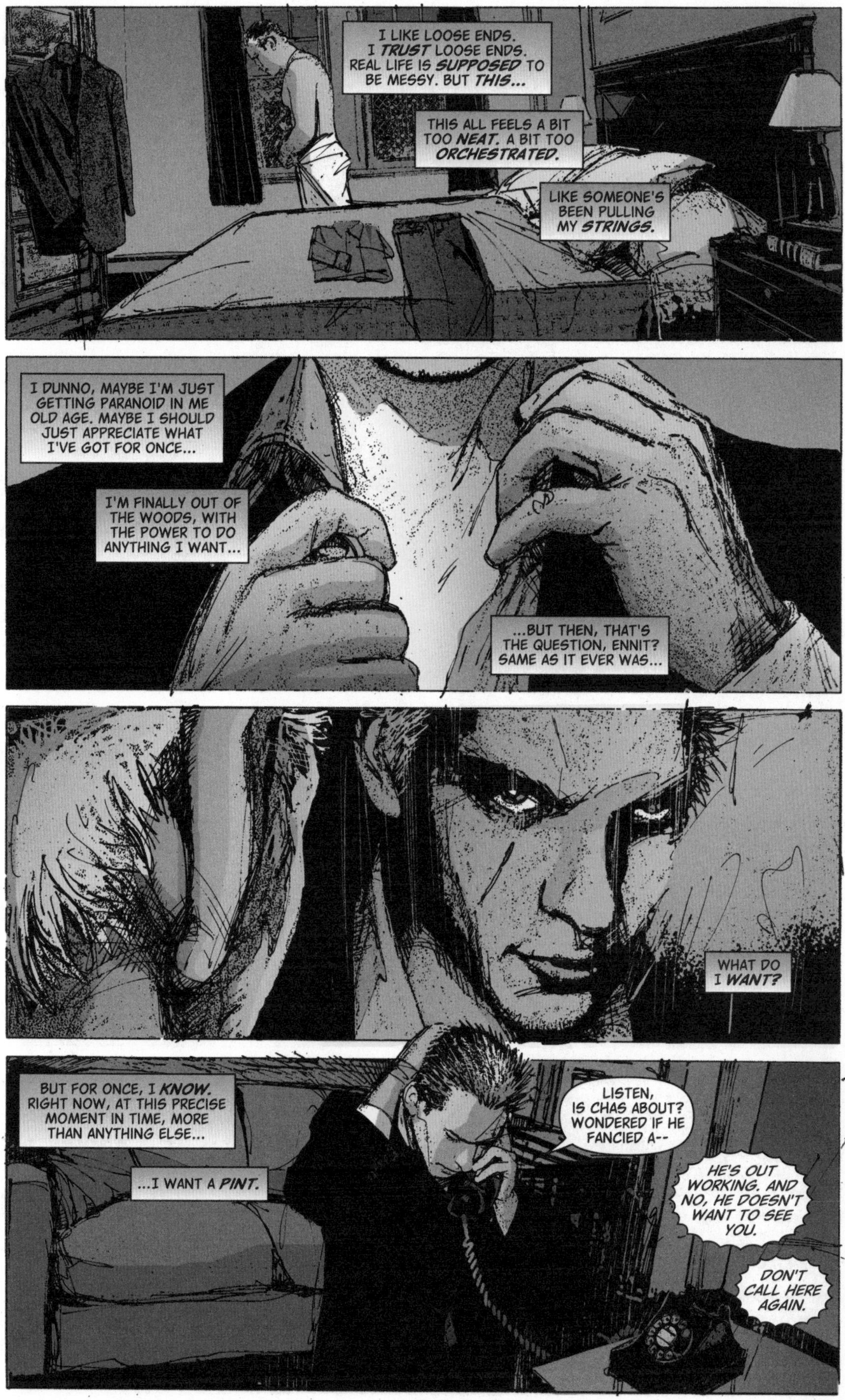

I LIKE LOOSE ENDS. I TRUST LOOSE ENDS. REAL LIFE IS SUPPOSED TO BE MESSY. BUT THIS...
THIS ALL FEELS A BIT TOO NEAT. A BIT TOO ORCHESTRATED.
LIKE SOMEONE'S BEEN PULLING MY STRINGS.
I DUNNO, MAYBE I'M JUST GETTING PARANOID IN ME OLD AGE. MAYBE I SHOULD JUST APPRECIATE WHAT I'VE GOT FOR ONCE...
I'M FINALLY OUT OF THE WOODS, WITH THE POWER TO DO ANYTHING I WANT...
...BUT THEN, THAT'S THE QUESTION, ENNIT? SAME AS IT EVER WAS...
WHAT DO I WANT?
BUT FOR ONCE, I KNOW. RIGHT NOW, AT THIS PRECISE MOMENT IN TIME, MORE THAN ANYTHING ELSE...
...I WANT A PINT.
LISTEN, IS CHAS ABOUT? WONDERED IF HE FANCIED A--
HE'S OUT WORKING. AND NO, HE DOESN'T WANT TO SEE YOU.
DON'T CALL HERE AGAIN.

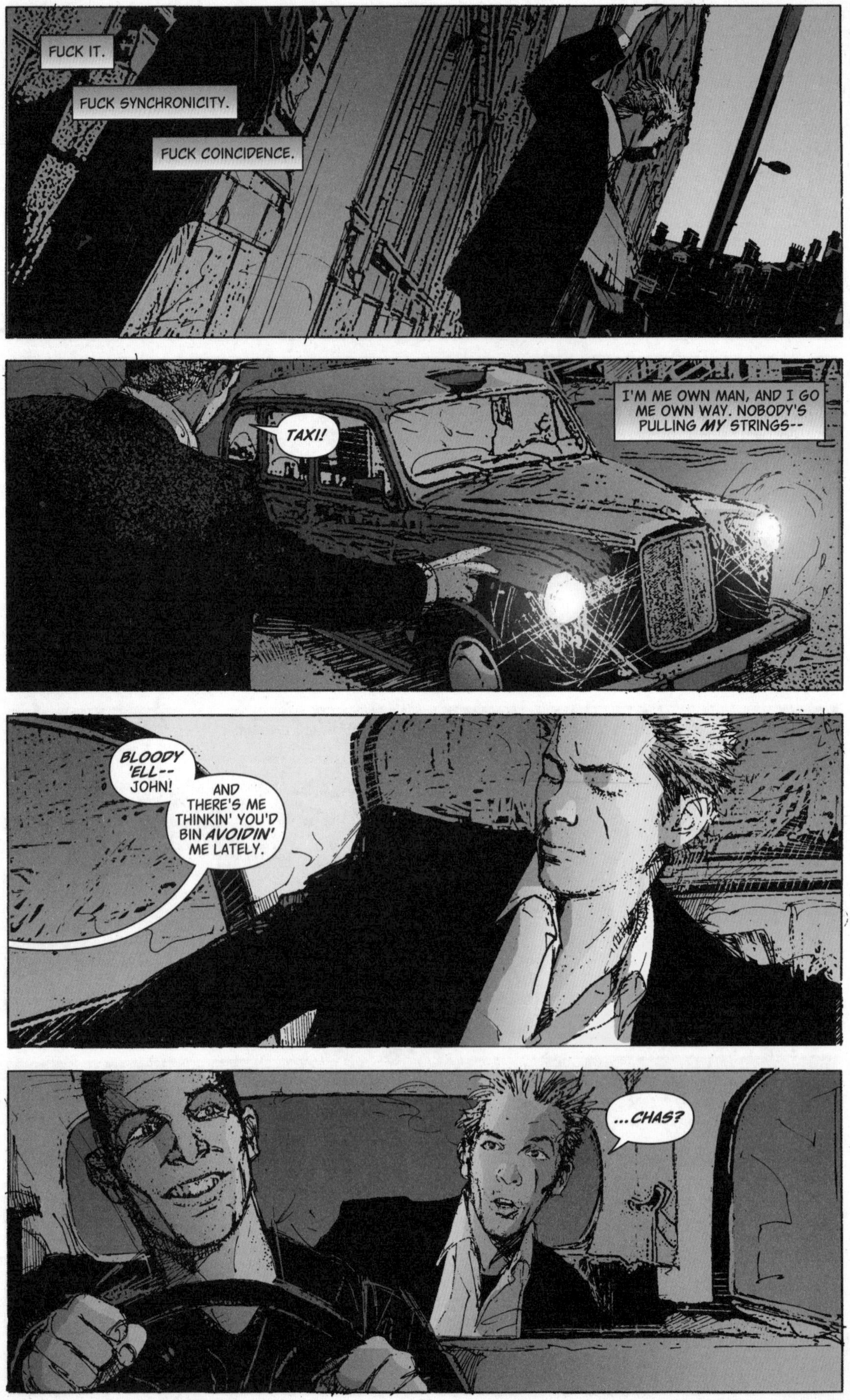
FUCK IT.
FUCK SYNCHRONICITY.
FUCK COINCIDENCE.
TAXI!
I'M ME OWN MAN, AND I GO ME OWN WAY. NOBODY'S PULLING MY STRINGS--
BLOODY 'ELL-- JOHN!
AND THERE'S ME THINKIN' YOU'D BIN AVOIDIN' ME LATELY.
...CHAS?

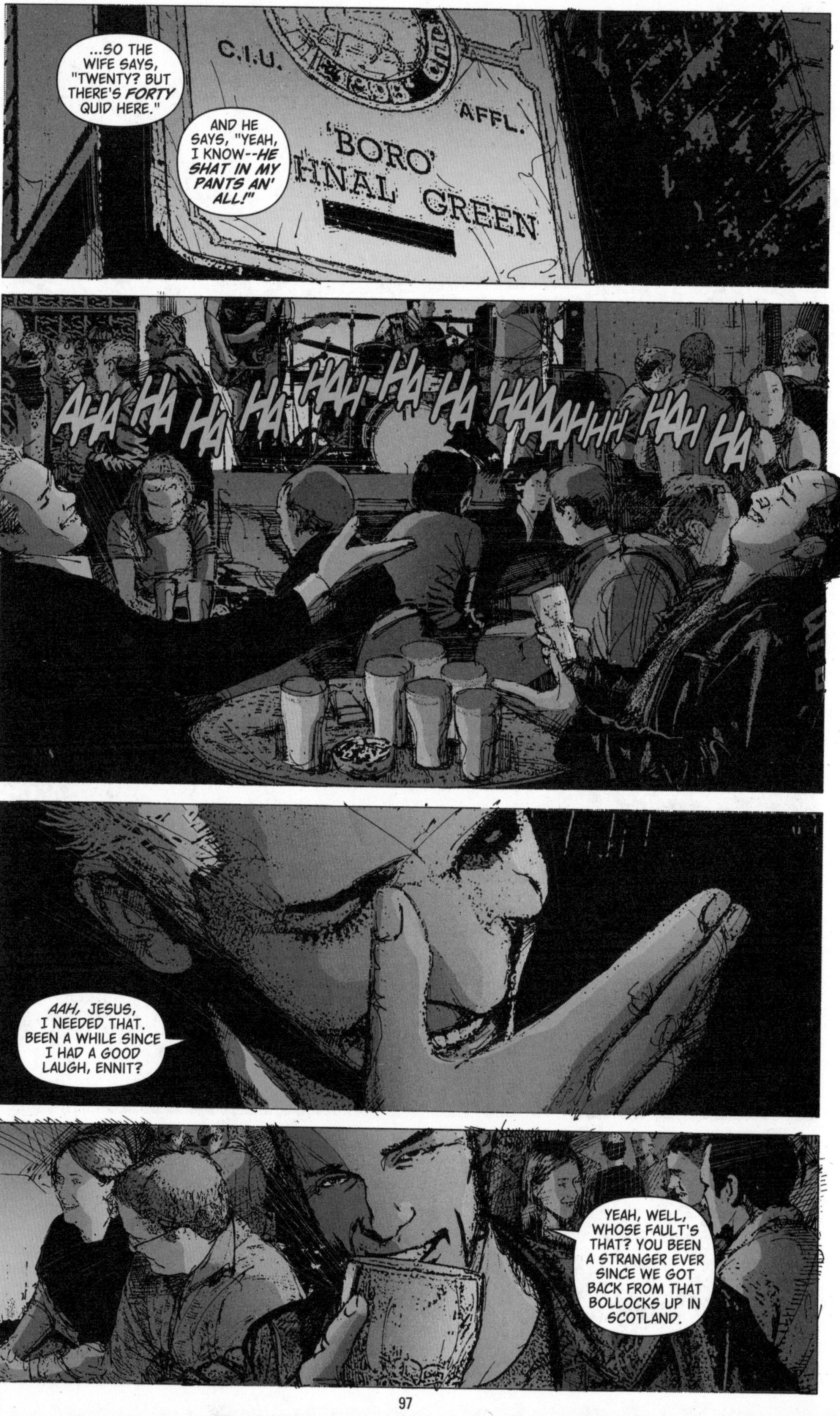
C.I.U.
AFFL.
'BORO'
HNAL GREEN
[redacted]
...SO THE WIFE SAYS, "TWENTY? BUT THERE'S *FORTY* QUID HERE."
AND HE SAYS, "YEAH, I KNOW--*HE SHAT IN MY PANTS AN' ALL!*"
AHA HA HA HA HAH HA HA HAAAHHH HAH HA
AAH, JESUS, I NEEDED THAT. BEEN A WHILE SINCE I HAD A GOOD LAUGH, ENNIT?
YEAH, WELL, WHOSE FAULT'S THAT? YOU BEEN A STRANGER EVER SINCE WE GOT BACK FROM THAT BOLLOCKS UP IN SCOTLAND.

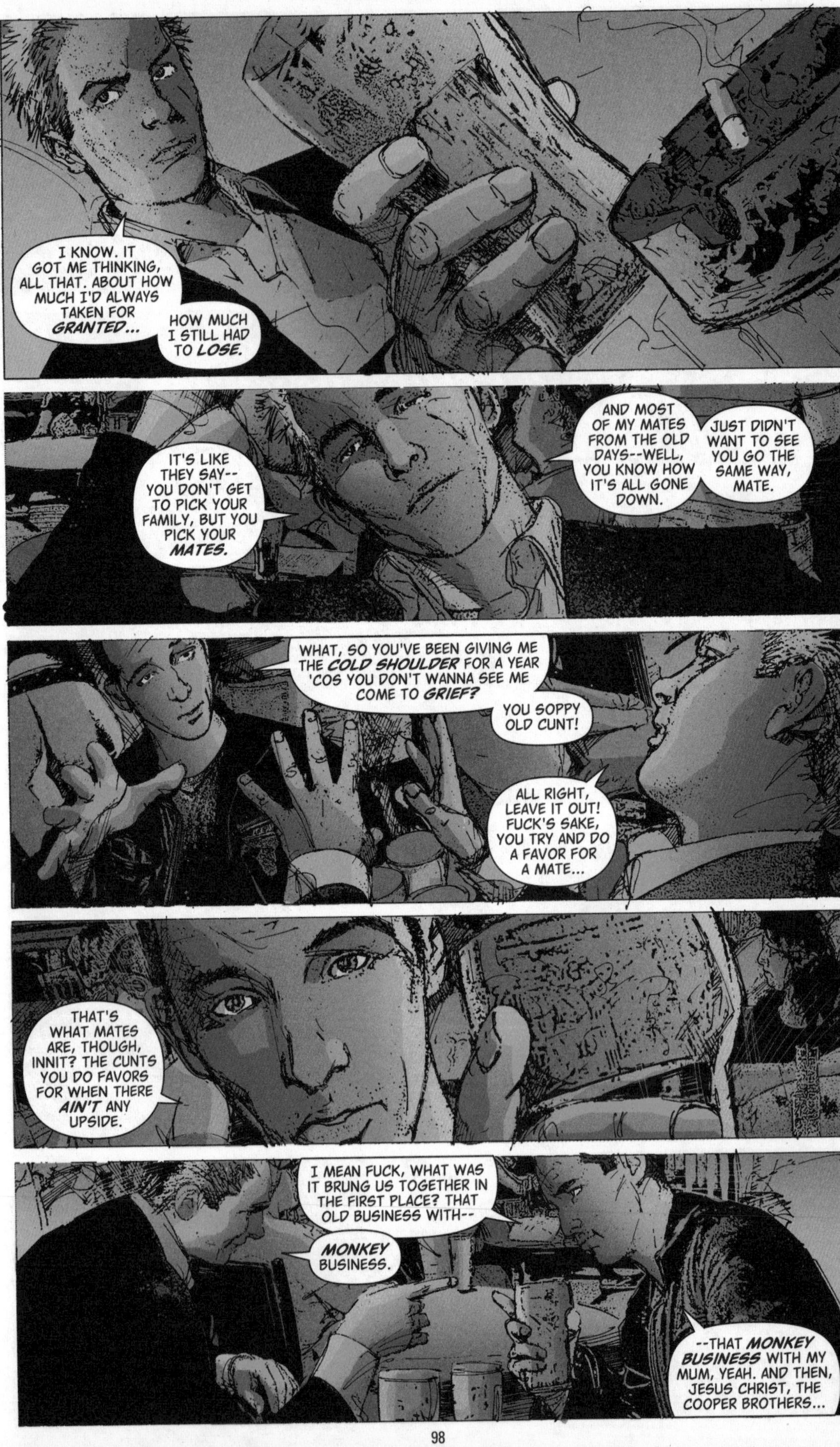
I KNOW. IT GOT ME THINKING, ALL THAT. ABOUT HOW MUCH I'D ALWAYS TAKEN FOR GRANTED...
HOW MUCH I STILL HAD TO LOSE.
IT'S LIKE THEY SAY--YOU DON'T GET TO PICK YOUR FAMILY, BUT YOU PICK YOUR MATES.
AND MOST OF MY MATES FROM THE OLD DAYS--WELL, YOU KNOW HOW IT'S ALL GONE DOWN.
JUST DIDN'T WANT TO SEE YOU GO THE SAME WAY, MATE.
WHAT, SO YOU'VE BEEN GIVING ME THE COLD SHOULDER FOR A YEAR 'COS YOU DON'T WANNA SEE ME COME TO GRIEF?
YOU SOPPY OLD CUNT!
ALL RIGHT, LEAVE IT OUT! FUCK'S SAKE, YOU TRY AND DO A FAVOR FOR A MATE...
THAT'S WHAT MATES ARE, THOUGH, INNIT? THE CUNTS YOU DO FAVORS FOR WHEN THERE AIN'T ANY UPSIDE.
I MEAN FUCK, WHAT WAS IT BRUNG US TOGETHER IN THE FIRST PLACE? THAT OLD BUSINESS WITH--
MONKEY BUSINESS.
--THAT MONKEY BUSINESS WITH MY MUM, YEAH. AND THEN, JESUS CHRIST, THE COOPER BROTHERS...

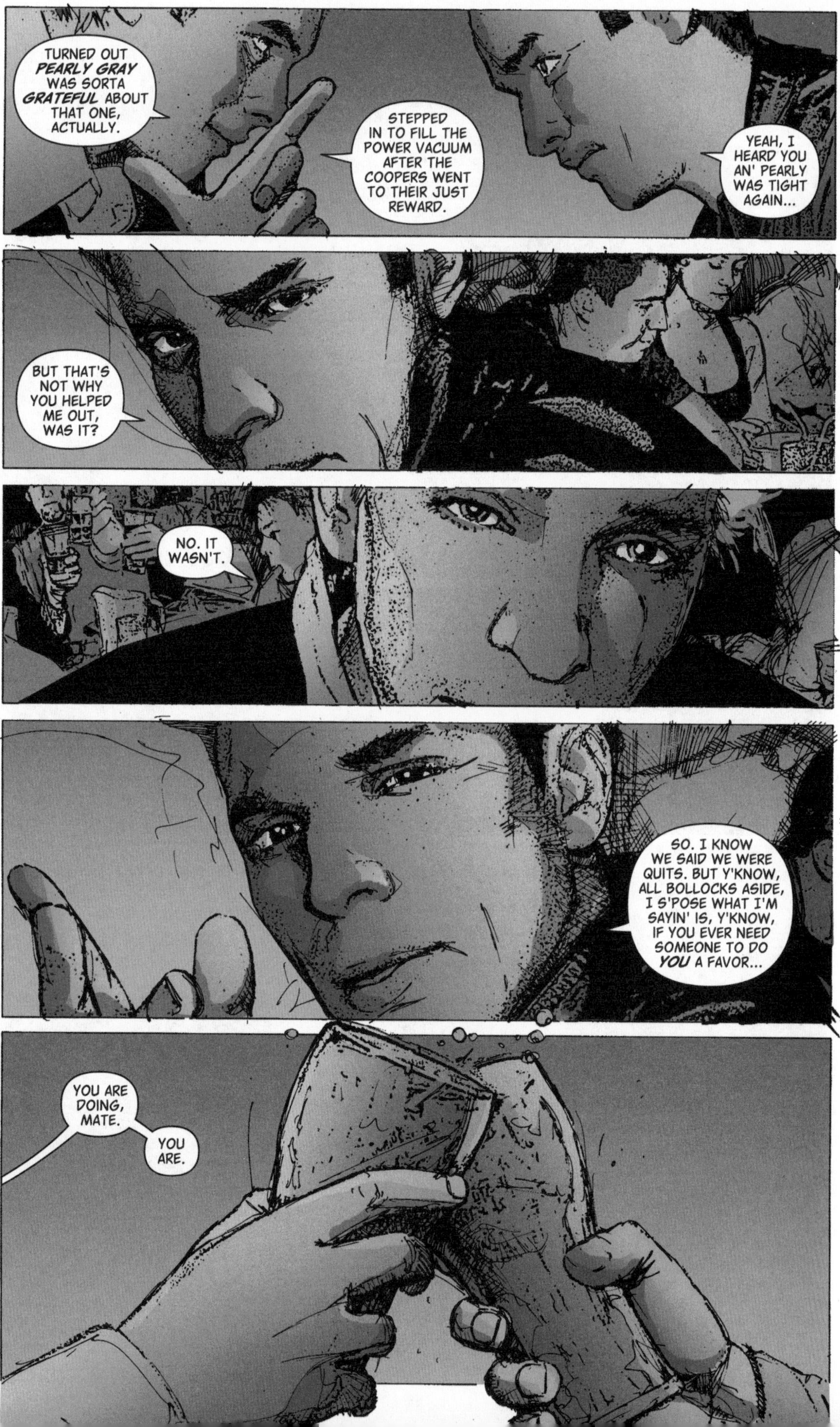
TURNED OUT PEARLY GRAY WAS SORTA GRATEFUL ABOUT THAT ONE, ACTUALLY.
STEPPED IN TO FILL THE POWER VACUUM AFTER THE COOPERS WENT TO THEIR JUST REWARD.
YEAH, I HEARD YOU AN' PEARLY WAS TIGHT AGAIN...
BUT THAT'S NOT WHY YOU HELPED ME OUT, WAS IT?
NO. IT WASN'T.
SO. I KNOW WE SAID WE WERE QUITS. BUT Y'KNOW, ALL BOLLOCKS ASIDE, I S'POSE WHAT I'M SAYIN' IS, Y'KNOW, IF YOU EVER NEED SOMEONE TO DO YOU A FAVOR...
YOU ARE DOING, MATE.
YOU ARE.

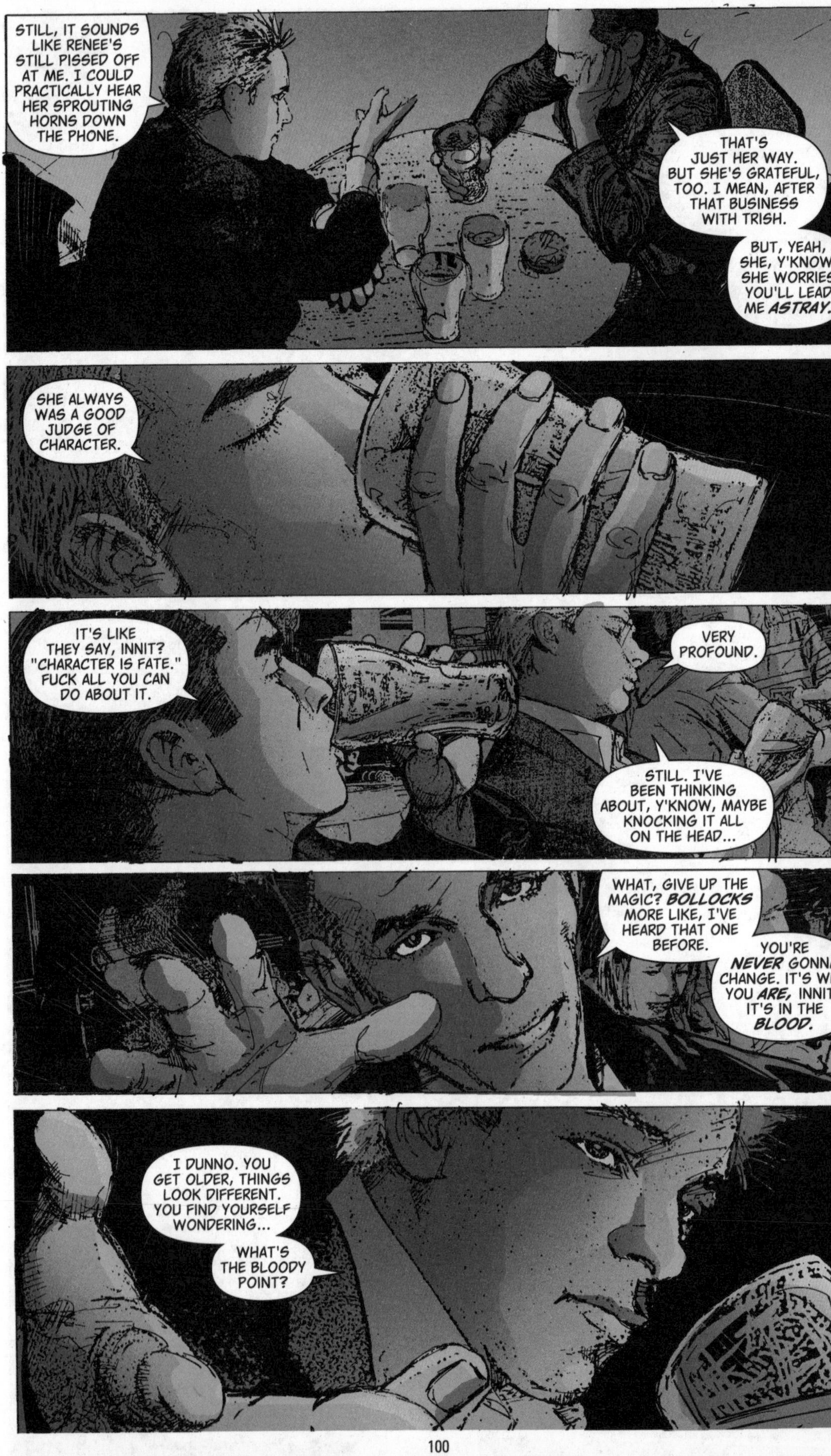
STILL, IT SOUNDS LIKE RENEE'S STILL PISSED OFF AT ME. I COULD PRACTICALLY HEAR HER SPROUTING HORNS DOWN THE PHONE.
THAT'S JUST HER WAY. BUT SHE'S GRATEFUL, TOO. I MEAN, AFTER THAT BUSINESS WITH TRISH.
BUT, YEAH, SHE, Y'KNOW. SHE WORRIES YOU'LL LEAD ME ASTRAY.
SHE ALWAYS WAS A GOOD JUDGE OF CHARACTER.
IT'S LIKE THEY SAY, INNIT? "CHARACTER IS FATE." FUCK ALL YOU CAN DO ABOUT IT.
VERY PROFOUND.
STILL. I'VE BEEN THINKING ABOUT, Y'KNOW, MAYBE KNOCKING IT ALL ON THE HEAD...
WHAT, GIVE UP THE MAGIC? BOLLOCKS MORE LIKE, I'VE HEARD THAT ONE BEFORE.
YOU'RE NEVER GONNA CHANGE. IT'S WHO YOU ARE, INNIT? IT'S IN THE BLOOD.
I DUNNO. YOU GET OLDER, THINGS LOOK DIFFERENT. YOU FIND YOURSELF WONDERING...
WHAT'S THE BLOODY POINT?

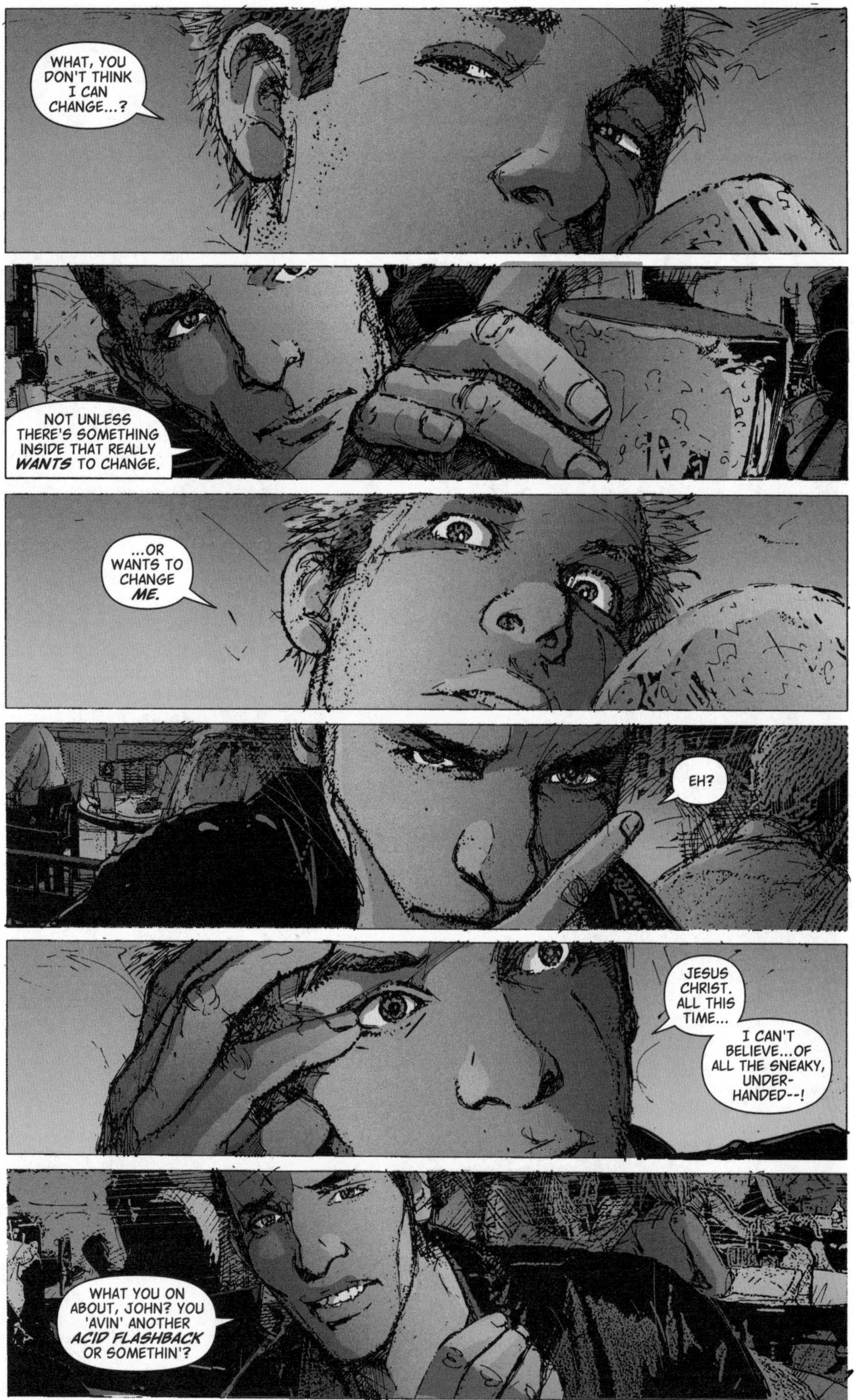
WHAT, YOU DON'T THINK I CAN CHANGE...?
NOT UNLESS THERE'S SOMETHING INSIDE THAT REALLY *WANTS* TO CHANGE.
...OR WANTS TO CHANGE *ME.*
EH?
JESUS CHRIST. ALL THIS TIME...
I CAN'T BELIEVE...OF ALL THE SNEAKY, UNDER-HANDED--!
WHAT YOU ON ABOUT, JOHN? YOU 'AVIN' ANOTHER *ACID FLASHBACK* OR SOMETHIN'?

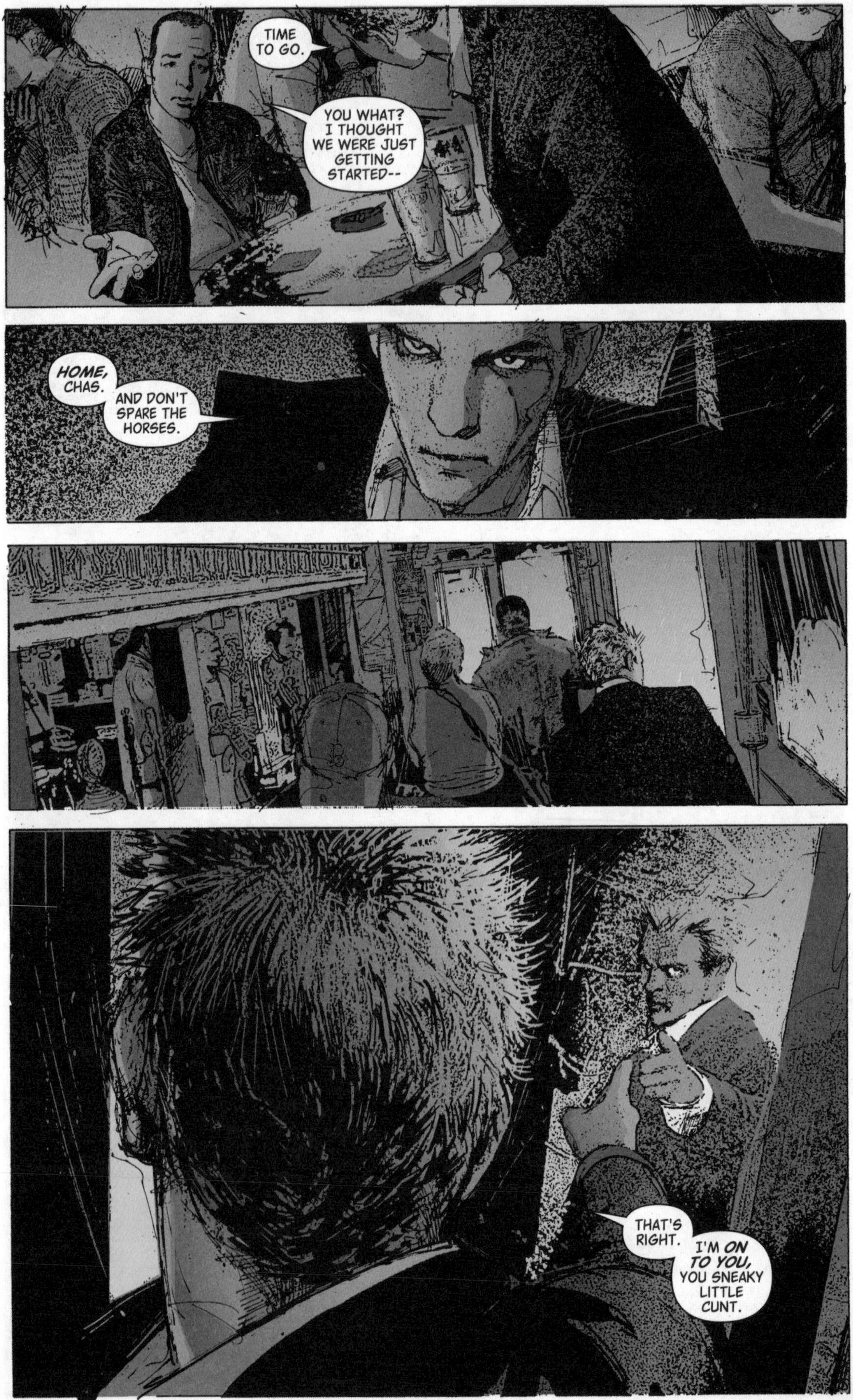

TIME TO GO.
YOU WHAT? I THOUGHT WE WERE JUST GETTING STARTED--
HOME, CHAS.
AND DON'T SPARE THE HORSES.
THAT'S RIGHT.
I'M ON TO YOU, YOU SNEAKY LITTLE CUNT.

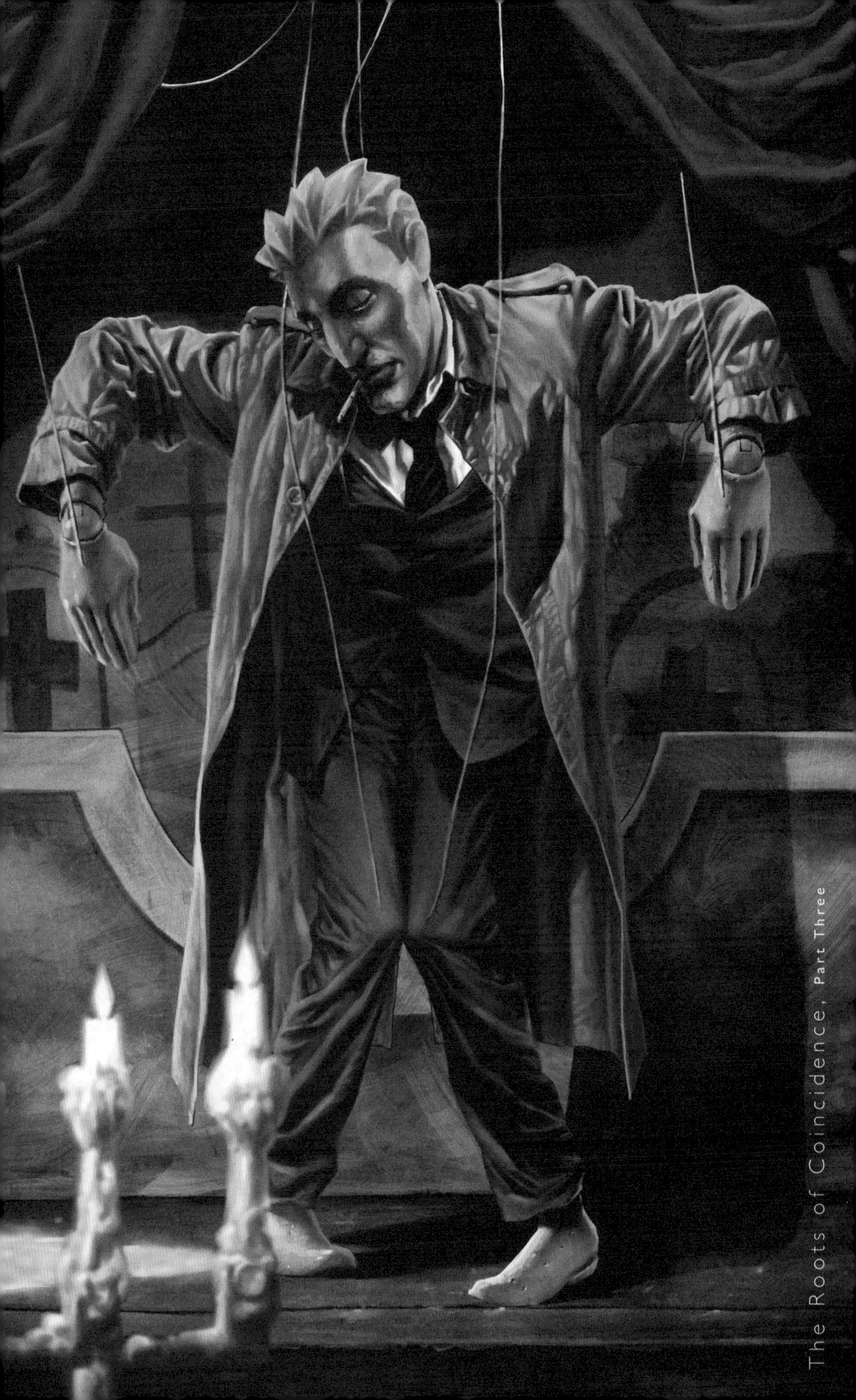

The Roots of Coincidence, **Part Three**

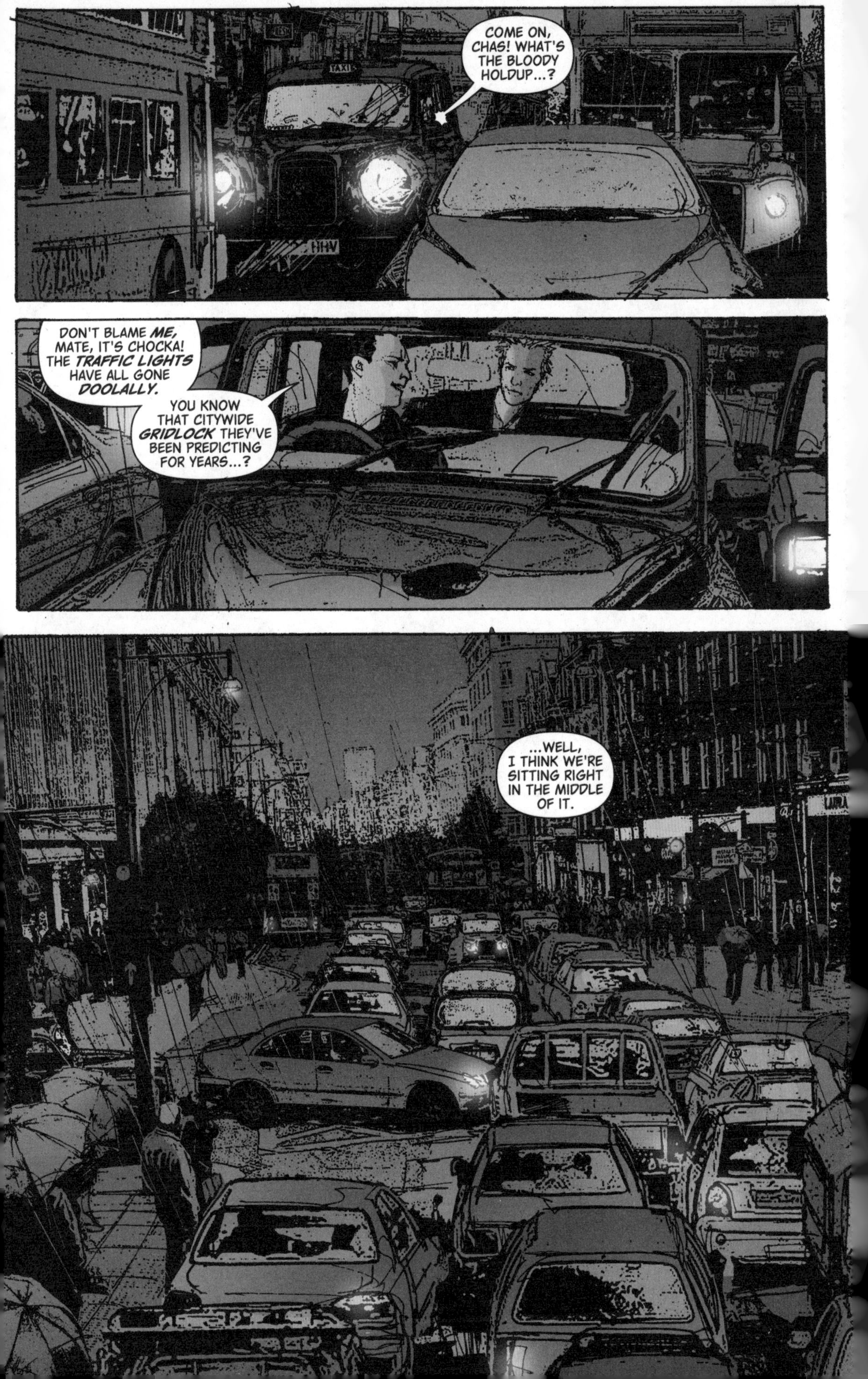
COME ON, CHAS! WHAT'S THE BLOODY HOLDUP...?
DON'T BLAME ME, MATE, IT'S CHOCKA! THE TRAFFIC LIGHTS HAVE ALL GONE DOOLALLY.
YOU KNOW THAT CITYWIDE GRIDLOCK THEY'VE BEEN PREDICTING FOR YEARS...?
...WELL, I THINK WE'RE SITTING RIGHT IN THE MIDDLE OF IT.

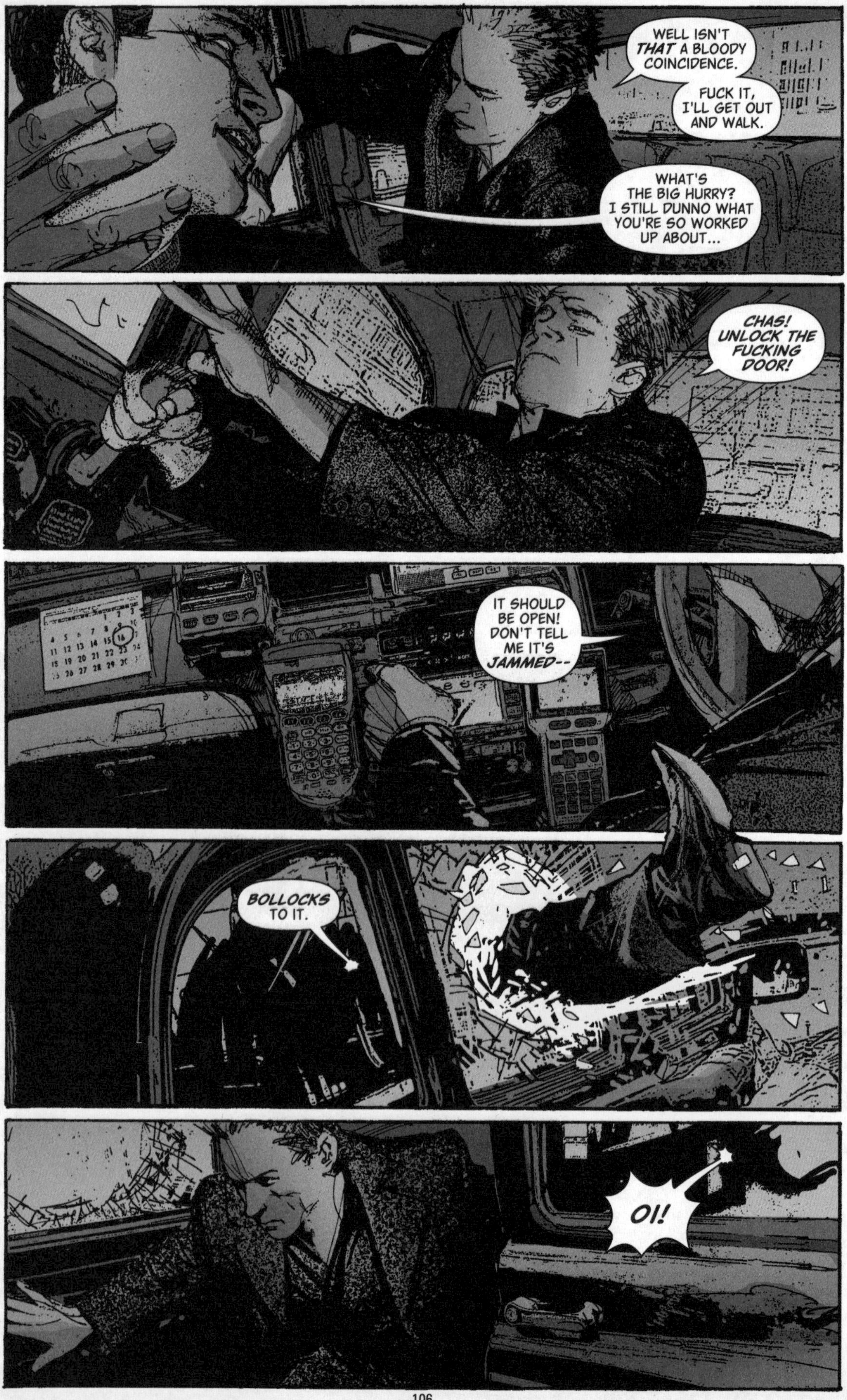

WELL ISN'T *THAT* A BLOODY COINCIDENCE.
FUCK IT, I'LL GET OUT AND WALK.
WHAT'S THE BIG HURRY? I STILL DUNNO WHAT YOU'RE SO WORKED UP ABOUT...
CHAS! UNLOCK THE FUCKING DOOR!
IT SHOULD BE OPEN! DON'T TELL ME IT'S *JAMMED--*
BOLLOCKS TO IT.
OI!

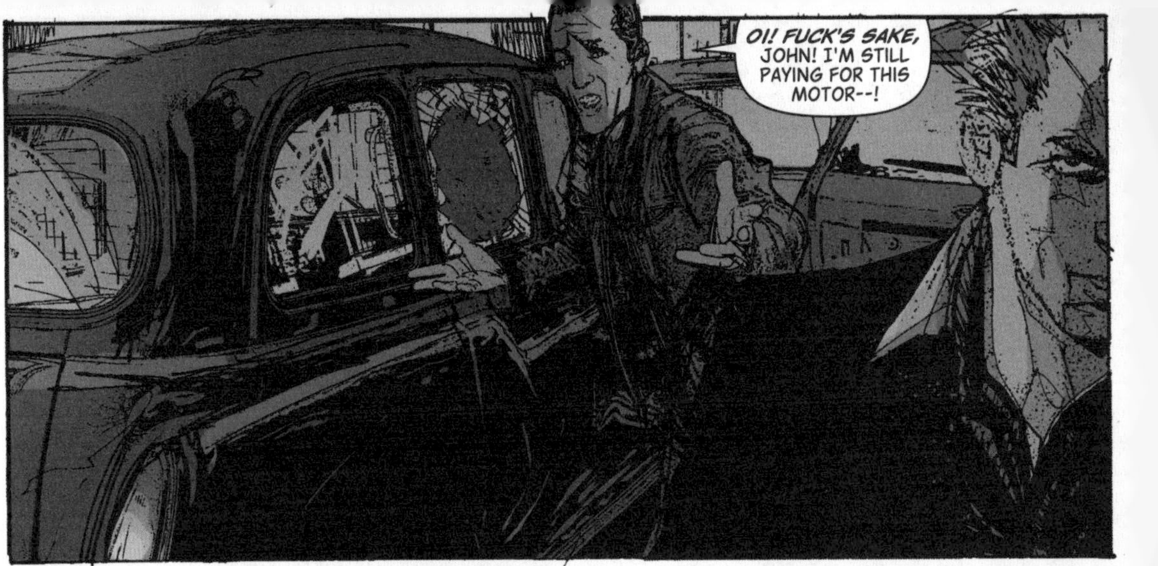
OI! FUCK'S SAKE, JOHN! I'M STILL PAYING FOR THIS MOTOR--!

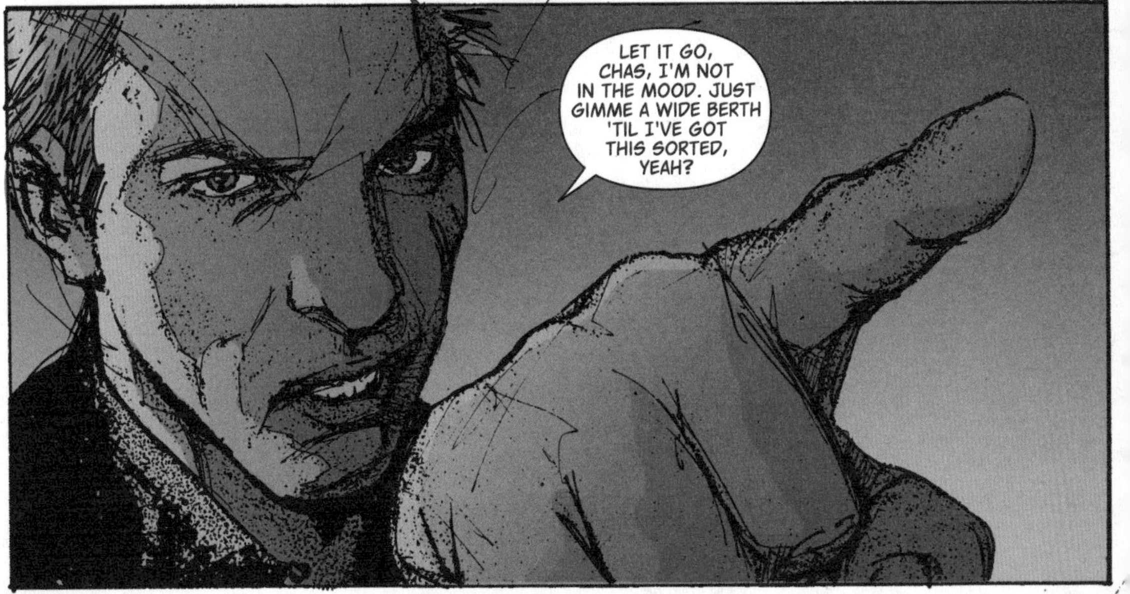
LET IT GO, CHAS, I'M NOT IN THE MOOD. JUST GIMME A WIDE BERTH 'TIL I'VE GOT THIS SORTED, YEAH?

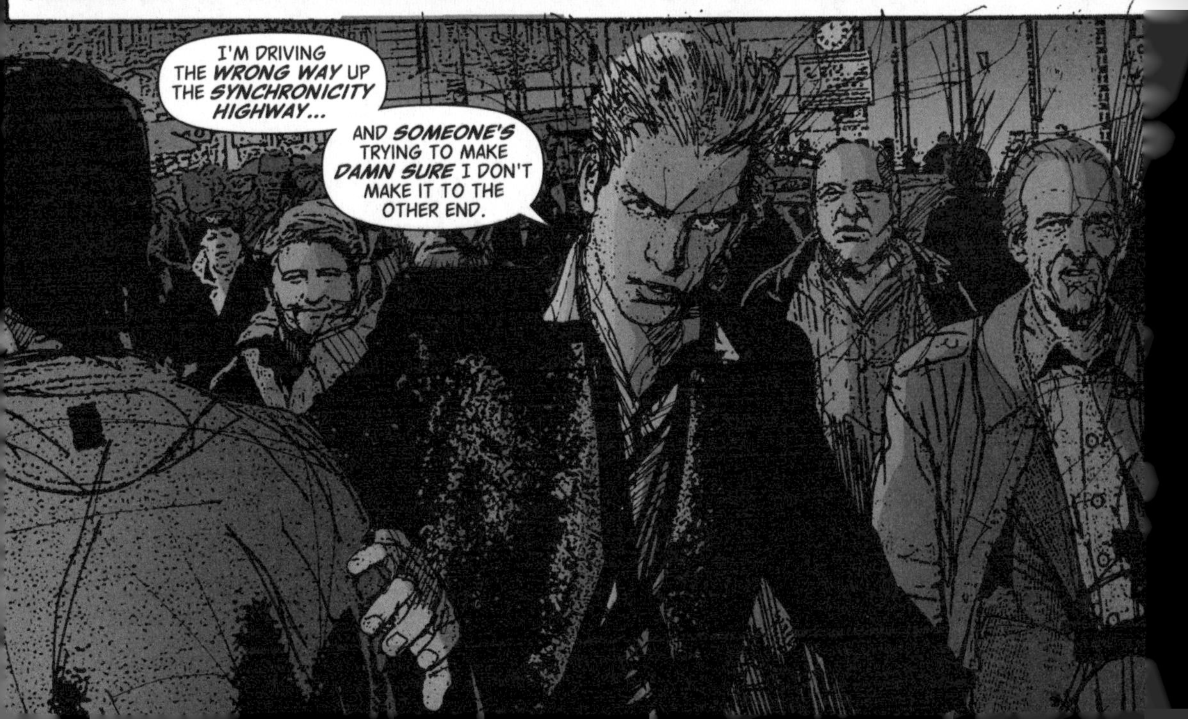
I'M DRIVING THE WRONG WAY UP THE SYNCHRONICITY HIGHWAY...
AND SOMEONE'S TRYING TO MAKE DAMN SURE I DON'T MAKE IT TO THE OTHER END.

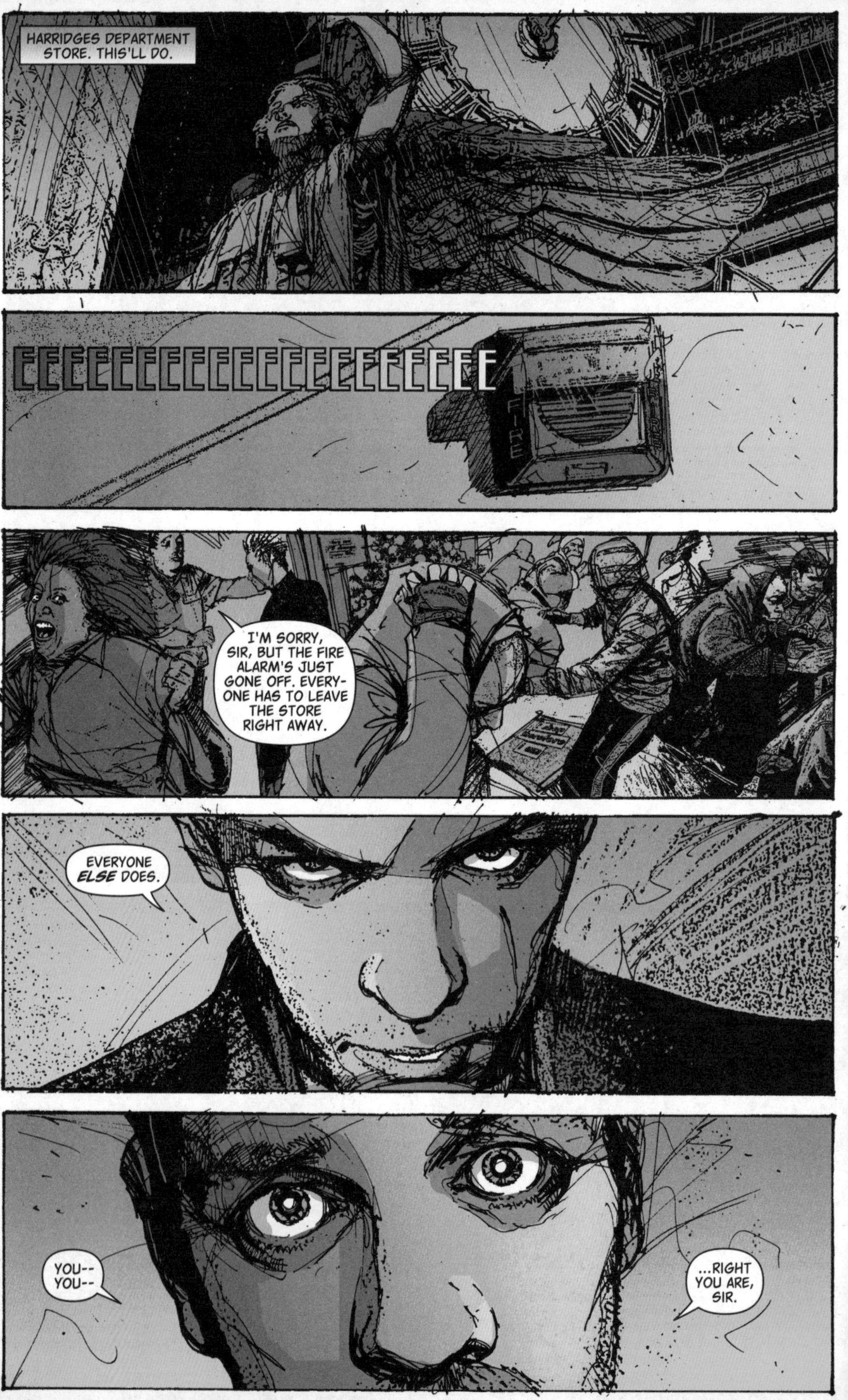
HARRIDGES DEPARTMENT STORE. THIS'LL DO.
EEEEEEEEEEEEEEEEEEEEEE
FIRE
I'M SORRY, SIR, BUT THE FIRE ALARM'S JUST GONE OFF. EVERY-ONE HAS TO LEAVE THE STORE RIGHT AWAY.
EVERYONE *ELSE* DOES.
YOU-- YOU--
...RIGHT YOU ARE, SIR.

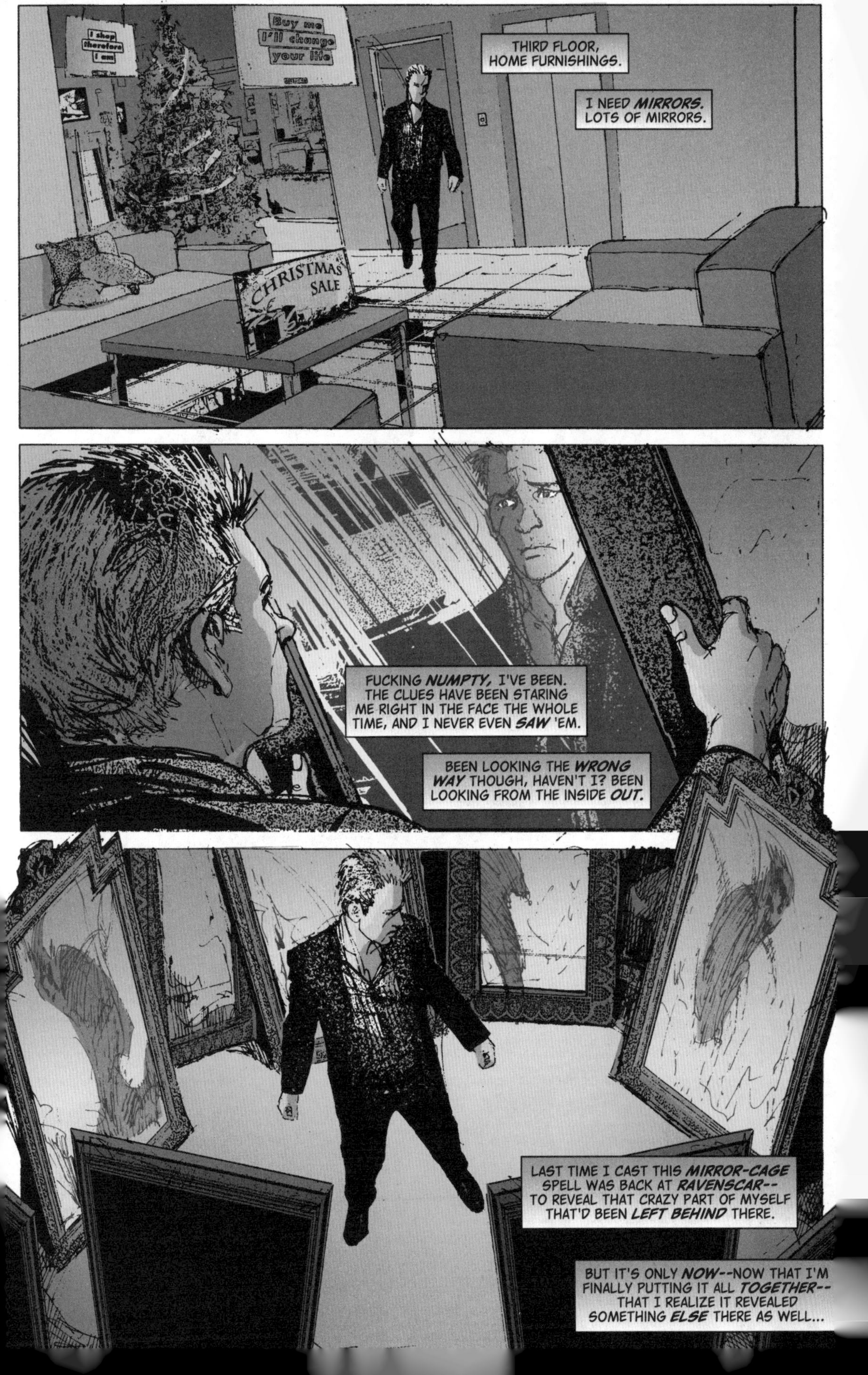
I shop therefore I am
Buy me I'll change your life
THIRD FLOOR, HOME FURNISHINGS.
I NEED MIRRORS. LOTS OF MIRRORS.
CHRISTMAS SALE
FUCKING NUMPTY, I'VE BEEN. THE CLUES HAVE BEEN STARING ME RIGHT IN THE FACE THE WHOLE TIME, AND I NEVER EVEN SAW 'EM.
BEEN LOOKING THE WRONG WAY THOUGH, HAVEN'T I? BEEN LOOKING FROM THE INSIDE OUT.
LAST TIME I CAST THIS MIRROR-CAGE SPELL WAS BACK AT RAVENSCAR-- TO REVEAL THAT CRAZY PART OF MYSELF THAT'D BEEN LEFT BEHIND THERE.
BUT IT'S ONLY NOW--NOW THAT I'M FINALLY PUTTING IT ALL TOGETHER-- THAT I REALIZE IT REVEALED SOMETHING ELSE THERE AS WELL...

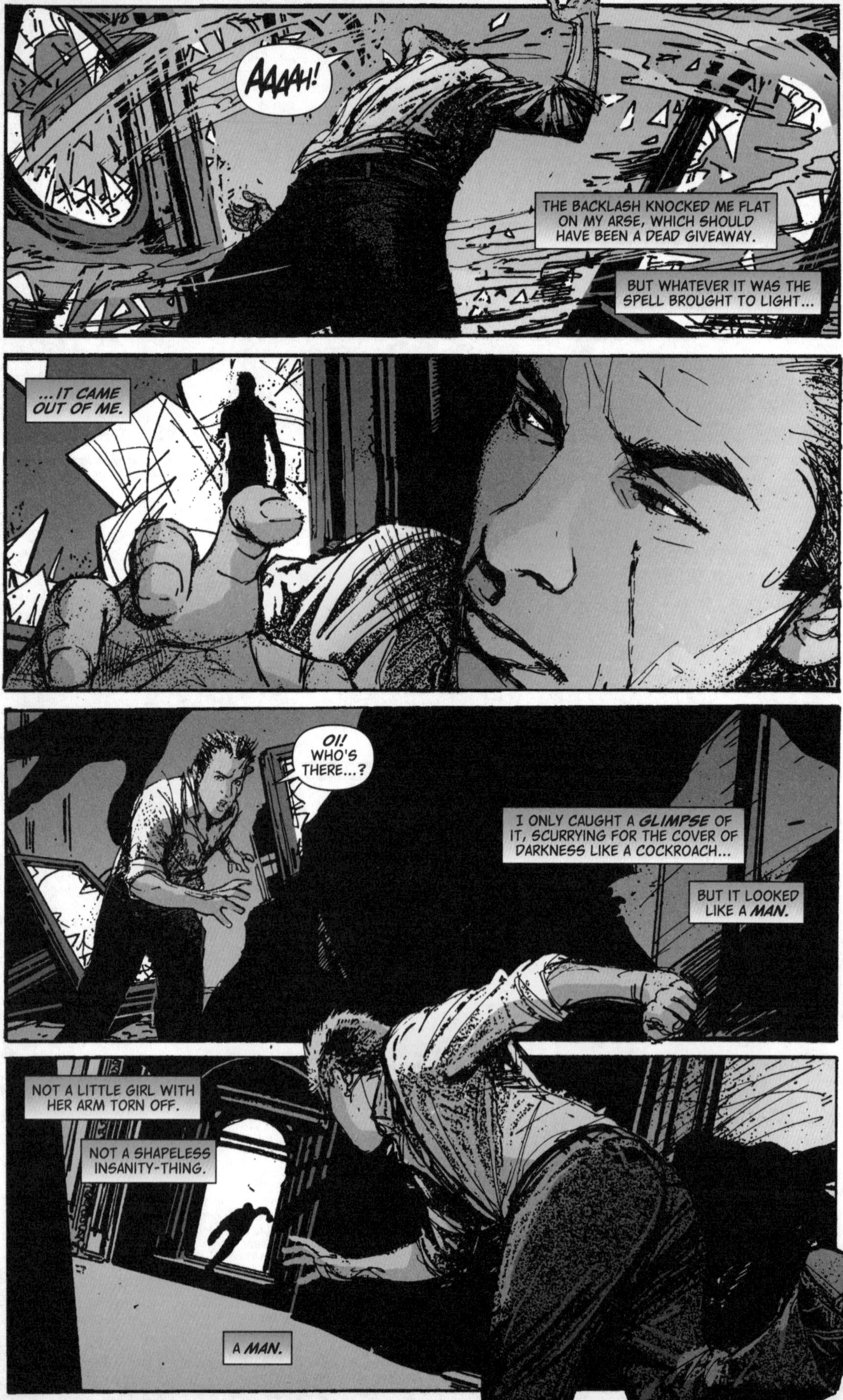
AAAAH!
THE BACKLASH KNOCKED ME FLAT ON MY ARSE, WHICH SHOULD HAVE BEEN A DEAD GIVEAWAY.
BUT WHATEVER IT WAS THE SPELL BROUGHT TO LIGHT...
...IT CAME OUT OF ME.
OI! WHO'S THERE...?
I ONLY CAUGHT A GLIMPSE OF IT, SCURRYING FOR THE COVER OF DARKNESS LIKE A COCKROACH...
BUT IT LOOKED LIKE A MAN.
NOT A LITTLE GIRL WITH HER ARM TORN OFF.
NOT A SHAPELESS INSANITY-THING.
A MAN.

AND IN THAT BRIEF MOMENT THE FIGURE STOOD REVEALED, MAKO CAUGHT A *GLIMPSE* OF IT FROM HALF A WORLD AWAY.

I SAW A CAGE OF MIRRORS. A RAVEN AND A SCAR.

AND THEN I SAW *HIM.* JUST FOR A MOMENT. BUT HIS FACE WAS HIDDEN FROM ME, A FLEEING SHADOW...

AND THEN HE WAS GONE.

HE FOLLOWED IT TO ENGLAND, THINKING IT WAS *ME.*

BUT IT HAD *HIDDEN* AGAIN. THROWN A *CLOAKING SPELL* AROUND ITSELF--AND *ME* WITH IT.

I CANNOT SEE. THERE IS A SHADOW ABOUT YOU.

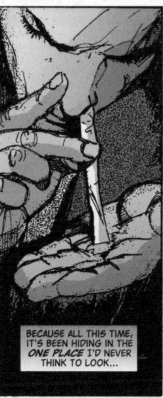

BECAUSE ALL THIS TIME, IT'S BEEN HIDING IN THE *ONE PLACE* I'D NEVER THINK TO LOOK...

...*INSIDE ME.*

ALL RIGHT, YOU SLIPPERY LITTLE BUGGER.

ENOUGH OF THIS *SNEAKING AROUND* SHIT.

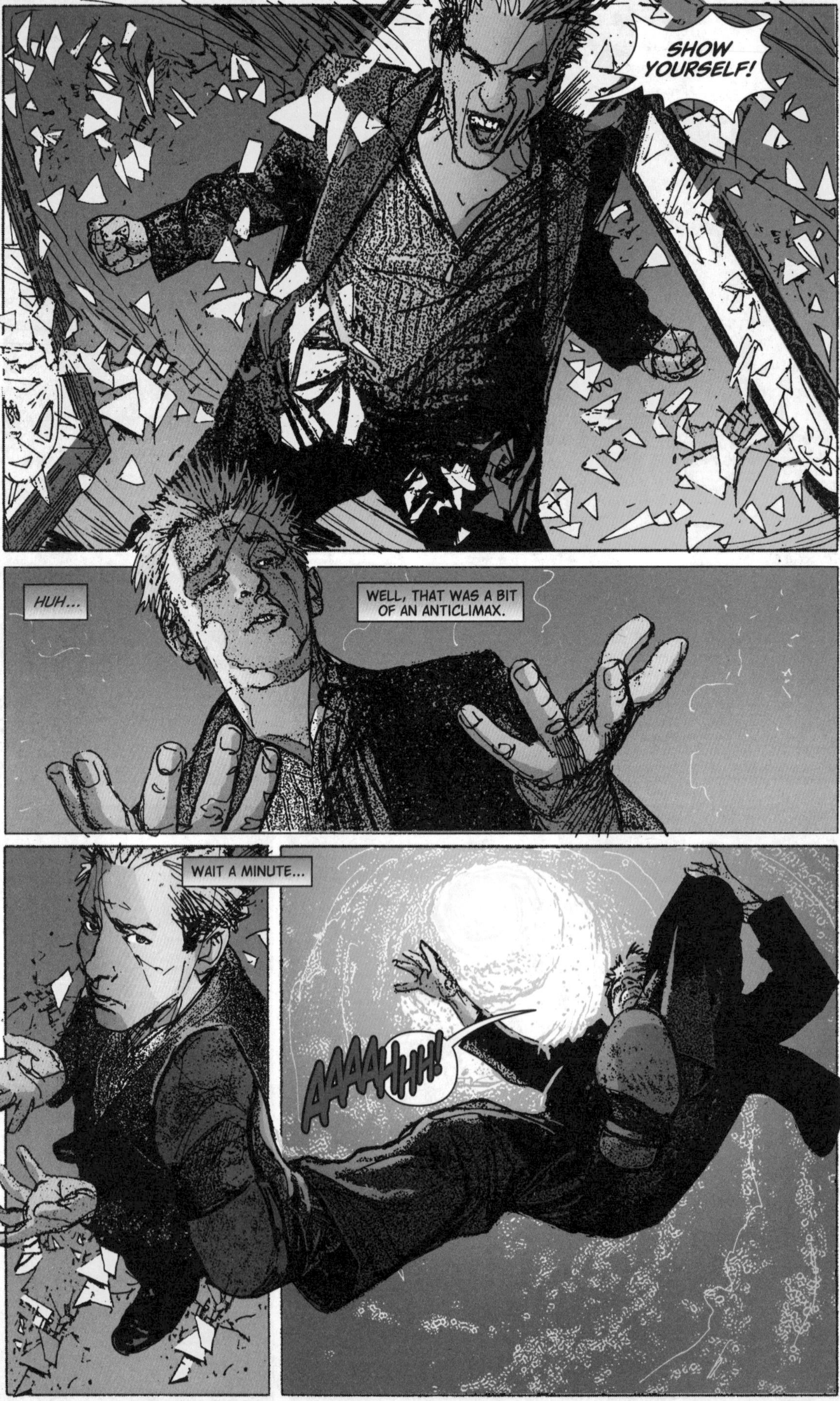
SHOW YOURSELF!
HUH...
WELL, THAT WAS A BIT OF AN ANTICLIMAX.
WAIT A MINUTE...
AAAAHHH!

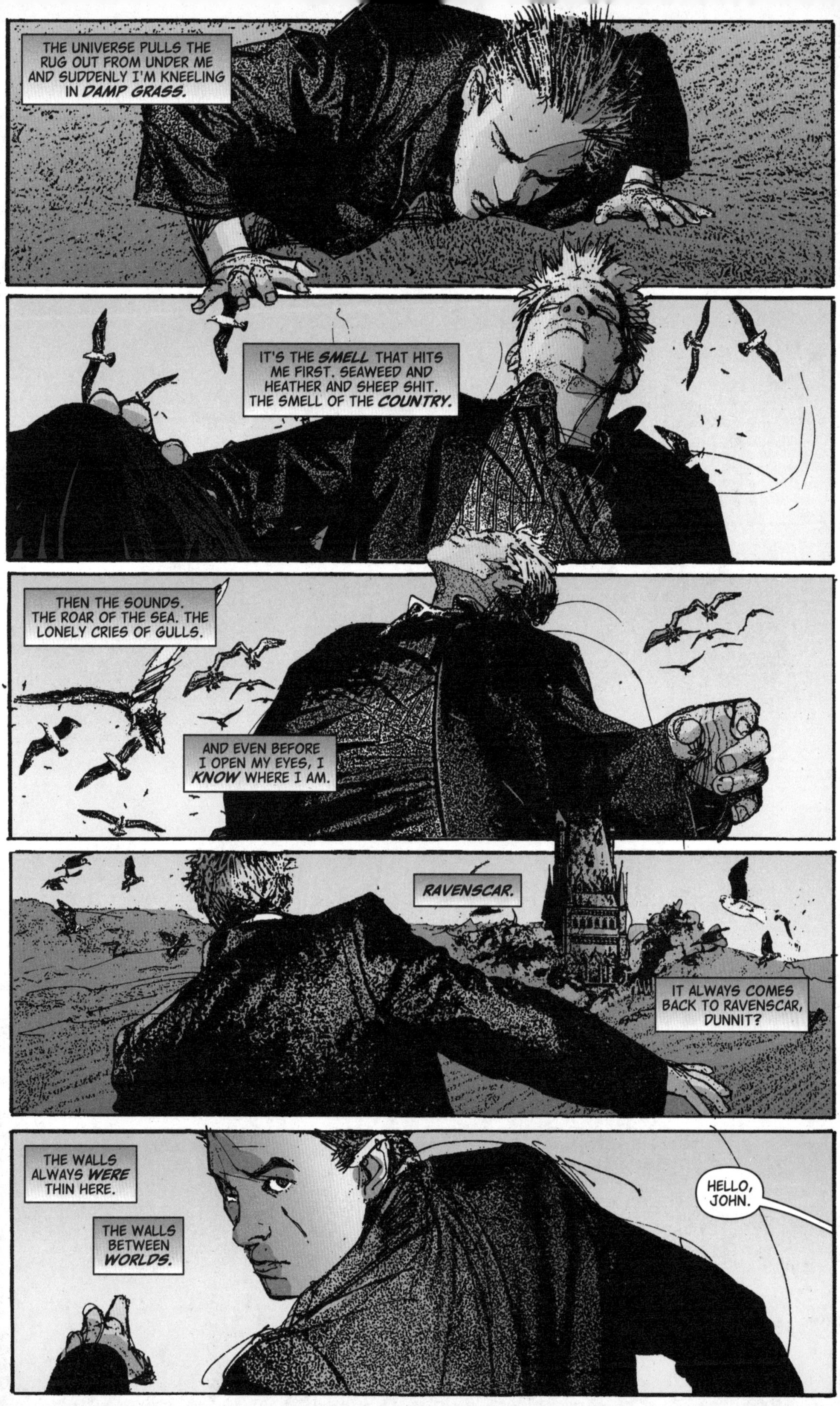
THE UNIVERSE PULLS THE RUG OUT FROM UNDER ME AND SUDDENLY I'M KNEELING IN DAMP GRASS.
IT'S THE SMELL THAT HITS ME FIRST. SEAWEED AND HEATHER AND SHEEP SHIT. THE SMELL OF THE COUNTRY.
THEN THE SOUNDS. THE ROAR OF THE SEA. THE LONELY CRIES OF GULLS.
AND EVEN BEFORE I OPEN MY EYES, I KNOW WHERE I AM.
RAVENSCAR.
IT ALWAYS COMES BACK TO RAVENSCAR, DUNNIT?
THE WALLS ALWAYS WERE THIN HERE.
THE WALLS BETWEEN WORLDS.
HELLO, JOHN.

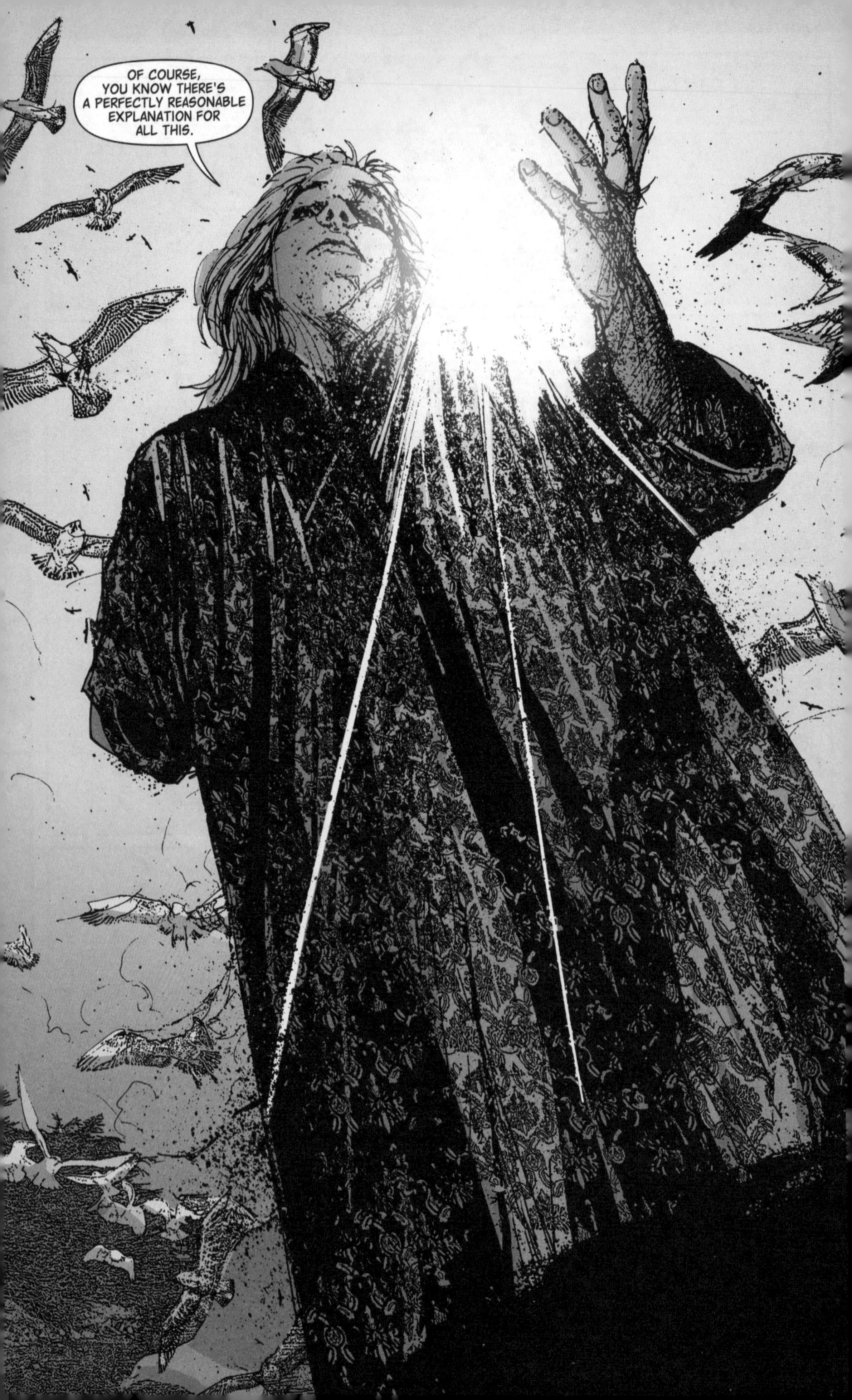
OF COURSE, YOU KNOW THERE'S A PERFECTLY REASONABLE EXPLANATION FOR ALL THIS.

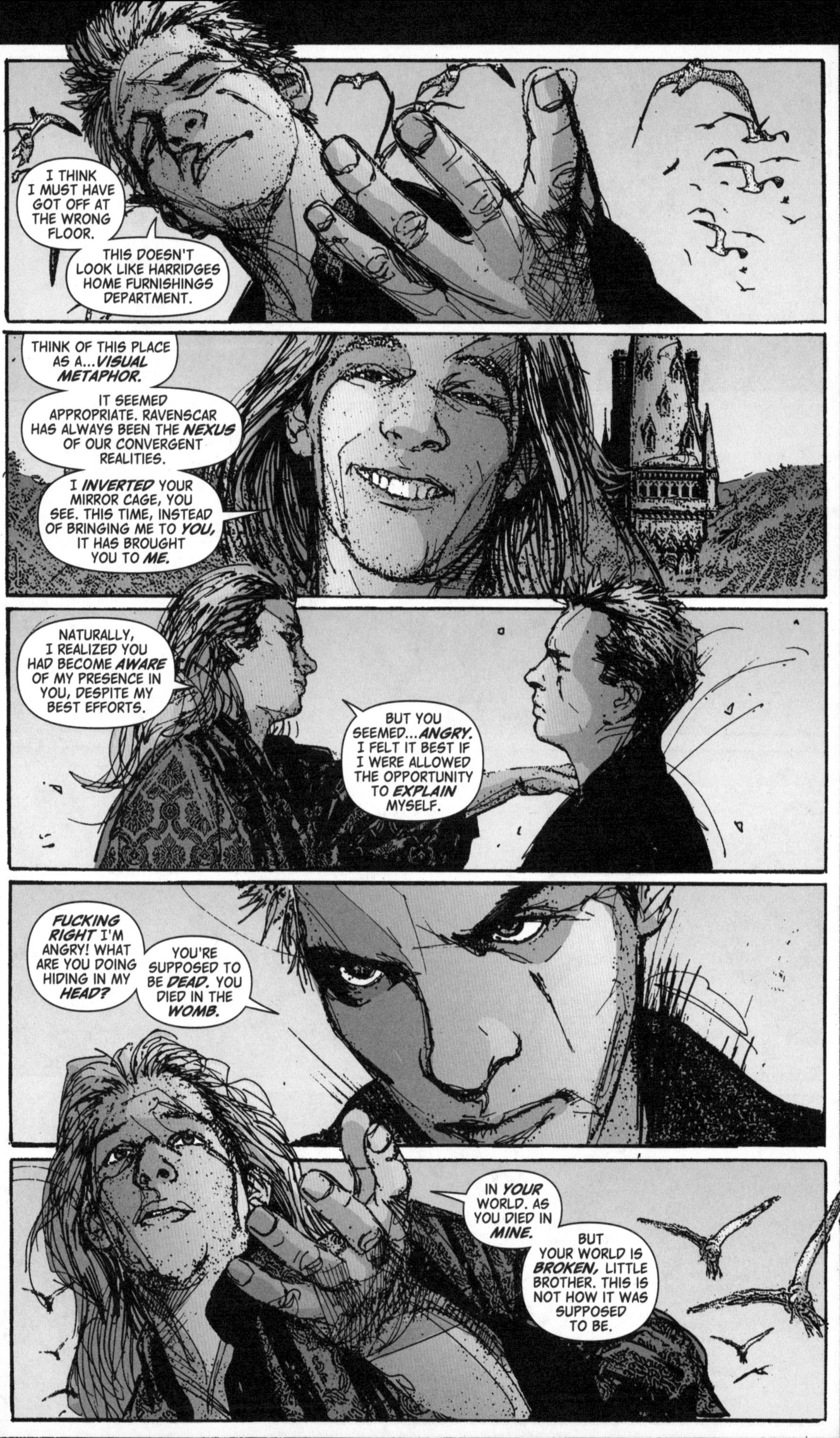
I THINK I MUST HAVE GOT OFF AT THE WRONG FLOOR.
THIS DOESN'T LOOK LIKE HARRIDGES HOME FURNISHINGS DEPARTMENT.
THINK OF THIS PLACE AS A...VISUAL METAPHOR.
IT SEEMED APPROPRIATE. RAVENSCAR HAS ALWAYS BEEN THE NEXUS OF OUR CONVERGENT REALITIES.
I INVERTED YOUR MIRROR CAGE, YOU SEE. THIS TIME, INSTEAD OF BRINGING ME TO YOU, IT HAS BROUGHT YOU TO ME.
NATURALLY, I REALIZED YOU HAD BECOME AWARE OF MY PRESENCE IN YOU, DESPITE MY BEST EFFORTS.
BUT YOU SEEMED...ANGRY. I FELT IT BEST IF I WERE ALLOWED THE OPPORTUNITY TO EXPLAIN MYSELF.
FUCKING RIGHT I'M ANGRY! WHAT ARE YOU DOING HIDING IN MY HEAD?
YOU'RE SUPPOSED TO BE DEAD. YOU DIED IN THE WOMB.
IN YOUR WORLD. AS YOU DIED IN MINE.
BUT YOUR WORLD IS BROKEN, LITTLE BROTHER. THIS IS NOT HOW IT WAS SUPPOSED TO BE.

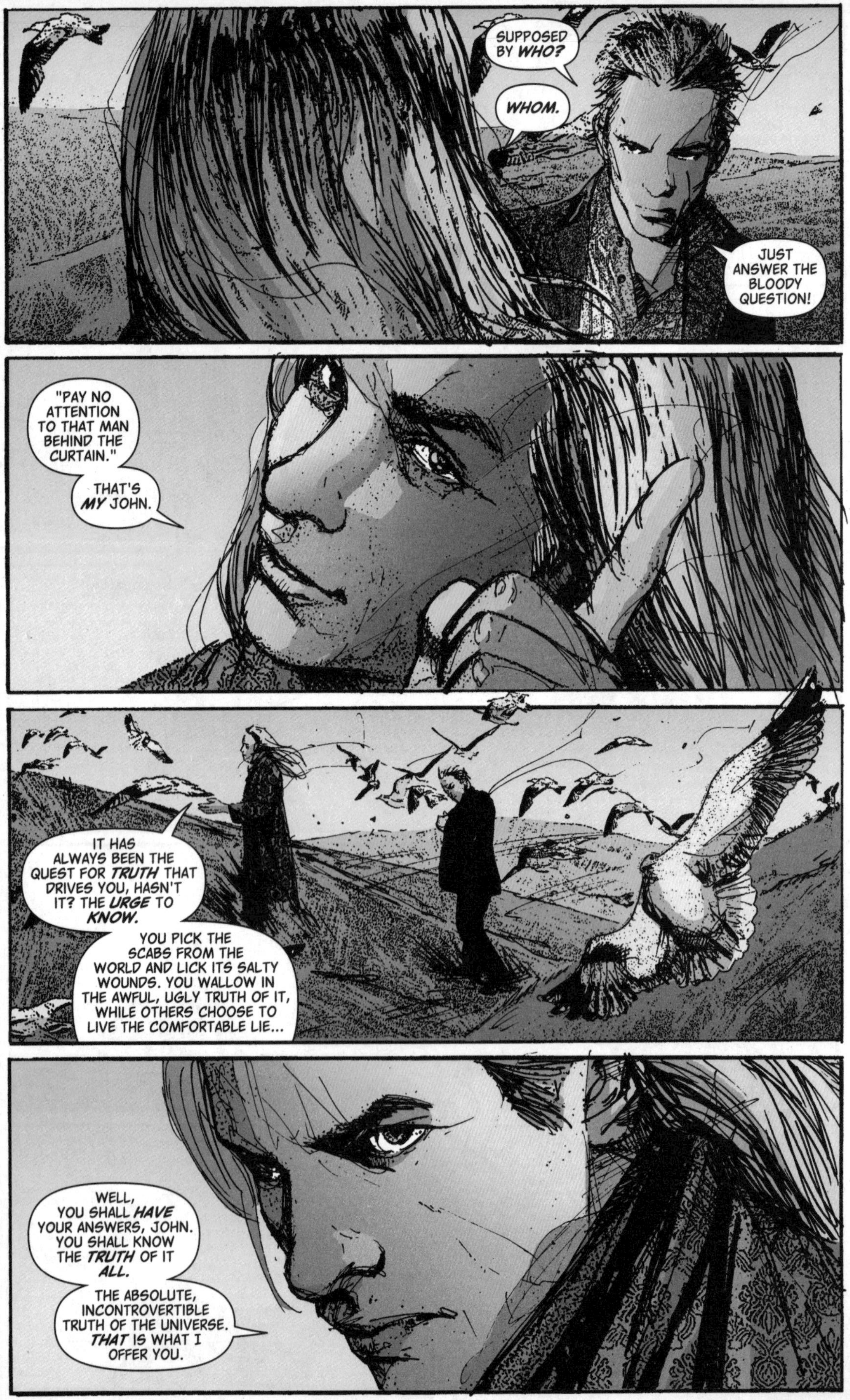
SUPPOSED BY WHO?
WHOM.
JUST ANSWER THE BLOODY QUESTION!
"PAY NO ATTENTION TO THAT MAN BEHIND THE CURTAIN."
THAT'S MY JOHN.
IT HAS ALWAYS BEEN THE QUEST FOR TRUTH THAT DRIVES YOU, HASN'T IT? THE URGE TO KNOW.
YOU PICK THE SCABS FROM THE WORLD AND LICK ITS SALTY WOUNDS. YOU WALLOW IN THE AWFUL, UGLY TRUTH OF IT, WHILE OTHERS CHOOSE TO LIVE THE COMFORTABLE LIE...
WELL, YOU SHALL HAVE YOUR ANSWERS, JOHN. YOU SHALL KNOW THE TRUTH OF IT ALL.
THE ABSOLUTE, INCONTROVERTIBLE TRUTH OF THE UNIVERSE. THAT IS WHAT I OFFER YOU.

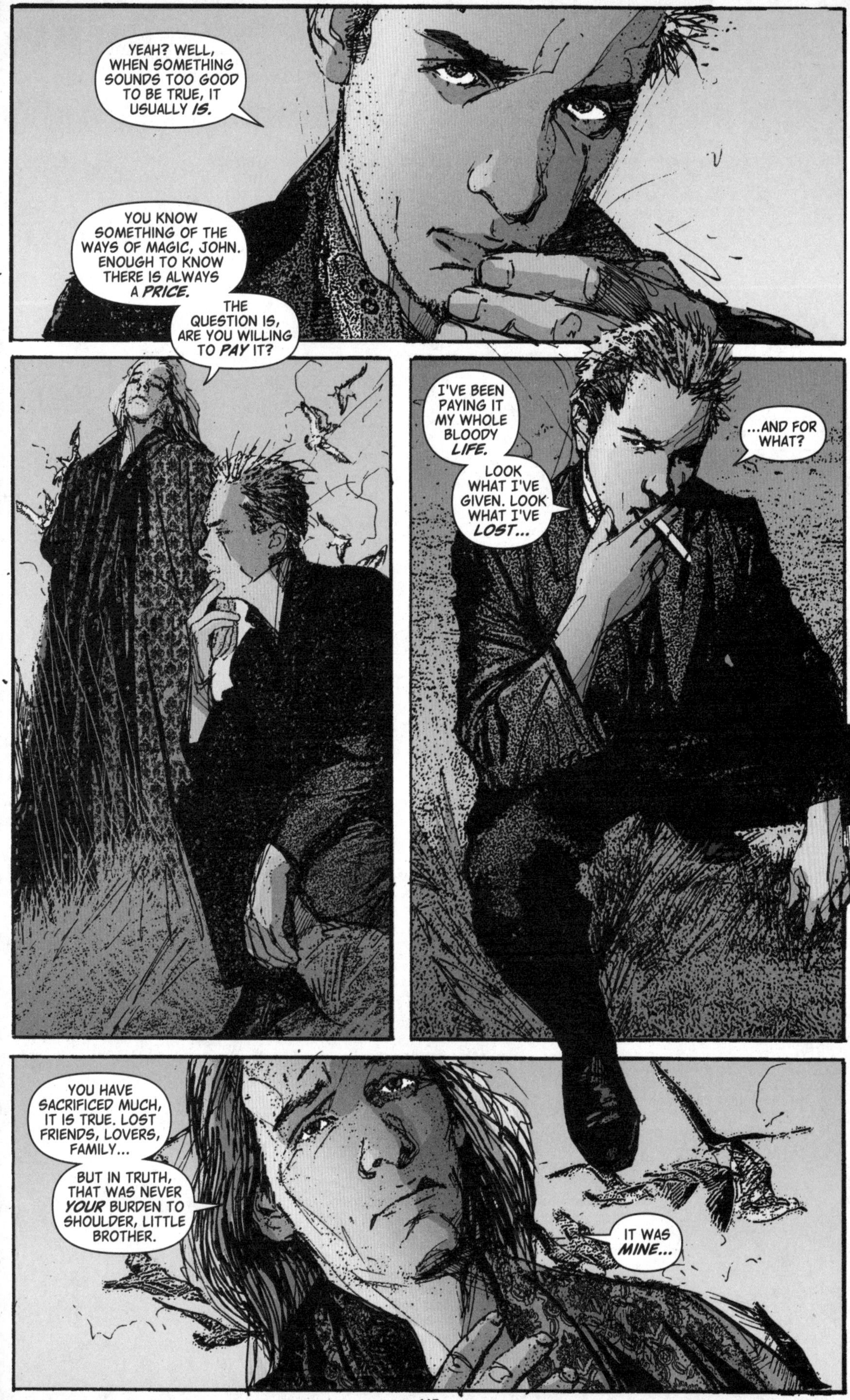
YEAH? WELL, WHEN SOMETHING SOUNDS TOO GOOD TO BE TRUE, IT USUALLY *IS.*
YOU KNOW SOMETHING OF THE WAYS OF MAGIC, JOHN. ENOUGH TO KNOW THERE IS ALWAYS A *PRICE.*
THE QUESTION IS, ARE YOU WILLING TO *PAY* IT?
I'VE BEEN PAYING IT MY WHOLE BLOODY *LIFE.*
LOOK WHAT I'VE GIVEN. LOOK WHAT I'VE *LOST...*
...AND FOR WHAT?
YOU HAVE SACRIFICED MUCH, IT IS TRUE. LOST FRIENDS, LOVERS, FAMILY...
BUT IN TRUTH, THAT WAS NEVER *YOUR* BURDEN TO SHOULDER, LITTLE BROTHER.
IT WAS *MINE...*

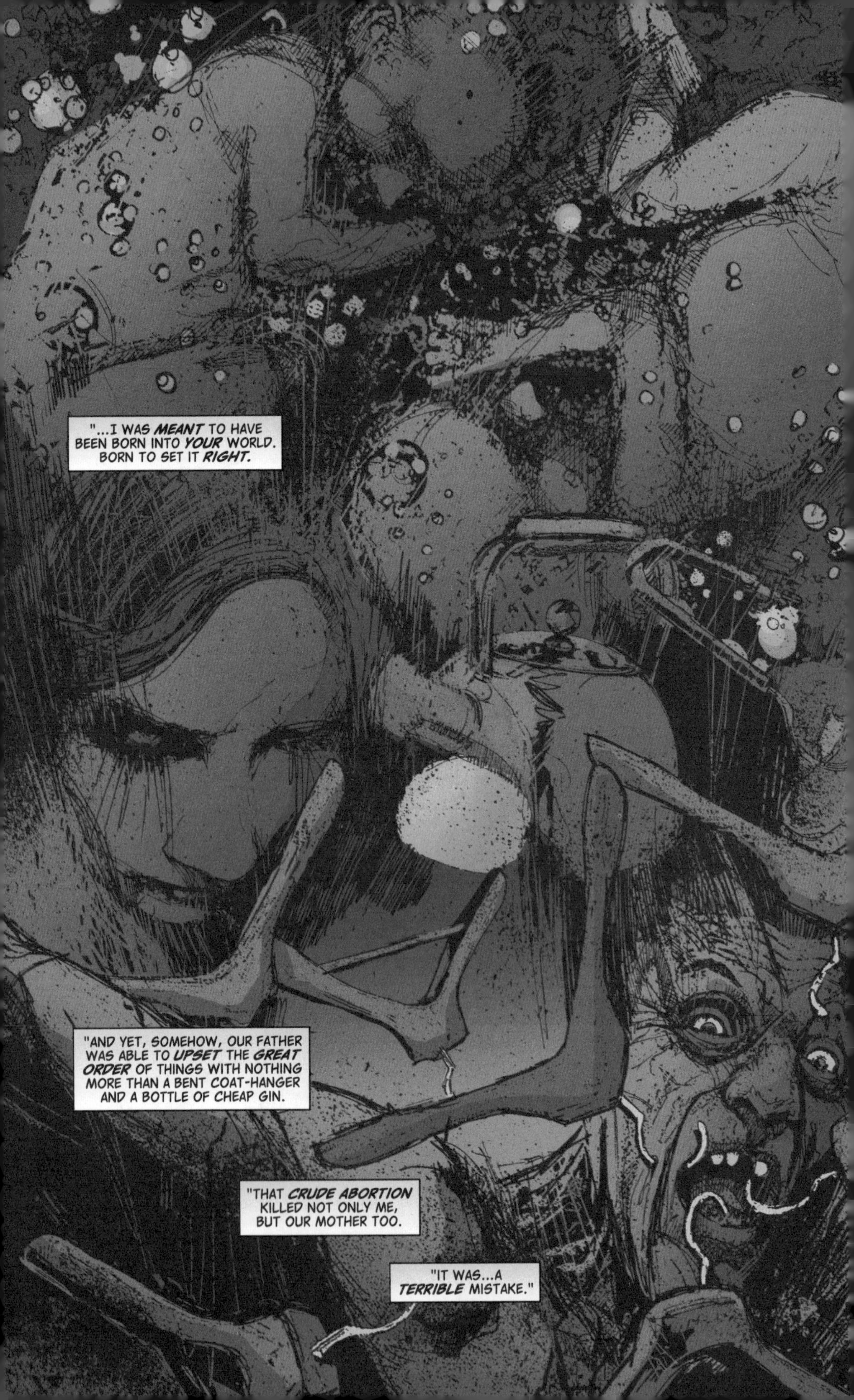
"...I WAS MEANT TO HAVE BEEN BORN INTO YOUR WORLD. BORN TO SET IT RIGHT.
"AND YET, SOMEHOW, OUR FATHER WAS ABLE TO UPSET THE GREAT ORDER OF THINGS WITH NOTHING MORE THAN A BENT COAT-HANGER AND A BOTTLE OF CHEAP GIN.
"THAT CRUDE ABORTION KILLED NOT ONLY ME, BUT OUR MOTHER TOO.
"IT WAS...A TERRIBLE MISTAKE."

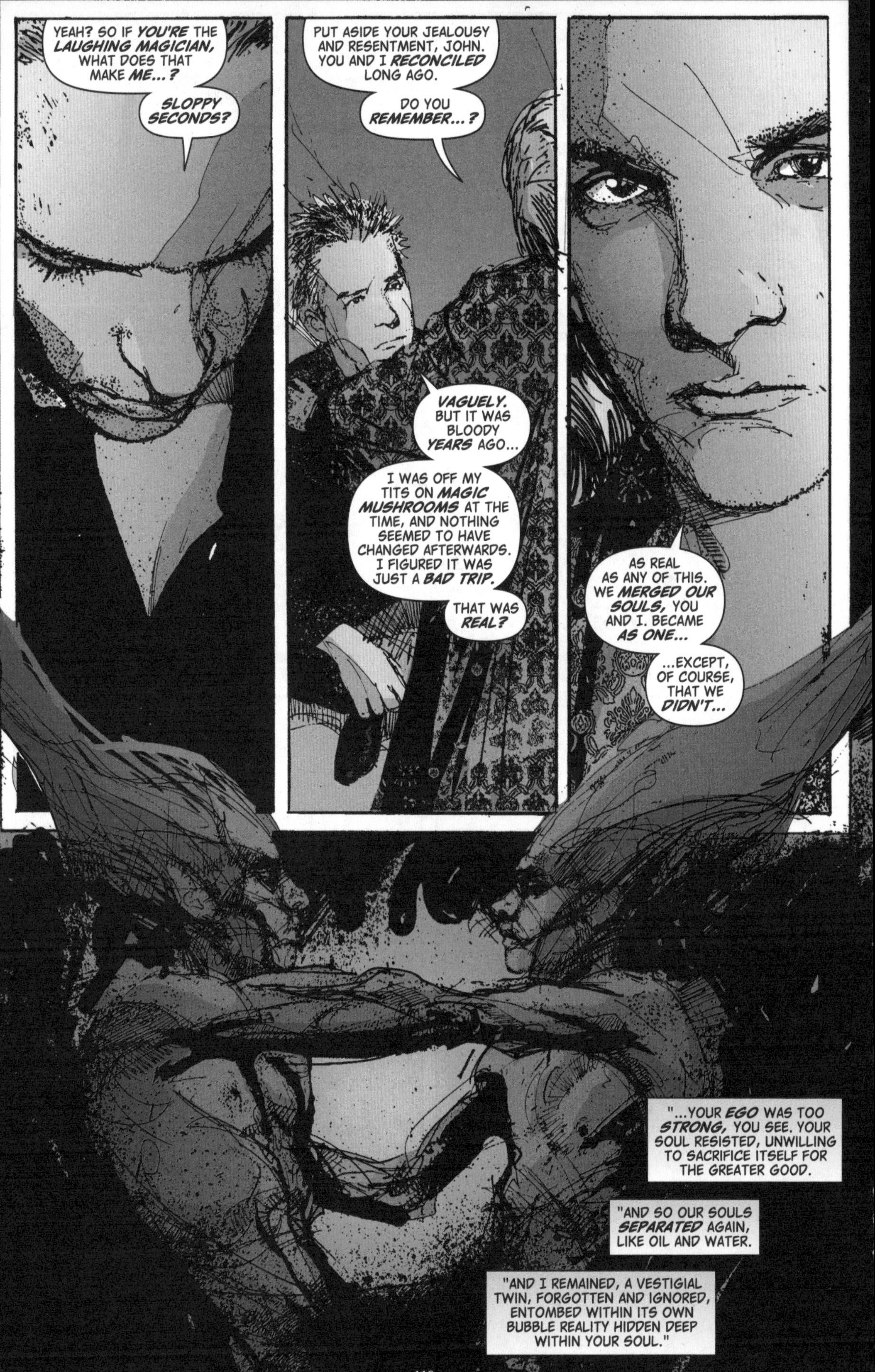
YEAH? SO IF YOU'RE THE LAUGHING MAGICIAN, WHAT DOES THAT MAKE ME...?
SLOPPY SECONDS?
PUT ASIDE YOUR JEALOUSY AND RESENTMENT, JOHN. YOU AND I RECONCILED LONG AGO.
DO YOU REMEMBER...?
VAGUELY. BUT IT WAS BLOODY YEARS AGO...
I WAS OFF MY TITS ON MAGIC MUSHROOMS AT THE TIME, AND NOTHING SEEMED TO HAVE CHANGED AFTERWARDS. I FIGURED IT WAS JUST A BAD TRIP.
THAT WAS REAL?
AS REAL AS ANY OF THIS. WE MERGED OUR SOULS, YOU AND I. BECAME AS ONE...
...EXCEPT, OF COURSE, THAT WE DIDN'T...
"...YOUR EGO WAS TOO STRONG, YOU SEE. YOUR SOUL RESISTED, UNWILLING TO SACRIFICE ITSELF FOR THE GREATER GOOD.
"AND SO OUR SOULS SEPARATED AGAIN, LIKE OIL AND WATER.
"AND I REMAINED, A VESTIGIAL TWIN, FORGOTTEN AND IGNORED, ENTOMBED WITHIN ITS OWN BUBBLE REALITY HIDDEN DEEP WITHIN YOUR SOUL."

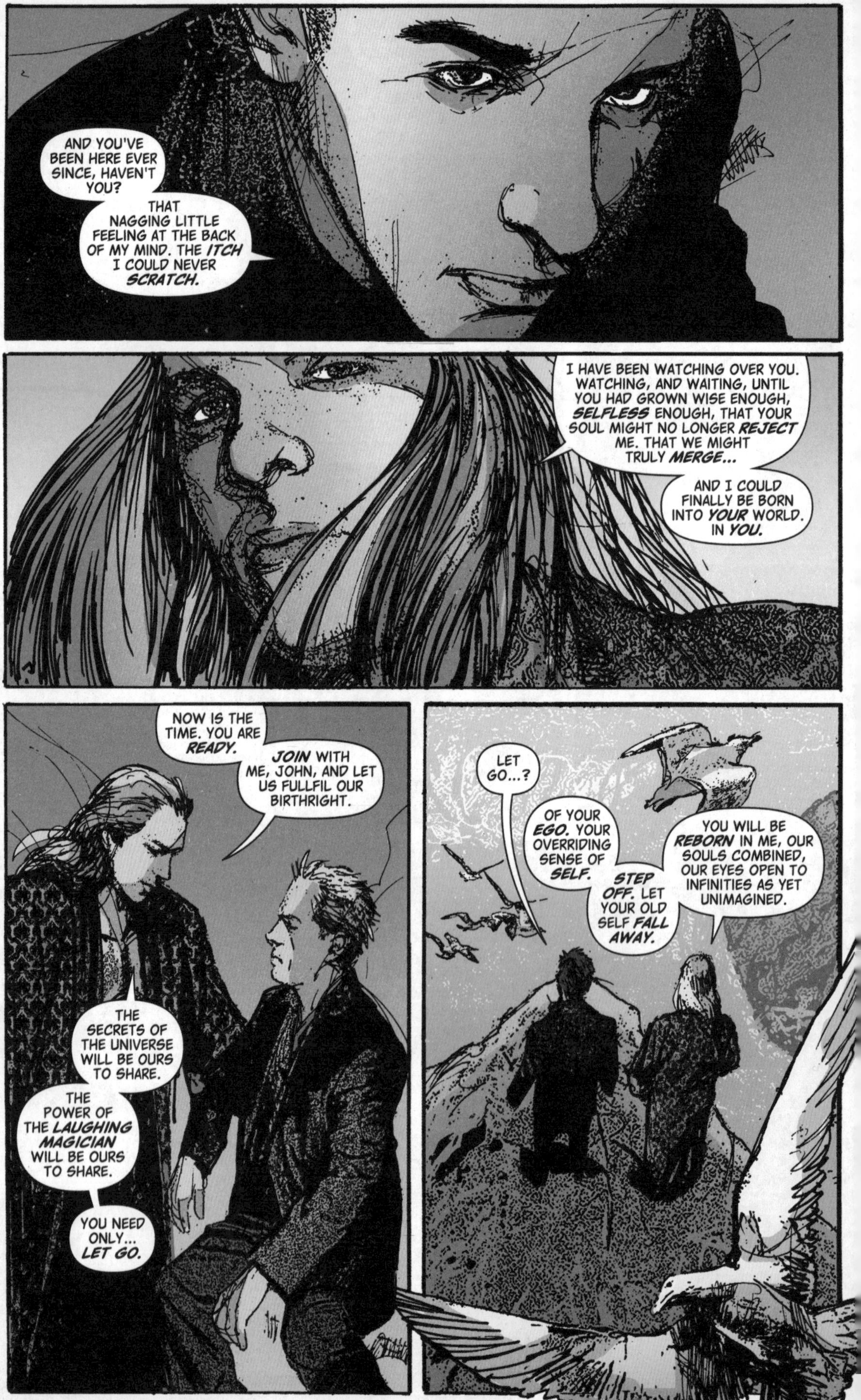

AND YOU'VE BEEN HERE EVER SINCE, HAVEN'T YOU?
THAT NAGGING LITTLE FEELING AT THE BACK OF MY MIND. THE ITCH I COULD NEVER SCRATCH.
I HAVE BEEN WATCHING OVER YOU. WATCHING, AND WAITING, UNTIL YOU HAD GROWN WISE ENOUGH, SELFLESS ENOUGH, THAT YOUR SOUL MIGHT NO LONGER REJECT ME. THAT WE MIGHT TRULY MERGE...
AND I COULD FINALLY BE BORN INTO YOUR WORLD. IN YOU.
NOW IS THE TIME. YOU ARE READY.
JOIN WITH ME, JOHN, AND LET US FULLFIL OUR BIRTHRIGHT.
THE SECRETS OF THE UNIVERSE WILL BE OURS TO SHARE.
THE POWER OF THE LAUGHING MAGICIAN WILL BE OURS TO SHARE.
YOU NEED ONLY... LET GO.
LET GO...?
OF YOUR EGO. YOUR OVERRIDING SENSE OF SELF.
STEP OFF. LET YOUR OLD SELF FALL AWAY.
YOU WILL BE REBORN IN ME, OUR SOULS COMBINED, OUR EYES OPEN TO INFINITIES AS YET UNIMAGINED.

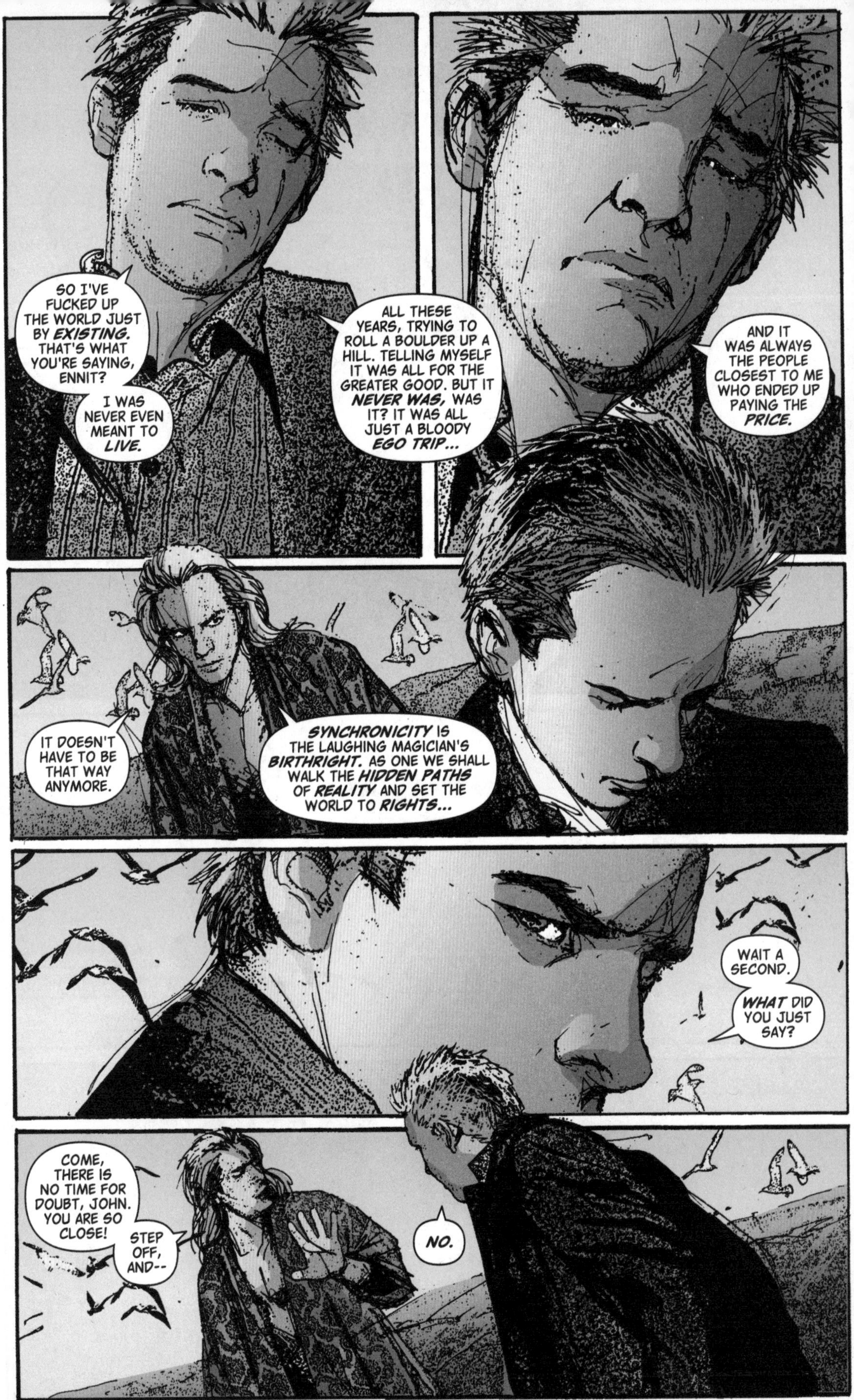
SO I'VE FUCKED UP THE WORLD JUST BY EXISTING. THAT'S WHAT YOU'RE SAYING, ENNIT?
I WAS NEVER EVEN MEANT TO LIVE.
ALL THESE YEARS, TRYING TO ROLL A BOULDER UP A HILL. TELLING MYSELF IT WAS ALL FOR THE GREATER GOOD. BUT IT NEVER WAS, WAS IT? IT WAS ALL JUST A BLOODY EGO TRIP...
AND IT WAS ALWAYS THE PEOPLE CLOSEST TO ME WHO ENDED UP PAYING THE PRICE.
IT DOESN'T HAVE TO BE THAT WAY ANYMORE.
SYNCHRONICITY IS THE LAUGHING MAGICIAN'S BIRTHRIGHT. AS ONE WE SHALL WALK THE HIDDEN PATHS OF REALITY AND SET THE WORLD TO RIGHTS...
WAIT A SECOND.
WHAT DID YOU JUST SAY?
COME, THERE IS NO TIME FOR DOUBT, JOHN. YOU ARE SO CLOSE!
STEP OFF, AND--
NO.

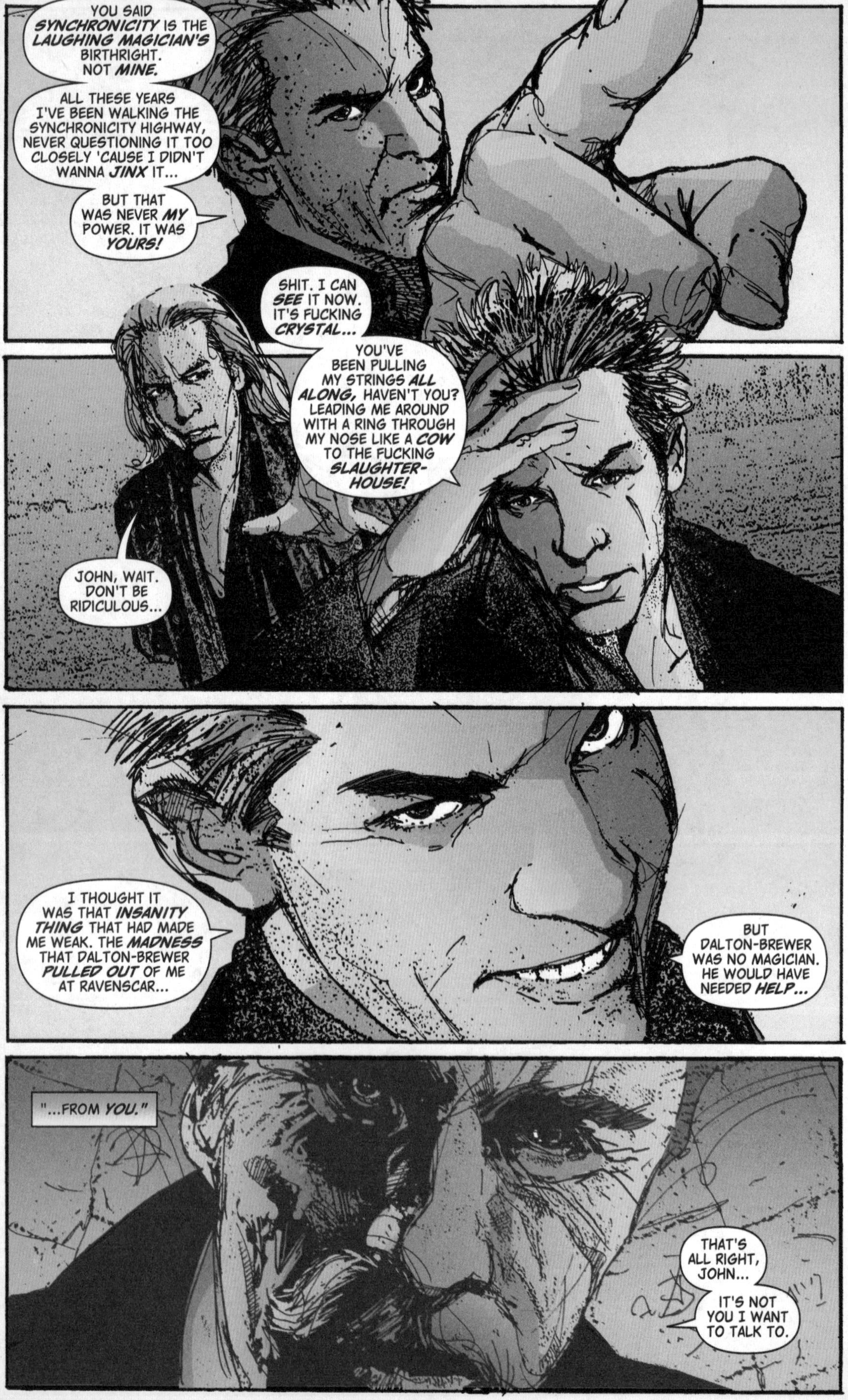
YOU SAID SYNCHRONICITY IS THE LAUGHING MAGICIAN'S BIRTHRIGHT. NOT MINE.
ALL THESE YEARS I'VE BEEN WALKING THE SYNCHRONICITY HIGHWAY, NEVER QUESTIONING IT TOO CLOSELY 'CAUSE I DIDN'T WANNA JINX IT...
BUT THAT WAS NEVER MY POWER. IT WAS YOURS!
SHIT. I CAN SEE IT NOW. IT'S FUCKING CRYSTAL...
YOU'VE BEEN PULLING MY STRINGS ALL ALONG, HAVEN'T YOU? LEADING ME AROUND WITH A RING THROUGH MY NOSE LIKE A COW TO THE FUCKING SLAUGHTER-HOUSE!
JOHN, WAIT. DON'T BE RIDICULOUS...
I THOUGHT IT WAS THAT INSANITY THING THAT HAD MADE ME WEAK. THE MADNESS THAT DALTON-BREWER PULLED OUT OF ME AT RAVENSCAR...
BUT DALTON-BREWER WAS NO MAGICIAN. HE WOULD HAVE NEEDED HELP...
"...FROM YOU."
THAT'S ALL RIGHT, JOHN...
IT'S NOT YOU I WANT TO TALK TO.

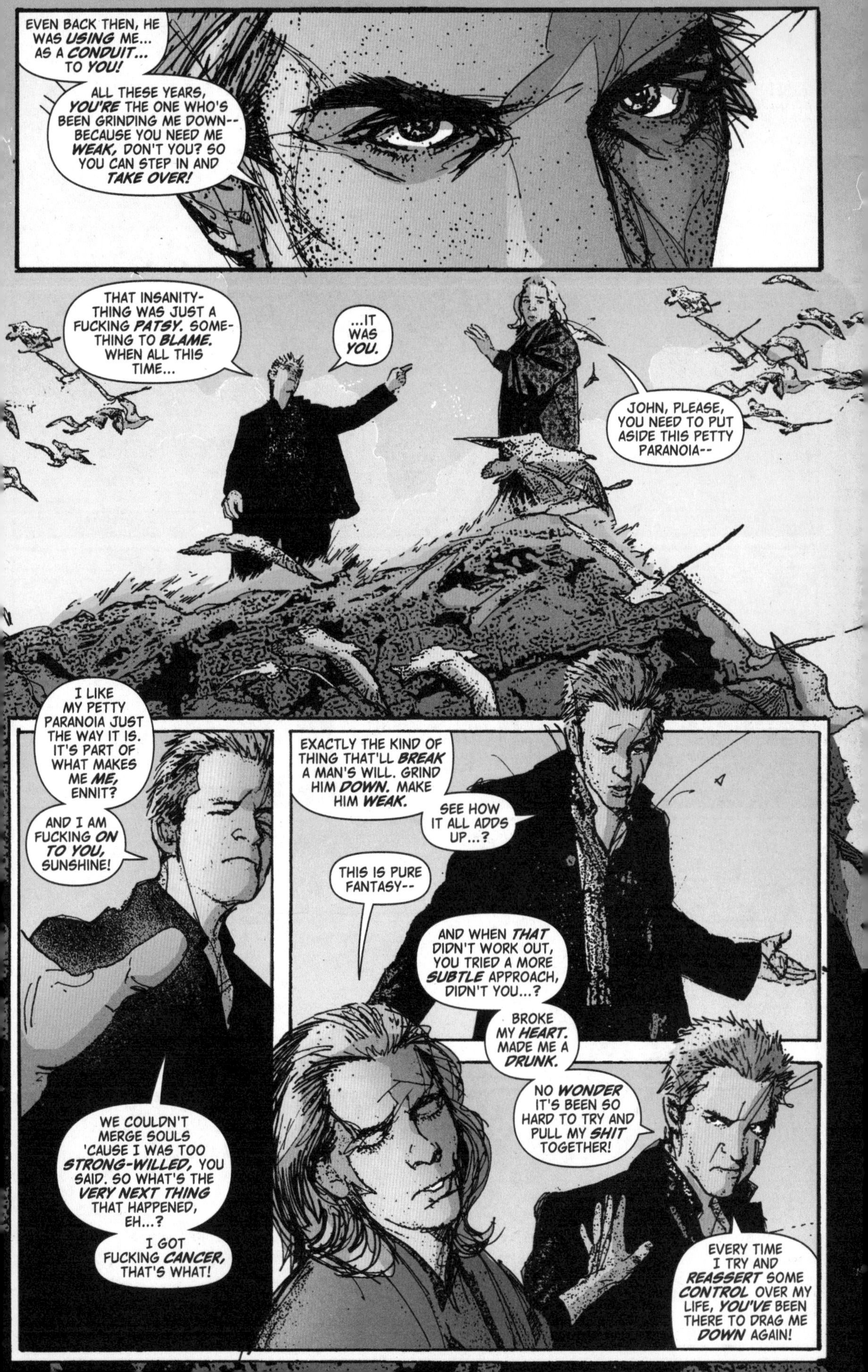
EVEN BACK THEN, HE WAS USING ME... AS A CONDUIT... TO YOU!
ALL THESE YEARS, YOU'RE THE ONE WHO'S BEEN GRINDING ME DOWN-- BECAUSE YOU NEED ME WEAK, DON'T YOU? SO YOU CAN STEP IN AND TAKE OVER!
THAT INSANITY-THING WAS JUST A FUCKING PATSY. SOME-THING TO BLAME. WHEN ALL THIS TIME...
...IT WAS YOU.
JOHN, PLEASE, YOU NEED TO PUT ASIDE THIS PETTY PARANOIA--
I LIKE MY PETTY PARANOIA JUST THE WAY IT IS. IT'S PART OF WHAT MAKES ME ME, ENNIT?
AND I AM FUCKING ON TO YOU, SUNSHINE!
WE COULDN'T MERGE SOULS 'CAUSE I WAS TOO STRONG-WILLED, YOU SAID. SO WHAT'S THE VERY NEXT THING THAT HAPPENED, EH...?
I GOT FUCKING CANCER, THAT'S WHAT!
EXACTLY THE KIND OF THING THAT'LL BREAK A MAN'S WILL. GRIND HIM DOWN. MAKE HIM WEAK.
SEE HOW IT ALL ADDS UP...?
THIS IS PURE FANTASY--
AND WHEN THAT DIDN'T WORK OUT, YOU TRIED A MORE SUBTLE APPROACH, DIDN'T YOU...?
BROKE MY HEART. MADE ME A DRUNK.
NO WONDER IT'S BEEN SO HARD TO TRY AND PULL MY SHIT TOGETHER!
EVERY TIME I TRY AND REASSERT SOME CONTROL OVER MY LIFE, YOU'VE BEEN THERE TO DRAG ME DOWN AGAIN!

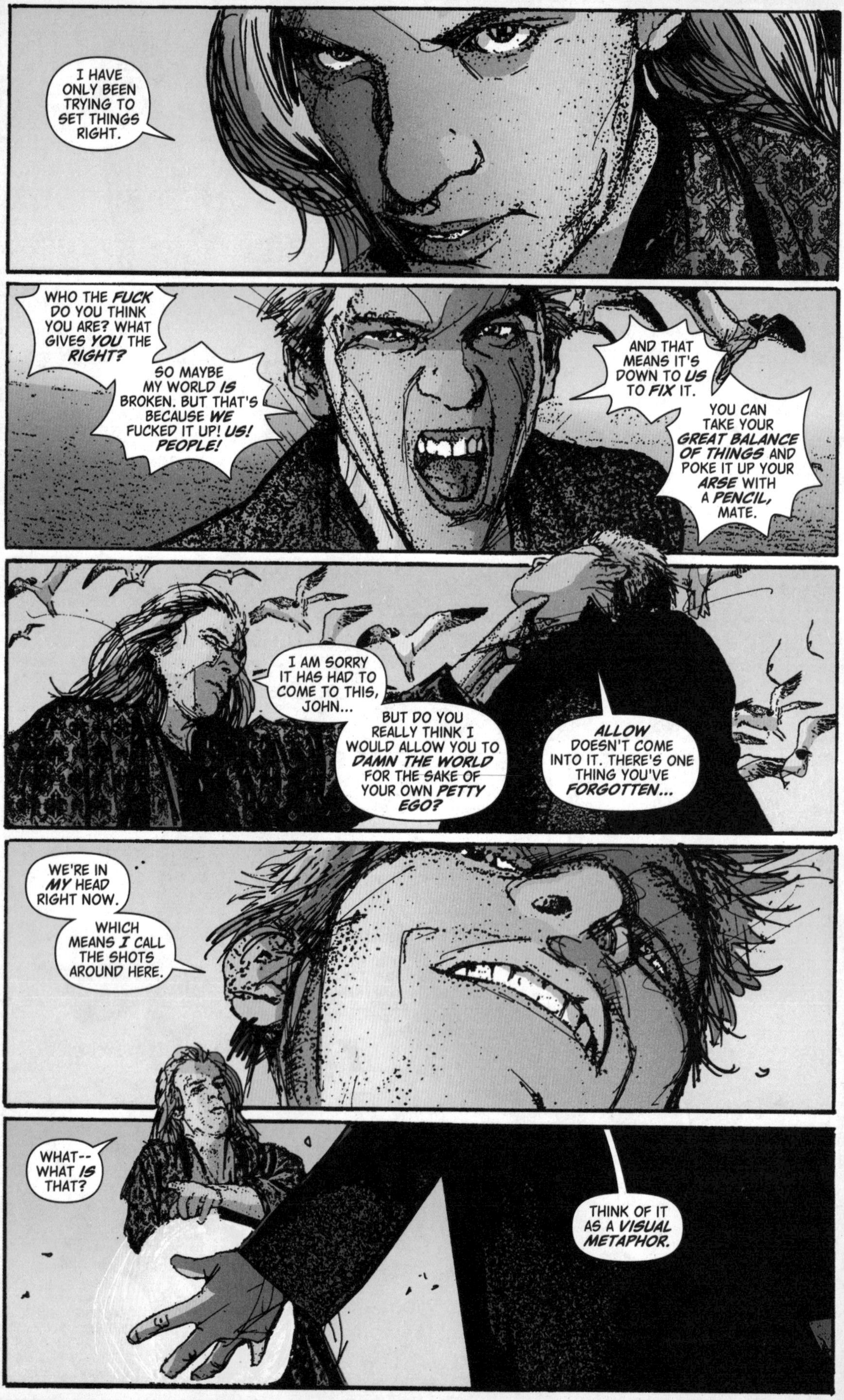
I HAVE ONLY BEEN TRYING TO SET THINGS RIGHT.
WHO THE FUCK DO YOU THINK YOU ARE? WHAT GIVES YOU THE RIGHT?
SO MAYBE MY WORLD IS BROKEN. BUT THAT'S BECAUSE WE FUCKED IT UP! US! PEOPLE!
AND THAT MEANS IT'S DOWN TO US TO FIX IT.
YOU CAN TAKE YOUR GREAT BALANCE OF THINGS AND POKE IT UP YOUR ARSE WITH A PENCIL, MATE.
I AM SORRY IT HAS HAD TO COME TO THIS, JOHN...
BUT DO YOU REALLY THINK I WOULD ALLOW YOU TO DAMN THE WORLD FOR THE SAKE OF YOUR OWN PETTY EGO?
ALLOW DOESN'T COME INTO IT. THERE'S ONE THING YOU'VE FORGOTTEN...
WE'RE IN MY HEAD RIGHT NOW.
WHICH MEANS I CALL THE SHOTS AROUND HERE.
WHAT-- WHAT IS THAT?
THINK OF IT AS A VISUAL METAPHOR.

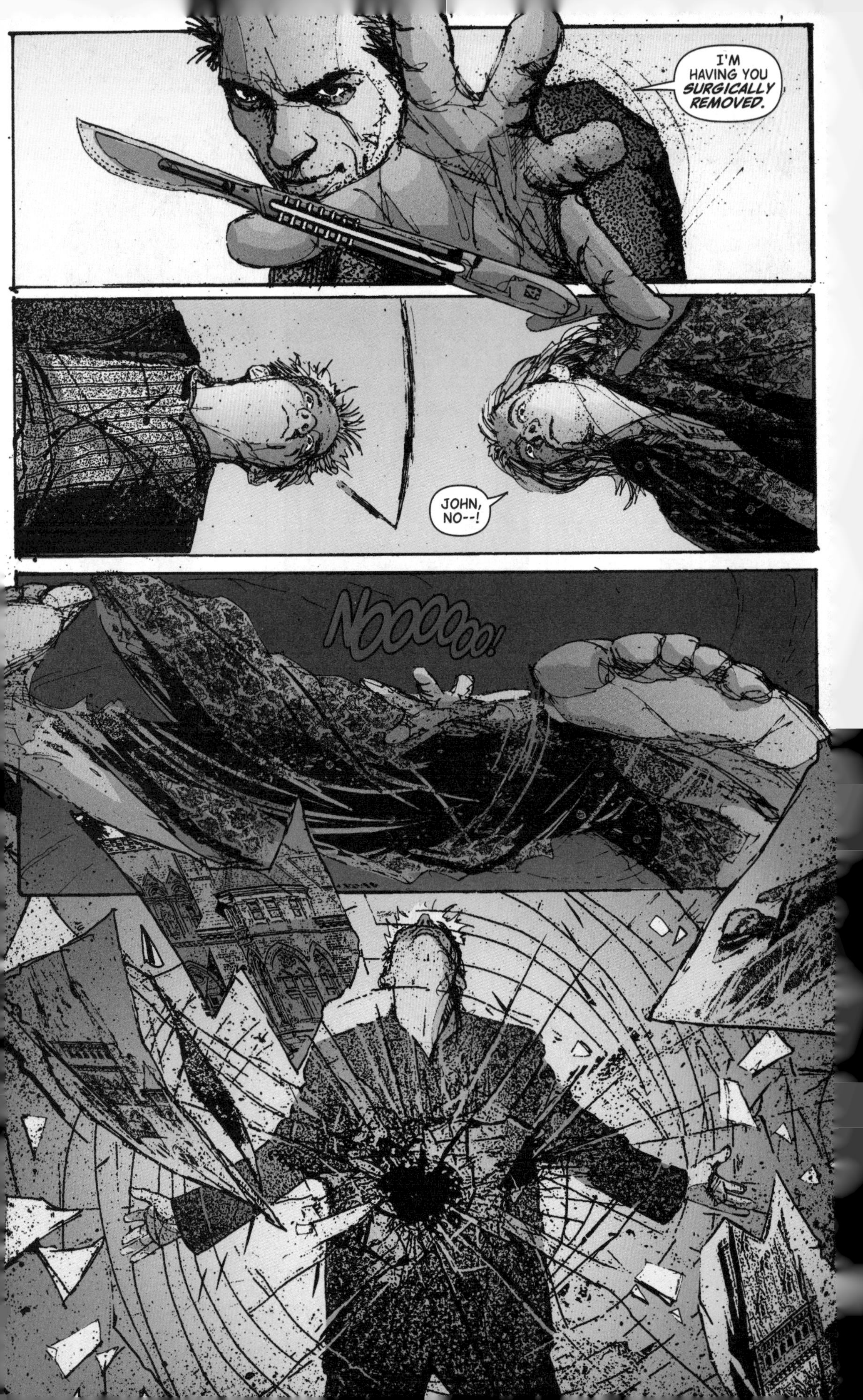
I'M HAVING YOU SURGICALLY REMOVED.
JOHN, NO--!
NOOOOOO!

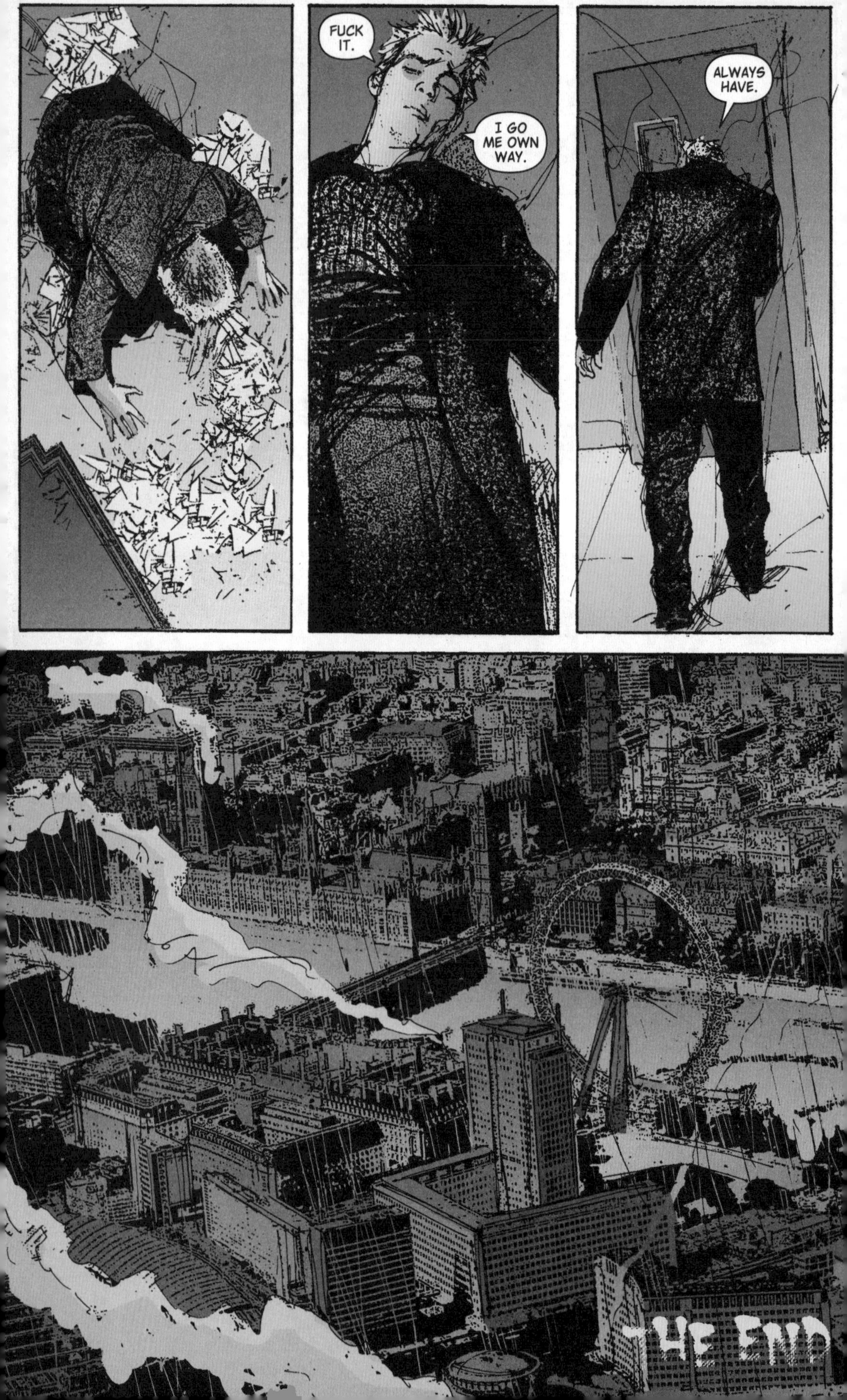
FUCK IT.
I GO ME OWN WAY.
ALWAYS HAVE.
THE END

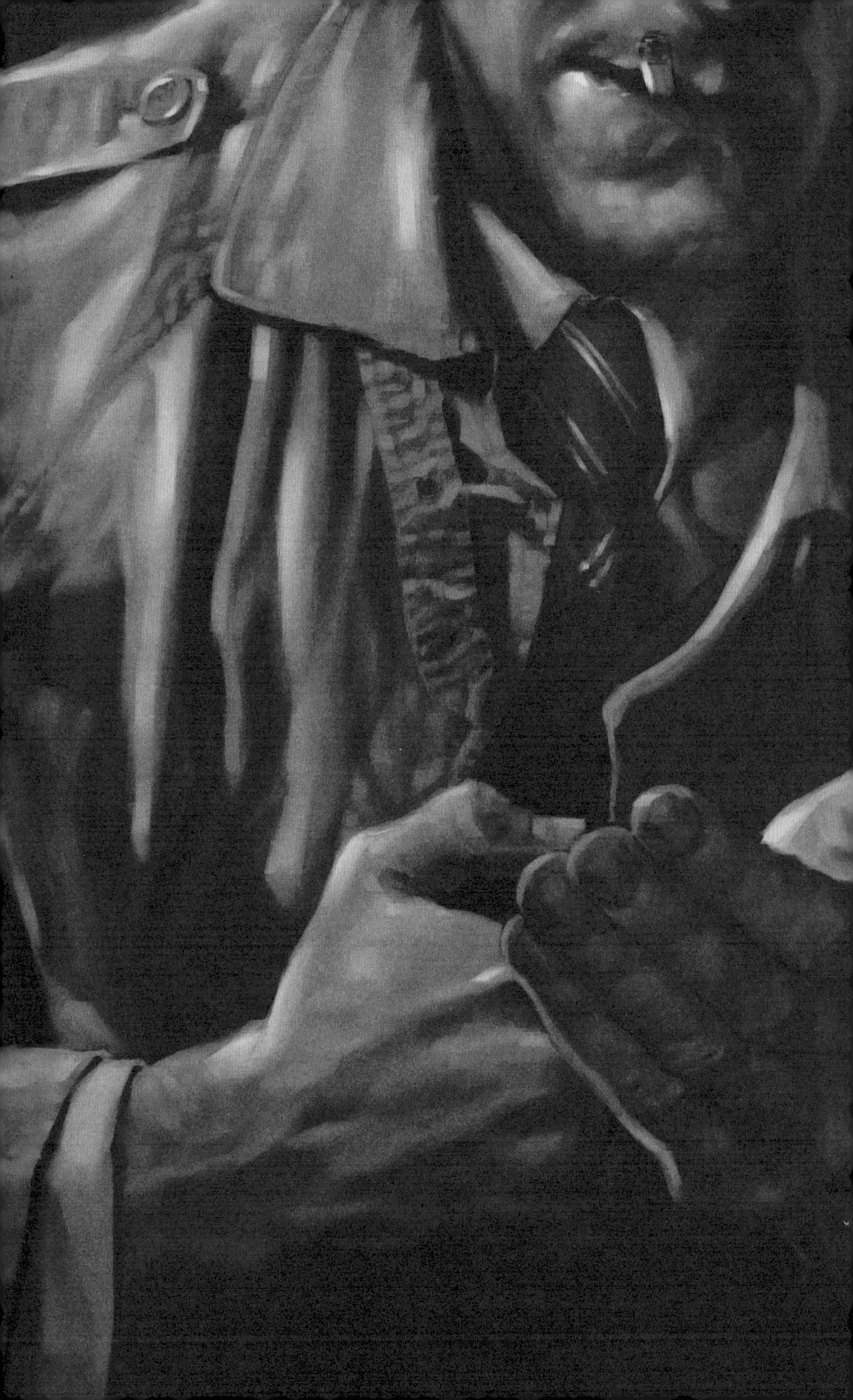